Published by Createspace, a DBA of On-Demand Publishing,
LLC. 4900 LaCross Road, North Charleston, SC 29406, USA

This book is dedicated to Aisling and Fiona for their support and love, to Shane, the Miracle Man, and to Séan, who we love and miss very much.

Prologue

Gar

The voice over the intercom announced the next stop:

Muine Bheag, Bagenalstown.

I looked at Fin and he looked back at me, eyebrows raised.

Here we go, I thought.

This was our stop. After a one-hour train ride, and eighteen years of separation, we were finally going to meet our mother again. I could feel the butterflies fluttering in my stomach. We followed our elder brother Shane towards the door of the carriage.

Shane pulled the door open, the sun spilled in, and we stepped out onto the platform.

I squinted and then I saw her; older, greyer but unmistakable: it was our Mam.

Chapter 1

Gar

Our mother was born in the early 1950s and was brought up in rural Carlow in a small two-bedroomed cottage surrounded by farmland a couple of miles away from the nearest town. The cottage was small but bursting with life as our mother was one of thirteen siblings. When we stayed there as children, it was crowded enough with four of us in one bedroom (two to a bed) so I struggled to imagine what it must have been like when my mother was growing up there.

In 1973, when our mother was in her early twenties, she worked in Butlin's Holiday Camp, just outside Dublin city. It was while working at Butlin's that she met our father, who had just turned eighteen years of age and was holidaying in Butlin's. Things moved quickly and they got married in January 1974. By June of that year our older brother Shane was born and the three of them moved into the front bedroom of our father's parents' two-bedroom house in Crumlin.

After five years of married life in one room, I was born in 1979 to add my writhing humanity to the cramped proceedings. The living arrangement continued like that for another two years until my younger brother Fin was born in 1981 and shortly after Fin arrived in the world we moved out of our grandparents' front bedroom in Crumlin and into the relative splendour of a three-bedroom council house of our own in Tallaght.

I lived in Tallaght from the age of two to the age of seven and my memories are of a happy time. As a relatively new estate there were plenty of construction sites around the area to keep three young boys in adventure-filled contentment. There were also other young families like ours, so there were lots of kids to hang around with.

The neighbours on our road shared a strong sense of community and one of my most vivid memories was of the street parties that were held every summer. There were a couple of neighbours who were lorry drivers and who would block off the street on the appointed day by parking their lorries at either end of the street. Once that was done, a collective effort began of bringing out tables and chairs and lining them up in the middle of the road. Tablecloths were draped down the length of the line of tables and pots and bowls of food were produced until the tables were heaving. Much to our delight there were always far too many bowls of jelly and trifle prepared and we would gorge ourselves until jelly came out of our ears.

The house next door to us was unoccupied for a few months until one day a family of settled travellers moved in. This was met with trepidation from our parents and curiosity from us. We gazed out of the upstairs windows at the sight of naked traveller children playing in their front garden. We had never seen kids on the road playing with no clothes on and were fascinated by the sight of them running around the garden chasing the half dozen Jack Russell terriers that moved in with them.

****

Although we could discern grumbles from the parents on the road, as a child I had no automatic prejudice against the travellers. That all changed though when one of the traveller kids stole my Big Wheel. A Big Wheel was a moulded plastic tricycle with two small blue wheels at the back, a red plastic chassis and the bright blue big wheel at the front. The Big Wheel was my pride and joy. I was therefore distraught when one of the traveller kids shoved me off my Big Wheel and tore off down the road on it before I realised what was happening. Once the horror of what had transpired sank in, I did what any sensible five-year-old with an older brother would do and ran into the house screaming my older brother's name. Shane heard my cries and chased after the boy and took the Big Wheel back, much to my delight. My big brother, the hero, had saved the day and not for the last time.

As a child in Tallaght, Shane sometimes got into trouble with the authorities. A low point for him was when he was brought home in a Garda car having stolen Kit-Kat bars from the local Dunnes Stores. Fin and I cowered in the kitchen as the Gardaí called at the door and brought Shane in.

During our childhood we would occasionally visit our mother's family down in Carlow, staying in our grandparents' cottage with no sanitation and an outhouse, which horrified and fascinated in equal measure. Instead of a toilet, there was simply a large black bucket usually half full of faeces and clods of tissue paper floating in urine.

We had to squat over this bucket and take careful aim. In summer (which is when we visited most) there was usually a swarm of flies around the bucket to keep us company. Pretty soon we learnt to stuff our noses with tissue paper before setting foot in the outhouse which blocked out the worst of the smell. We also learned to squat quickly and skilfully to avoid the dreaded splash-back and also to avoid looking directly into the bucket. It was something of a relief to get back to Dublin and the miracle of modern plumbing.

Despite this unpleasant feature, for us Dublin lads coming down from the concrete suburbs of Tallaght, the country fields were full of adventure. We dared each other to run through the bull's field trying to avoid the cow pats (and the bull). We double dared each other to stand atop the cylindrical hay bales and try not to fall off while the other kids pushed the hay bale down the hill.

****

By the time Fin was getting ready to start junior infant's class; I was already through senior infants and getting ready to start first class while Shane was finishing off primary school and getting ready to start secondary school. It was at this time in 1986 that we moved out of our council house in Tallaght and into a private house in Knocklyon, a new middle-class estate on the edge of Dublin suburbia.

I enjoyed the early years living in our new home. We three brothers were popular kids on our road as we were good at football, climbing trees and digging tunnels through the hayfields which were right opposite our house.

At this time our housing estate was the last of the suburbs before you hit the hayfields and the Dublin Mountains. We were on the edge of civilisation and as kids that was perfect as we got the best of both worlds. The adults were not as keen at having hayfields next door as we were, especially when the autumn harvest brought swarms of field mice into the estate trying to escape the combine harvester. As recent arrivals from Tallaght we were fascinated by the daily find of multi-coloured spotted field mice washed up in the drains at the back of the house. Picking them up by the tail and putting them in the bin was a pleasurably gruesome task that I enjoyed.

Within a year or two of us moving in, the nuns who owned the hayfields behind our house sold the valuable real estate for development. We got one final tsunami of mice when the JCBs moved in and after that the mice never troubled us again as the fields were paved over and a large housing estate was built in the seemingly interminable sprawl of the suburbs into the Dublin Mountains.

By 1988, Shane was fourteen years of age in secondary school while Fin and I were still in primary school so Shane was very much the older brother. On the one hand this was great as he was the Great Protector and no-one ever messed or bullied me when Shane was around. On the other hand, he would take advantage of his position as big brother and would regularly help himself to a disproportionate share of whatever food there was to be divided between us. If there were six Weetabix left, Shane would take three for himself and give us three between the two of us:

Taxes are high, he'd say, chuckling to himself.

But Shane always looked out for us. As long as Shane was around; I didn't worry about being bullied.

Just as long as he was around.

Fin

When I look back to Tallaght, my most vivid memories are that of my Mam doting on me, caring for me and doing everything she could to ensure my happiness. I was the youngest, the baby, and it would probably be fair to say that I received a bit more attention than Gar and Shane from our Mam as the youngest child often does.

When I hurt my foot and declared to Gar, Shane and my Mam that I had a headache in my foot, she consoled me while Gar and Shane laughed. When our father made a curry that I found too hot to eat, I cried while I ate it. My Mam asked my father to stop making me eat it. He ignored her and ordered me to keep eating, seeming to think it would be beneficial to me in the long run. My father would regularly say, derogatively, that my Mam '*mollycoddled*' me. Although it seems like an entirely natural thing, he made it clear that he thought my Mam *mollycoddling* me was a bad thing.

5

I had good times too with my father. On one occasion he recorded the three of us singing on a tape recorder. Shane was singing "Yellow Submarine" with the words changed to "stork margarine" and Gar and I found this hilarious.

In the early years in our new home, I was often left behind when Shane and Gar were taken to the park or elsewhere, being considered 'too young' to go. I was always annoyed, wanting to be involved with what my older brothers were doing. Usually my Mam would cheer me up by playing with me and talking to me and listening to me. I would mostly forget then that the others had even gone out. One time, Shane and Gar had gone with our Mam to pick blackberries and I stayed in the house with my father. I was upset that I couldn't go to pick blackberries and he told me we'd have a better time at home. He was listening to *Rubber Soul* by *The Beatles* and he rubbed my head as I sang along to *Nowhere Man*.

On one occasion shortly before Christmas, when our parents had gone out, Shane woke us out of bed and brought us into the spare room to show us where our father had hidden two bikes that we were going to get "from Santa" for Christmas. We were delighted with the bikes although this did spell the end of any lingering belief in Santa. Over the Christmas holidays, my father and mother brought me and Gar along to a nearby park where they taught us how to ride our bikes. We later admitted to them that Shane had shown us the bikes beforehand so there was no pretence of Santa in our house the following Christmas. Although I was a bit upset at there being no Santa, I felt extremely grateful to my father, who I was led to believe had not only bought our bikes but set them up to a high level.

On weekend mornings, our Mam would often cook breakfast and serve it to our father in bed. I used to go up and he would give me some of his breakfast and I would sit in the bed with him and ask him about all the pictures in the newspaper he read. One time, my father was going to an Ireland rugby match and because I couldn't go, he told me to look out for him on the television. I was so naïve; I looked at the players faces expecting to see my Dad. I thought he was going to be an Ireland player that day, why not?

In 1987, I broke my leg in school. My father had to leave work to drive me to the hospital. Before we left for the hospital, he constructed some sort of support from a tin whistle that Shane owned and then he drove me to the hospital. He told me many times afterwards that the tin whistle had saved my leg from further damage and I felt grateful for that.

Naturally I wanted dearly to get on with my father and I did for the most part in these earlier years. He seemed to want me to be happy. He used to call me from wherever I was in the house when songs I liked came on television. Paul McCartney, *We All Stand Together*; Dire Straits, *The Walk of Life* and Peter Gabriel's *Sledgehammer* were amongst my favourites. My father would watch them with me and Gar and higher up the volume. He seemed to be proud that his young sons had the same taste in music as him, although truthfully it was the videos I was more impressed by.

Besides these happy episodes, there were other times when he made me feel sad as a child and made me feel more distant from him. When I wrote a song at the age of five or six called "*Sam and his Dog*", I sang it proudly to my family. My Mam laughed at the lyrics and told me it was great which was encouraging. Shane told me it was good, then poked fun at me over it, as older brothers do. But my father told me bluntly that he considered it to be a copy of *"Hey Bulldog'"* by the *Beatles*, who he was obsessed with. I protested that I wasn't copying any song but he said it was a copy and he didn't like it. Shane kept the piece of paper with the song wrote on it in his room and occasionally would take it out and start singing it to me laughing. But I didn't find it funny and was miserable about the song that my father told me I copied so I sneaked into Shane's room one evening and tore it up.

I wanted my father's approval and I wanted to spend quality time with him. One afternoon, I was watching Snoopy on TV and he came in with a cup of coffee. As he took his first sip of coffee, he asked me did I want a cup too. I said that I did, even though I disliked the taste of coffee. It was just that I didn't want to pass up this moment with my father. I struggled to drink a few sips of the coffee but I tried to hide the fact. Instead I sat looking quite content watching Snoopy with my Dad, drinking Nescafe.

Possibly the most idyllic father-son moment my father and I shared occurred one time when he was playing his guitar. I was enthusiastic about music and upon hearing the guitar I ran into where our father was playing in the spare bedroom. He asked me did I want to sing along. I was delighted and I sang *"Across the Universe"* as my father strummed the chords. He told me I was singing it well and I felt so proud that my father was telling me I was good at something.

But when I asked if I could play the guitar, I was told in no uncertain manner that I was never to touch his guitar and if I did I would be in serious trouble. As disappointed as I was with this, I thought there must be a good reason for it.

Chapter 2

Gar

I have many happy memories from my childhood, kicking around the rugby ball with Shane and my father in the park, going for hikes in the Dublin Mountains with my parents and spending happy days in the local library with our mother reading and renting out *Asterix, Tintin, Billy Bunter* and *Biggles* books. When our father came home from work, he would take off his shoes, have a cup of tea and we would watch the *Real Ghostbusters* cartoon with him.

In 1988, my father brought me to see the parade of a giant Gulliver through the streets of Dublin and I was amazed by the size of the giant. That same year we jumped around the sitting room in delight when Ray Houghton scored against England in Euro '88 and hid behind the couch barely able to watch the remaining eighty minutes or so as Ireland held on for a famous win.

But those happy memories from my childhood are clouded by unhappy memories of my parents fighting. Often when these fights were going on, I would be upstairs in the bedroom with Fin listening to arguments in the darkness; shouting and screaming, doors slamming, silence and our mother's tears. On many of these nights, Shane, who as the older brother had his own room across the hall, would secretly cross into our room and snuggle up onto our beds where we would whisper together.

I had a recurring nightmare that one night my parents would call me down into the hall, tell me they were splitting up, and ask me to choose which parent I wanted to live with. In my nightmare I knew what I would do: I would throw myself on the ground between them and grab one leg each and say-

I'm not going to decide. You have to stay together.

I reasoned that the only possible response would be for them to say - *OK, you win, we're all staying put together.*

What I did not know at that time was that it was not just about our father and our mother, there was a third party involved, and she had been involved for many years.

Fin

Despite the fights, I was in denial about my parents' troubles. Unlike Gar, I tried to ignore them, hoping they would just go away. I had a friend whose parents always seemed to be fighting and I hoped this was just normal adult behaviour.

Sometimes the fighting would cease for a while and things could be fine. One afternoon when I was worrying about my parents, I came in from playing outside to find them sitting in the living room together listening to the Police song, *"Message in a Bottle"*. Both of them were happy and they were singing along together. They did not resemble a couple on the verge of separation in any way, rather a happy couple in love. I told myself that this meant things were fine. But in reality, an argument was always lurking around the corner.

One Friday evening, our father was grooming himself in front of the mirror in the hall getting ready to go out. As he stood admiring himself in full view of my Mam and me, our Mam lost her patience and shouted at him, asking him if he was sure he looked alright for *meeting up with his girlfriend?* I could sense the awkwardness and I was struck by the look our father gave our Mam. He looked and spoke to her as if she had betrayed him by mentioning *his girlfriend* in front of one of the children. A shouting match ensued.

At the time, I didn't know who was in the wrong but I felt more disconnected from my father. When he left, I sat on my Mam's knee and we watched television as she held me. I didn't want to leave my Mam's arms that evening.

As the arguments between them became more regular and tumultuous, people outside our house started to notice. On one occasion, I was playing with a deck of cards in the sheltered area between our house and the neighbour's house. I was with the boy who lived next door and another boy from down the road. We each suggested card games that we knew how to play. There were easy ones such as Snap and more complex ones such as Gin Rummy. All the time my parents' argument could be heard coming from the living room area and through the wall to where we were, with varying degrees of loudness.

As we began to run low on ideas for games, the boy next door suggested we play a game called *'Happy Families'*. He was smirking as he said it. I naively asked what the rules were and the boy answered with mock surprise:

Have you never played Happy Families before?

The boy then laughed and went home. The other boy also left and I sat pondering the situation, not wishing to enter the house where my parents were arguing, so instead I just sat there under the shelter wondering why my parents fought so much.

Chapter 3

Gar

One afternoon, when I was eight or nine years' old my father asked me did I want to go to the park to throw the rugby ball around. I agreed enthusiastically and held the rugby ball in the back seat as we drove towards the park. On the way, my father suddenly pulled the car in to the left-hand kerb where a glamorous young woman was walking in the same direction as the car. Our father rolled down the window on the passenger side of the car and called out her name. She turned and acknowledged our father and me in the back seat.

Our father asked her where she was going. He told her we were on our way to the park and asked her did she want to come with us. She seemed nervous at this suggestion. It was palpable even to me as an eight-year-old. She hesitated, but after some persuasion she got into the car. We were introduced, I was told her name was Caroline but beyond that I was not given any more explanation.

So off we went to the park - me, my father and his mistress. Caroline stopped in the shop and bought bags of crisps for me which went down very well. I thought she was one of our father's friends, a bit younger than our Mam and that was that. By this stage of their affair, our father clearly had no inhibitions about being seen in public with her and with us.

When we first met Caroline she was around twenty-one years of age and our father was twelve years her senior.

****

Following this first meeting with Caroline, we began to meet her on more and more regular occasions. In 1988, we spent time with Caroline and our father at the Dublin Millennium celebrations when a mock Viking invasion was staged at Clontarf.

On St. Stephen's Day that year, our father told me and Fin to get in the car as we were going to visit our Nanny and Grandad in Crumlin but for reasons not made clear, our mother would not be coming with us. As we drove towards Crumlin our father announced that we were actually going to pop in to see his friend Caroline who lived in a rented house in Templeogue. We then spent the day with our father and our father's new friend playing Monopoly, drinking Coke, eating crisps and chocolate marshmallows. Although we enjoyed the treats and the attention, it felt strange being away from our mother for the day with this woman we hardly knew.

Our father made it clear to us that he wanted us to like his new friend and generally acted happy and friendly when we were with her. Sometimes, however, he acted mean towards her in front of us, which presented a confusing picture.

One such occasion occurred after we had been to rugby training one Sunday afternoon. At around the same time as our father introduced us to Caroline, our father got us involved in mini-rugby in De Le Salle Palmerston RFC where we played every Sunday morning. Caroline and our father watched us on the side-lines and socialised with the other parents in the clubhouse afterwards. I don't believe the other children's parents ever met my mother and I don't know what my father told them about her. However, they must have wondered how two boys (ten and eight years old) had a twenty-two-year-old, somewhat glamorous, *'mother'*. To give an idea of how young looking she was, our father used to boast about how Caroline used to gain entrance to rugby matches *on the schoolgirl ticket*.

Sometimes after training, we would visit our Nanny and Grandad (our father's parents) in Crumlin. We were very close to our grandparents and enjoyed these visits. On one such visit though, things were not going well between Caroline and our father. In the car journey to our grandparents' house they had been screaming and shouting at each other, not an uncommon sight for us to behold, even at this early stage.

On this occasion, the fighting reached a climax just as the car stopped outside our grandparents' house. The argument continued even as we all got out of the car and stood on the pavement outside the house. I recall Caroline raising her voice and our father referring to the fact that they were outside his parents' house but she raised her voice again. Our father told her to be quiet again but she kept talking. Our father seemed to lose patience. He had been drinking from a can of 7-Up which he held in his hand. As we watched, he raised the can over Caroline's head and slowly and methodically drained the dregs of the 7-Up over her head and onto her hair. Caroline had long, black curly hair and as we watched, the sparkling fluid bounced off her curls and onto her face. Fin and I stood there motionless, not daring to speak.

Our father turned and walked towards our grandparents' house. After a minute or two Caroline followed behind, drying her eyes with one hand and carrying an apple pie in the other. We followed suit and the afternoon proceeded as if nothing had happened.

Up to this point our father had seemed to want us to like Caroline. I was therefore very confused and somewhat disturbed to watch him humiliate her and degrade her in front of us. In order to not make my father angry, I wanted to like Caroline too.

Our father and Caroline had many fights in the years that followed, with our father never slow to use his aggression towards her. Unfortunately for me and Fin, Caroline seemed to deal with this by channelling that aggression towards us.

Fin

I was not surprised by the 7-Up incident because it was no different to how I had seen our father act towards our Mam. Seeing him behave this way to Caroline led me to increasingly dislike him. Later on in the day, after that incident, our father tried to joke about it. Caroline seemed confused but acted like she thought she should show that she saw a funny side to the whole thing. It was more awkward than any of our previous meetings with her and I remained quiet and sombre throughout. Caroline seemed concerned by this and tried to cheer me up. On the way home, we stopped and she went into the shop. When she returned she threw a packet of crisps each to myself and Gar. There was nothing like a bag of crisps to make me forget my worries and I ate them gleefully. Unbeknownst to me, before I had even met Caroline, it transpired that she had been buying crisps every week for us.

Every Friday evening, Gar, Shane and I got our pocket money from our Mam and bought biscuits and other treats in the local supermarket. When we got home we watched *The Two Ronnies* on TV with our Mam. This was always the highlight of the week for me. Our father was not present at this Friday night ritual. He would either not return from work or come home and get dressed up and go back out.

When it came to giving us treats, sometimes my father would share one of his chewing gums with me or give me a square of his *Yorkie* bar and I was quite satisfied with this. I didn't consider him to be mean or anything but he wasn't the kind of father who would stop in a shop and buy us sweets off his own bat.

So I was pleasantly surprised one Saturday morning when my father told me to go out to the car to check if there was something in it I might like. I went out and was delighted to find a packet of crisps. This new treat of a bag of crisps on a Saturday morning became a weekly thing and for me it was a welcome delight. It was not just because I liked savoury snacks but I also appreciated what I thought was a kind, thoughtful, fatherly gesture.

I used to play on the road with my friend every Saturday morning and our play was usually interrupted when his father drove by bringing with him a packet of Opal Fruits or Fruit Pastilles for my friend. I was envious of my friend but now I could proudly tell him that *my father was getting me crisps every week.*

It felt good to think that my father was thinking of me and Gar on his way home from wherever he was. It felt good to think that he was making the effort to stop and buy us something nice. We showed our delight obviously and our father happily accepted our gratitude. After some months had passed and we had met Caroline a few times, our father, who was trying to get us to like her, told us that it was in fact Caroline who had bought us the crisps that we found on those Saturday mornings *because she was so fond of us.* This annoyed me as it meant my father had lied to me and that he was not as thoughtful or considerate as I had believed him to be. I didn't want to have to tell my friends that my father had lied to me every week, whatever the reason.

Around the same time, I found my father becoming more distant and preoccupied and I felt like I was the last thing on his mind. As he became more distant, I became closer to my Mam. I would happily sit on her lap for hours and watch television. My father was against this and used to order my Mam to stop *mollycoddling* me. The more I saw him shout at or upset my Mam, the more I resented him and felt

15

closer to my Mam. The more I showed affection towards my Mam, the more he seemed to resent me and the divide between us grew.

I observed my friends' relationships with their fathers as I reached eight or nine years of age and knew they were different to mine. Some of my friends would naturally hug their fathers unprompted. By now, I didn't in any way feel compelled to hug my father. I didn't understand why this was and really thought it was perhaps somehow my fault.

****

As the relationship between our parents got worse, so did our living conditions. I knew we weren't a rich family but until this time we had been provided for fairly adequately and I don't remember ever wanting for anything. However, around the time that Caroline came on the scene, things changed and we seemed to live in a state of near poverty. The only clothes we had were ragtag charity clothes, purchased for little or nothing in charity shops. We spent many an afternoon with our Mam rummaging around *Fred's Fashions* (the St. Vincent de Paul charity shop). This wasn't really something that bothered me as fashion wasn't that important to me at that age but what did bother me was the lack of heat in our house and the lack of food. I spent many cold winter days and nights huddled in the kitchen with my Mam. We would sit close to a standalone gas heater holding our hands in front of it for heat. The rest of the house would be Baltic so I didn't venture out of the kitchen even to watch TV. I used to drink glasses of milk and I noticed that the glasses my Mam gave me were half milk, half water. I gave out to my Mam at the time, complaining that I wanted proper glasses of milk like I had been getting previously.

There was not enough food in the house either and when I told my Mam I was hungry; she would often give me a cup of tea that wouldn't alleviate the hunger. I could tell that she was sad about the situation and sometimes my complaining would visibly bring her close to tears so I stopped complaining.

****

Shortly after this, I realised for certain that my parents were getting separated and that we were moving out of our home. I was sitting in

16

the back of the car talking to Gar while my parents drove around visiting houses for us and our Mam to move in to. My Mam and my father had gone inside to view one particular house and left us outside in the car with the radio playing. Gar was usually a good person for me to ask about things that I wasn't sure about. *"Girls just wanna have fun"* by Cyndi Lauper came on the radio.

Why does she say girls just want to have fun when boys want to have fun too? I asked.

She's not saying only girls want to have fun, she is saying that that's all they want to do, Gar said, who sounded more perturbed than usual at my asking him a stupid question.

All I want to do is have fun too and I'm not a girl? Why would anyone not want to have fun? What's the point of this song, it's stupid! I responded

Gar sighed.

I knew Gar was annoyed at something and it wasn't me, despite me testing him. My questions were more stupid than usual though, since I was building up to the real question I wanted to ask him.

What's the reason for us being here Gar? What are they doing in that house?

I think we're going to live with Mam here, he sighed again, *and Dad's going to stay in our house.*

He looked devastated.

I had come to a similar conclusion although I was more worried about who we were going to live with.

How d' ya know, did they tell you? I asked

I heard them, Gar said.

That piece of evidence was further backed up when our Mam and father appeared and invited us to come in and look at the house. As we looked around the small house, in a location I cannot remember, I quietly asked our Mam if it was me, Gar and her that would live in the house. She nodded sheepishly. It appeared as if she was afraid to even talk about it in front of our father. I was delighted that it was going to be the three of us. In fact, I thought this was an ideal situation. Shane used to tease me constantly, as older brothers sometimes do. Gar didn't as much and we played together as we were so close in age and got on quite well.

I didn't think I would miss my father in any way. And of course, my Mam would be there. It was more positives than negatives for me. I kept these thoughts to myself as I knew somehow that if I showed delight, my father would be angry. I'd like to say I didn't want to hurt his feelings but that would be a lie. Another reason for curbing my enthusiasm was Gar's demeanour. I could tell he wasn't at all happy with how this was working out. I tried to cheer him up.

I think it will be grand livin' here Gar; the shop is right beside us.

Gar just looked at me and I knew if I said another word, he might start crying so I just looked the other way.

As it turned out, that small house wasn't chosen. We looked at other properties to rent and it became apparent to me that my father was very keen for Gar and me to move out with our Mam. He openly promoted the idea and was as pleasant towards our Mam and us as I had ever seen him. He seemed eager for her to settle on a property to rent and I heard him try to convince my Mam that different properties were perfect for us. He talked to our Mam in an unusually nice tone that bore no resemblance to the contemptuous tone he usually used towards her.

It was eventually decided my Mam would rent a house in an estate in Firhouse where Gar, my Mam and I would live, 30 minutes' walk away from the house in Knocklyon. I was relatively pleased with the outcome, happy to be with my Mam and not my father.

Chapter 4

Gar

In 1989, within three years of us moving out of Tallaght, our father and mother were legally separated. Our father stayed in the house with Caroline. Shane, who was sixteen at the time, stayed with our father and Caroline in the family home.

I have some happy memories of the year that Fin, our mother and I spent living together, our mother sitting out the back reading a book while Fin and I played in the garden. I remember evenings spent watching *Only Fools and Horses* and *The Two Ronnies* with our mother. We would eat bowls of biscuits and laugh together. When it was time for bed, every evening we would kneel down together in the sitting room and say our prayers. Our mother always told us to pray by first thanking God for what we had before requesting from him what we wanted. I tried to follow her example when I prayed.

During the summer of 1989, I played for Knocklyon under-11's Community Games rugby team. We trained twice a week on Tuesday and Thursday nights and the training took place on nearby football pitches, which were almost equidistant from my mother's house and my father's house. My father told me that I should stay with him after these training sessions and not go back to my mother's house. I was reluctant to do this as I didn't feel good about not returning to my mother's house but my father persisted until I felt that I had I had better do what he said or I would be in trouble. So I started going to his house after training and I was rewarded with sweets and Club Orange. I felt a bit sad though thinking of Fin and my mother in the house without me.

Over that summer, we won the Dublin and Leinster Community Games championships and I played in every game. The All-Ireland finals took place in Mosney in September, where we played the Ulster champions in the semi-final. We won and advanced to the final against the Munster champions. Caroline and my father came along to Mosney to watch me play. A few hours before the final, I was taken to one side by our coaches and told that I was being dropped for the final match. I was upset at this as I had played in every game so far that season and thought I deserved to play in the final. However, I had found myself getting distracted during games and not being able to focus. The coach, aware of the sensitive situation of dropping someone for the big final, asked me, as kindly as he could:

Is that OK, Gar?

I nodded as if it was fine but inside I really just wanted to bawl my eyes out. I did what any ten-year-old child would do and went looking for my mother. Unfortunately for me I had only my father and Caroline for comfort. I told them what had happened and cried my head off, gurgling and snotting in anguish. Caroline, who was twenty-two at this stage, looked at me like she did not know what to say and my father half-heartedly attempted a joke.

I was afraid that my father thought that I had let him down by not getting picked in the final.

The team won the final without me and a few weeks later we were paraded around the local housing estates with the trophy and all of the boys hanging out of the car windows with our medals. Despite not playing in the final, I was very proud of our achievements which were recorded on the front page of the local parish newsletter.

In that same summer of 1989, while we were living with our mother, Shane, Fin and I went on a camping holiday with our father and Caroline to France. Our father collected us from our mother's house and expressed his disgust that our mother had packed our clothes in black plastic bags. It was our first time abroad and we enjoyed the adventure although it felt strange sharing a family tent with our father and Caroline. The thin layer of canvas that separated our "rooms" in the tent meant that we heard everything that went on. We took to getting up early and leaving the tent as soon as we could.

Fin

I enjoyed life in the new house and threw myself enthusiastically into the move. Gar and I shared a large room with our beds on opposite sides and with a view out of the window in the middle of the room. I was excited about the new area that we now lived in. On the day we moved in, I stared excitedly out the window, thinking how much exploration could be done. Gar didn't seem quite so keen.

Our Mam seemed happy when we moved in. On the day we arrived, she gave me and Gar ten pence each and we went over to the shop that was across the road from the house. We quickly made the happy discovery that despite it being now almost time for the 1990 World Cup, the shop still sold *Mexico '86* chewing gum balls with *Mexico '86* stickers. They cost five pence each. I went all-in and got two of them as did Gar and we brought the stickers back and put them on our bedposts, the beginning of a *Mexico '86* sticker collection. On our way back, we ran around the church beside the shopping centre, which had some overgrown trees around it, and was quite exciting for a nine--year-old. I noted there was also a school right beside us. I was slightly worried that I would be moving school but was relieved when my Mam assured me that it wouldn't be necessary. There was a bus that stopped near our estate specifically for students living in the area that went to our school.

Ideal.

Before long, I had made friends with many of the other boys on the road. This was in contrast to Gar, who didn't really socialize outside in the estate. Looking back, particularly as time moved on, most of the times it seemed like my Mam and me were the only two that lived there. I remember Shane being there nearly as much as Gar, even though Shane was only visiting since he still lived 'full-time' in our old home. But Gar seemed to spend more and more time with our father, particularly as the year progressed.

There was no pressure really on me to go to my father's house except as it seemed to me in order to keep up appearances. I felt that my father didn't mind if I was there or not and there was usually a big rigmarole over how I would get to the house. On some occasions, Gar and Shane and I walked together which I thought was fun. It took around thirty minutes and there were a variety of routes we could take to mix it up. Occasionally my Mam would walk with me most of the way and other times, my father picked me up in his car.

On one of my early visits to my father's house, I arrived alone to find Caroline was the only person home. Since this was the lady that had given me crisps and lemonade, I was happy enough to hang out with her on my own. I did, however, find it a little odd that my father wasn't there given that I was supposed to be visiting him.

I noticed that Caroline was not the happy, friendly person she had appeared to be on our previous meeting and she seemed annoyed by my presence. I hadn't eaten lunch so I told Caroline I was hungry and this seemed to annoy her further. She asked angrily why my Mam hadn't given me lunch before I left the house. I responded by saying that it was too early for lunch before I left. She ranted something derogatory about my Mam as she opened a tin of spaghetti hoops. Despite the awkward atmosphere, I was keen to tuck into the spaghetti hoops which were a welcome variation on what I usually had for lunch.

After a few minutes of watching her stomp around the kitchen muttering obscenities, Caroline placed a plate of spaghetti hoops on toast in front of me. I was beginning to lose my appetite. When I finished it, I placed the knife and fork haphazardly on the plate. Caroline looked at my plate in disgust and questioned why I didn't know how to correctly place the knife and fork to show that I had finished a meal. I responded that nobody had ever showed me before.

She said firmly that she would *put manners on me* and turn me into a proper mannerly child. She went on to say how people wouldn't recognise me when she was finished with me. My interpretation of her rant was that she viewed me as being a bad child. It was upsetting but I couldn't decide if she was a good judge. I decided that she wasn't and that I would try to not take the negative comments to heart.

As she continued to shout at me, I remember feeling somewhat scared. She spoke in such a threatening manner. In my mind I compared her to the evil "whirligig witch" from a programme I used to watch around the time called *"Fortycoats"*. I didn't want to be around her. I got up from the table at the first chance I had and took my rugby ball outside. As I attempted place kicks at imaginary goalposts, I pondered the situation. I considered that the lemonade and crisps were really good treats but there were no treats today and instead I seemed to be meeting a very different woman. I decided I'd stay out on that green for as long as possible pretending to be Michael Kiernan until I was allowed to go home.

I couldn't wait to get back to my Mam.

On another occasion, I was supposed to be going up to my father's house during the week to spend the night. My Mam packed my sleepover gear and I got my schoolbag and uniform since I would be going to school directly from our father's house in the morning. My father was supposed to come up in his car to pick me up and bring me to his house. When he didn't arrive on time, we were not surprised. When a further hour passed, my Mam was a little concerned. Secretly I hoped that he wouldn't show up.

After another hour passed and it seemed ever more likely that my father wouldn't show up, my Mam called me over to her and sat me on her knee and cuddled me. I wasn't actually upset and I felt a bit guilty accepting the affection. I told her that I *was grand* and that I disliked my father anyway. My Mam said I had to think of all the nice things I could about my father. I couldn't understand why she was sticking up for the person who was usually quite mean to her. She rarely had anything bad to say about anyone, even him.

Some of my visits to my father were spent in the back of a car, while my father was teaching Caroline to drive. We would drive from my Mam's house to my father's house which would take a couple of hours instead of minutes while Caroline grappled with clutch control. By the time I arrived at my father's house, it was time for me to go to bed and then once I got up in the morning I went straight to school and back to my Mam's house. Even from a young age, I felt these visits were pretty pointless. Hardly a word would have been spoken to me by my father so it appeared to me that he was simply going through the motions and didn't care whether he saw me at all.

In our new home, our next-door neighbours had a son around the same age and we soon became good friends. His family were very welcoming to me and invited me in to their house regularly. We would play on the road or go to the local GIANT shopping centre where there was an 'Xtra-Vision', which was a video rental shop where we could look at different videos that we might want to see. We would sometimes look at the front pictures of the horror videos and laugh at how they were supposed to be scary but ultimately just amused us as nine-year-olds. The cover of "The Blob" was a personal favourite of mine.

Since Gar appeared to want to move back in with our father, I suspected that he and my father were having private conversations in my father's house when I was in my Mam's house. I concluded that Gar must know something that I didn't and I asked him about the possibility of us moving back in with our father. I argued with Gar that the benefits of living with our Mam far outweighed any benefits of living with my father and Caroline. We were already being put to use by Caroline on our visits, washing dishes and hanging out clothes. Our Mam never got us to do things like that, we merely had to clean up after ourselves and she was happy.

This was a persuasive and, I thought, conclusive argument for us to not want to live there.

Gar seemed to be convinced otherwise, however, and, it seemed to me, quite unreasonably so. His response to why we were better off living with my father and Caroline was simply that *we were just better off*. There was nothing to back it up. For someone who always backed up an argument with fact and reason, this was out of character for Gar and caused me a great deal of frustration. I knew that he was closer to our father than me but this didn't seem to me to be enough reason for him to want to move back with our father. It wasn't as if our father was lavishing him with gifts or anything. Our father was contemptuous to both of us, albeit he seemed to treat us with different levels of contempt.

What seemed clear to me from listening to my father was that there were two sides, akin to rival teams. He and Caroline were one team and Mam was the other. You could not be on both teams. When we moved in with our Mam, it appeared to me that Shane was on our father's team and Gar and I were on my Mam's. Now I feared that Gar had left our team and joined our father's. I knew that if this was true, Gar would feel a responsibility to do what our father said, no matter how it made him feel or whether he agreed with it or not.

I had noticed that he had become more distant with me since our move. When we first moved in with our Mam, we were as inseparable as we had always been throughout our childhood. We played *rounders* out the back garden and drew comics together. But as time went by and Gar spent more time with our father in his house and I stayed with my Mam, we grew apart. I made my own friends and the afternoons of me and Gar playing together became few and far between. He no longer seemed approachable to me. He didn't seem to be the same brother I had moved into the new house with. I noticed that in our Mam's house, he just seemed to be critical about everything there. He no longer liked our Mam's curry even though he used to have no problem with it before. Little things like that.

When Gar spoke of the possibility that we might be moving back in with our father, I refused to believe it. The reason for this was because a year previously, I believed that our father was quite content with us moving out of *his* house and in with our Mam. So I was confused at his apparent U-turn twelve months later that he now apparently wanted us to live with him again.

However, the fact that a move was imminent became clear when our father came to pick us up and a typical row developed between my father and my Mam at the front door of my Mam's house. My father was, as usual, the most vociferous and he was sounding as intimidating as ever. He was standing at the front door, shouting to my Mam that Gar and I would be better off living with him.

Our Mam stood a couple of steps back in the hallway. Gar and I stood in between them in the frame of the sitting room door. We had expected our father to arrive and for us to say goodbye to our Mam and go out to the car and drive off. However, the argument began and I attempted to skulk away to avoid witnessing it.

You.... get back here, my father shouted and motioned for me to return to where I had been standing. Gar was still rooted to the spot. My father was making the point that our school was a shorter walk from his house and that living with him would therefore be better for us. My Mam batted that argument away simply stating:

They need their mother.

It was very uncomfortable listening to it and I remember our Mam looking at us sympathetically and she said:

They don't need to hear all of this.

But our father retorted:

It's about them; they deserve to hear it.

He made it sound like he was doing us a favour. Our Mam seemed very uncomfortable arguing in front of us. As the argument escalated she seemed aghast and unable to get a sentence out. My father seemed to just get louder and more insistent.

I noticed Gar had tears in his eyes. I didn't.

Why don't we ask them who they want to live with? It's their lives, said our father matter-of-factly, while turning and ensuring to make eye contact with both of us.

Our Mam blurted something about us being *too young to make such decisions.* Knowing how persistent my father was, I began mentally preparing for his challenge. It was a no-brainer for me that I wanted to live with Mam, but this was a delicate situation. My concern wasn't that I might hurt my father's feelings, it was more that he might hurt me if I didn't give the answer he wanted. I was conscious of the fact that at the end of this argument, we were going to get into my father's car no matter what and it would just be the three of us in the car.

I was still hopeful, but not confident, that Gar might come to his senses and realise that living with Mam was the best option for him too. The importance of the situation was not lost on me; my future living arrangements were being decided right before my eyes. If I didn't stand strong here, that would be that.

The arguing continued and then despite my Mam's protestations, my father turned and said it:

Right then kids, who do ye want to live with? With her there, wherever you end up, he added disparagingly, *or back with me and Caroline and your brother Shane in our house?*
It was like a bad sales pitch.

Gar was now crying profusely and he hesitatingly walked towards our father, who looked like the cat that got the cream despite the fact that his eleven-year-old son was in tears. My father looked at me, making fierce eye contact, almost urging me to follow suit. In some ways, it seemed like the safest thing to do. My Mam would never give out to me if I did whereas I knew my father was liable to hold a grudge or worse still, hit me a smack when we got into his car. But I stood firm. Not firm enough to walk over to my Mam, but I figured I was standing close enough to her that they understood my choice. My father looked at me disgustedly.

He doesn't know what's good for him, because you're always mollycoddling him, but he'll learn as he gets older, he said.

He turned on his heel and led Gar with his arm around him out to the car. I looked at my Mam who was quiet at this point and visibly upset. My father shouted back seemingly impatiently *Are you coming or what Fin?*

I walked over to my Mam to give her a hug goodbye. Then I walked out and my father and Gar were already in the car and the engine was running. I quietly got in the back seat and said nothing. My father put the radio on and also said nothing. He seemed like he was annoyed with me but I was relieved that he wasn't shouting at me, rather just acting as if I wasn't there. I much preferred that. This silent treatment lasted until I went to school the next morning, although to my pleasant surprise, Caroline was extremely nice to me for that visit. None of this made any sense to me at the time.

Gar

The weeks leading up to us moving back in with our father were difficult. Our mother was extremely upset throughout this time. She and our father constantly fought and I recall her saying to him that she could no longer afford to pay the rent as he was not paying her any maintenance. I wasn't really sure what maintenance was but I heard the word used a lot around this time.

On the final day of living with my mother, as we waited for our father to come to collect me and Fin from the rented house we had lived in with her for the previous year, I walked into the sitting room to find my mother crying on the couch. I wanted to say something to console her but couldn't think of what to say. I told her I had seen a pair of underpants under the couch and asked her should I bring them with me? She didn't answer me and continued crying. She asked me to go over to her on the couch and she gave me a big hug.

Chapter 5

Gar

After we had moved back in with our father, our mother moved to a nearby estate and we only saw her intermittently, no more than a few hours every few weeks. She did not rent the whole house but only a room in the house so we did not visit her there but we would meet her in her friend's house (also nearby) or go for a walk together.

Throughout this time our father only referred to our mother in derogative terms. He coined a new word, "*Jo-ism*" (referencing our mother's first name, Josephine) – which he used to describe any negative attribute that Fin, Shane or I exhibited such as laziness, untruthfulness or stupidity. According to our father, these were all characteristics we could only have inherited from our mother. Shane and Fin were regularly accused of committing '*Jo-isms*'. Our father would say wistfully that if only Caroline had got Shane 'on time' she might have been able to help him but as Shane was already sixteen years old when our mother moved out and Caroline moved in, it was too late for Caroline *to kick the 'Jo-isms' out of him*. Meanwhile, he said Fin had been *mollycoddled* too much by our Mam, which led to Fin committing regular '*Jo-isms*'. Although I was only a child, I sensed that there was something wrong about my father portraying our mother in such a derogatory way. But I was far too afraid of him to even think of arguing with him.

Once a meeting with our mother was arranged, our father gave us instructions as to how we should behave towards our mother on these occasions. He told us that if she offered us a present we should not take it. He justified this by saying it was because it would upset Caroline (who was by now being portrayed to us as our new mother). He also seemed to suggest that we should regard any offer of a present from our mother as a kind of bribe that we should not accept.

Again, I sensed that there was something wrong with this instruction, but I feared my father so much that I did what I was told. This meant that when our mother produced a Beano comic book as a gift during one of our next visits, I told her I did not want it. She asked me why not? I could not look her in the eye nor give her a straight answer. She was never one to force us to do anything and so after Fin also refused to take it, she reluctantly and quietly put the present back in her bag.

I remember feeling shame that I had done something wrong but I was not sure what that something was.

When our mother tried to give us money, we refused to take this too. I felt conflicted, not just because I felt shame, but also because I could think of a million things I wanted to buy with the money she was offering. Despite this, and in fear of my father, I said no. When my mother looked at me I felt like she knew that we were only refusing her because our father had told us to. Why else do a couple of young boys refuse presents from their mother? As she put the money back in her purse, she looked tired and frustrated. I was sad and confused.

After these visits with our mother, which would last no more than a few hours, we reported back to our father that we had refused to take her presents. We were rewarded for our efforts. Even though it felt wrong to do these things, we were conflicted since our father commended us and he and Caroline gave us fizzy drinks and crisps.

Fin

As well as instructing us how to behave with our Mam, Caroline and our father ordered us, whenever we went to visit her, to wear clothes that Caroline, and not our Mam, had bought us. Caroline would inspect us before we left the house and ensure our hair was brushed flat on our heads with a side parting. This was different from our natural curly haired look we had under our Mam's care. Our father told us that if our Mam asked us why we looked different we were to say that *this was how Caroline dresses us.*

I felt that as I now lived with my father and Caroline, I was expected to be a willing member of *Team Dad*. I didn't ask nor want to be on his team but that is where I found myself. When he ordered me to do things, regardless of how it made me feel, I felt like I was trapped into complying. I didn't really care what way my hair was or what clothes I wore so complying with these orders was easy enough. But the more we complied, the more daring our father became with his orders and they soon escalated to a level I could not accept. On one occasion, as I was being inspected prior to visiting our Mam, he coolly stated his latest order to me:

If your mother goes to give you a hug, don't hug her back.

Usually I didn't dare talk back to him but when he said that to me I felt I wouldn't be able to carry out his order. I protested meekly that our Mam always hugged me the minute she saw me and I asked him *how I was expected to avoid her hugs?*

If she tries to hug you, just duck out of the hug, he answered, *it's for your own good, you need to stop letting her mollycoddle you. Don't hug your mother.*

I knew I wouldn't be able to do what he ordered but nodded as if I understood. The next time we visited Mam; I ignored his instructions and hugged my Mam anyway. Both Gar and Shane were there and witnessed me disobeying our father's instructions. On the walk home, Shane started mocking me, saying I was a Mammy's boy and how *she was always mollycoddling me.* He sounded like my father and I thought maybe he was under instructions from my father to police my behaviour and give me this speech if I disobeyed orders. After Shane mocked me, I walked behind Gar and Shane, fighting back tears.

Another time, Gar and I visited our Mam without Shane. As 'the policeman' wasn't there, I acted naturally with my Mam and hugged her. As we walked home, Gar said that he thought I had done something wrong. I pleaded with him that I hadn't and begged him not to tell our father. He seemed conflicted himself and he admitted that he didn't know why we couldn't accept hugs from our Mam either. I hoped this meant that he wouldn't be mentioning it to our father.

However, shortly after arriving home, my father was shouting for me. As I stood before him he roared at me that I needed to grow up and stop being *mollycoddled.* I felt bad but I didn't feel guilty. I decided that there must be something wrong with me giving my Mam hugs. Why else would Shane and my father condemn my actions? Why would Gar not keep the hugs secret unless they were wrong? It was all very confusing for me as a young boy but I knew I would have to work on it if I was going to survive in that environment.

Later I argued with Gar as to why he had told our father that I had accepted a hug from our Mam. He said awkwardly that my father just *got it out of him.* He said he didn't mean to say it.

30

The next time we met our Mam I felt as though I had no option but to comply with the non-acceptance of hugs from her. The only way I could do this was to convince myself that my father was right; I was a bad person if I accepted hugs or presents from my Mam. The problem was that I equally felt like I was a bad person if I didn't accept her hugs, since I knew that this would hurt my Mam. Furthermore, I wanted to accept the hugs and the presents. What ten-year-old boy doesn't?

Before the next visit, my father spoke to me in a friendly tone and told me that our Mam was *no good* as a mother to me. He said it was for my own good that I follow his instructions and that I would thank him for it when I was older. He made me feel like his previous anger was merely borne out of frustration that I just couldn't see how right he was.

For this particular visit, we were to meet our Mam outside a petrol station, a ten-minute walk from our house. As my Mam didn't drive we expected that she would probably take us somewhere close within walking distance. I was wearing a pair of blue jeans with a white patch on the knee, which had a design on it. These were "good jeans", which Caroline had bought me and told me to wear on this visit to Mam.

As we approached our Mam, she went to put her arm around me and I tried to manoeuvre out of the hug, as I had been instructed to do. But I couldn't look at my Mam when I did this so I focused on the patch on the jeans and just stared at the patch as I ducked out of the hug. I could hear my Mam asking me, in a hurt and concerned voice:

What's wrong?

I can still hear her say it as clear as day as I think about it now. It still makes me feel very sad.

I kept my head down staring at my knee patch, trying to tell myself in my head that she was a bad person. Gar and Shane said their 'Hello's' to her and presumably avoided her attempted hugs. I didn't watch. I just stared down at the patch. This was the first time I sincerely wanted my visit with my Mam to be over as soon as possible.

We walked up to a restaurant in a nearby shopping centre. While we were there, my Mam took out a comic book to give it to Gar. He declined the gift and she was visibly upset. The book was for both of us so she turned around and said:

Fin you'll take the comic book, won't you?

I looked at the ground and shook my head, indicating a negative response. I can't imagine the emotions she was feeling.

When the visit ended, I returned to my father's house and relayed to him that I had shrugged out of the hugs. He was absolutely thrilled. I was treated to a glass of red lemonade and a packet of crisps, as was Gar. I felt like I was learning how to live in this environment now and tried to forget the guilt caused by having upset my Mam. But deep down I was utterly saddened that I had to resort to this behaviour in order to survive. I began to realise that it was possible that I was trapped here until adulthood which seemed like an absolute lifetime away. I wasn't sure I could last that long living with my father.

The next time we visited Mam, she didn't attempt to hug me. She asked me did I want a hug and I looked at the ground and said *No*. She said that that was okay. This at least made the visit less awkward. My Mam was making me feel like she wasn't upset about me not returning or accepting her hugs. It seemed our Mam's approach was a very simple one: to make the visits as enjoyable an experience for us as possible, despite our father's negative influence.

Chapter 6

Gar

When we moved back in with our father, it soon became apparent that a policy of *'Erase and Replace'* was being implemented with great vigour by our father and Caroline. Every room in the house was ripped apart and refurbished with the effect that it removed all trace of our Mam. The visits with our Mam seemed to dwindle out as we were constantly discouraged from visiting her and told to act in certain ways when we did go to visit her. Our mother then told us that she had to go away for a period to find God. This was very confusing for us and our father interpreted it to us as meaning that our mother *had abandoned us.* He regularly repeated this comment which was usually followed up with him telling us how lucky we were to have Caroline and how she was a much better mother than our own mother. If we so much as flinched at that comment in a negative way, there was serious trouble and we were accused of being *ungrateful bastards.* But it was hard not to flinch because the reality was that Caroline was the exact opposite of motherly to us.

Very quickly we recognised that living with Caroline was going to be much different to living with our Mam. Caroline was a martinet. So much so, one of our uncles took to giving her the Nazi salute when he had a few drinks, much to everyone's amusement, except Caroline who was not amused.

We were given tasks to contribute to the household chores and failure to conduct those tasks meant you were on the receiving end of punishment. At the weekend and at special times we were given chocolate bars, crisps or other treats from the treat jar. There was no treat jar when we lived with our mother so when I saw the treat jar full of biscuits and sweets in the kitchen I was delighted. I regarded this as a welcome development but I soon discovered that although the treats were on display, it did not mean that we could just take a treat whenever we wanted. Caroline counted the biscuits and treats and they were dispensed by her entirely under her strict control.

Within a few weeks of the treat jar going on display, Caroline and our father summoned me, Fin and Shane to the kitchen and told us that a Penguin bar had gone missing from the jar. Caroline angrily demanded that the culprit confess who had stolen it and when she was met with silence; she and our father executed a kind of trial-by-ordeal. The trial took the form of an interrogation which was both verbal and physical, with our father employing a leather horsewhip that he had to whip us on the hands and backside accompanied by Caroline screaming at us to tell her who stole the bar. We were encouraged to tell them who the culprit was and would be rewarded for doing so. Eventually, after fruitless attempts to get us to confess or to rat on each other, they decided that Fin was responsible and he was punished with a pretty severe thrashing and sent to bed early. Years later, Shane admitted to us that he had actually taken the Penguin bar.

Caroline counted everything in the kitchen, even going to the trouble of counting the slices of bread in a sliced pan and counting the Weetabix in a packet to ensure she could keep track of what we ate. A great show was made every year when Caroline would make a Christmas pudding and a Christmas cake. These would be put in a biscuit tin in the press under the strict instruction that we were *not* to help ourselves to them – we were only to eat what we were permitted to eat by Caroline. This usually resulted in half of the cake and pudding mouldering in the biscuit tin until eventually in September or October, Caroline would throw them both out having deemed them gone off. We could only watch on in frustration, thinking about how we would have happily eaten them earlier in the year had we been permitted to do so.

****

Fin and I both wet the bed when we moved back in with our father and he employed physical punishment to try and knock this behaviour out of us. He used his horsewhip to punish us whenever we wet the bed. Ten lashes of the whip on the palm of my hand or on my backside was enough to reduce me to tears and leave a red welt on the palm of my hand or backside. It also had the effect of making me really, really not want to wet the bed but this desire did not necessarily translate into a dry bed in the morning. I tried to play mind games with myself to stop the bedwetting. Before falling asleep and after saying my prayers, I would repeat the mantra *I will not wet the bed* 200 times.

Unsurprisingly, this methodology had the exact opposite effect to what was desired.

One particular school morning, when I was in sixth class, I woke up with my pyjamas soaked through. I was afraid of my father finding out I had wet the bed so I simply put on my school uniform and went to school as if nothing had happened. Unfortunately, as I did not have a shower, the wetness from my leg soaked through my school trousers which I noticed when I got into school. I then spent most of the morning with my leg against a radiator in an effort to dry the trouser leg out. My strange behaviour did not escape the attention of some of my classmates; neither did the smell of dried urine that clung to me for the rest of the day.

****

It was during my final year in primary school in 1990 that I had my first romantic engagement with a girl when I attended a Halloween disco in the local parish hall. There were two girls there from my primary school class who were dressed as female Gardaí. One of their fathers was a Garda and they had borrowed the long jackets and hats from him. I found the idea of a girl dressed as a Garda very attractive so when one of the girls told me that the other girl fancied me I managed to work up the courage to give her a kiss in the corner of the parish hall.

I spent a weekend elated at this experience and had a few more snogs with this girl who lived in a nearby estate. Pretty soon Shane found out about this and thought it was hilarious and told our father about *Gar and his girlfriend*. My father was not happy with this development and told me in no uncertain terms that I needed to stop meeting this girl and *concentrate on my studies*. I obeyed my father and avoided the girl for a couple of weeks until she confronted me in front of others in the school playground. She asked me straight out why I was avoiding her. When I admitted it was because my father had told me not to see her any more she accused me of being a *'Daddy's boy'* and started taunting me with calls of *'Daddy's boy'* over and over again. With everything that was going on at the time I did not react well to this taunt and burst out crying and told her that *I was a 'Daddy's boy' because my Mam had abandoned me*. This created an awkward situation for everyone and unsurprisingly the girl in question never approached me again

At around this time, in early 1991, I was moving from primary school to secondary school so I sat entrance exams for two of the local secondary schools in the area. The first entrance exam I did was for Templeogue College, a non-fee paying local school. Caroline, who was still learning to drive and was a very nervous driver, gave me a lift to the school to sit the exam. On the way there, Caroline got lost and we ended up driving around a roundabout a number of times before we eventually arrived just in time for the exam. I sat the exam in something of a tizzy.

A few weeks later my father got a letter from the school saying that I had not got the required grades for the school to offer me a place. This was surprising as I was regularly top of my class in a number of subjects. Our father said he was disappointed with me but said that the reason I had not passed the examination was because of the journey to the exam which he claimed had not helped to settle my nerves. He said that to make sure I was settled the next time; he would personally drive me to the next entrance exam which was for the local fee-paying school, Terenure College.

I was very nervous on the drive to the school as my father left me in no doubt that having failed the other entrance exam that there was now considerable pressure to pass this entrance exam. When we arrived at the school, I found a desk and sat down in the middle of a large hall full of other kids my age chewing their pens in anticipation. When I got the papers I settled in well and was relieved that I could answer most of the questions easily. However, midway through the exam, I realised that I needed to go to the toilet. I tried to ignore it and hoped the feeling would go away but the need just intensified. I looked around to see if there was a sign for the toilet but could not see one anywhere. I also did not see anybody else asking to go to the toilet. I began to get worried. What if I was not allowed go to toilet? Maybe I could be expelled from the exam if I even asked? The teachers that were invigilating the exam seemed stern and unfriendly to me and I thought of my father. What would he say if I was expelled for asking to go to the toilet? At this stage I began to panic and in my state of fear I urinated on the seat in the middle of the examination hall. Once I started I could not stop the flow and felt the warmth of the urine spreading into the seat of my pants and down my leg. With crushing embarrassment, I realised that a pool of urine had collected on the floor under my chair and that the people sitting around me could see it. I started to cry.

When the bell sounded for the end of the first exam I sat at my chair for a while hoping everyone would leave the hall. When I thought most of the students were gone, I lifted my wet backside off the chair and saw a pool had formed on the chair and on the ground. I ran to the bathroom to try to dry myself off but with little success. I had arranged to meet my father during the interval and we stood and talked for half an hour. I made sure to stand with my back to the wall so that he could not see that I had wet my pants as I was afraid of what his reaction would be. As we stood there talking I saw a boy who had sat behind me pointing at me and laughing with some of his friends. I silently prayed my father didn't notice them or my cheeks turning bright red. At the end of the interval, I went back into the examination hall and sat back down on the wet seat. The urine was now cold and even more uncomfortable. After the exam, my father collected me and we went home where I got changed, seemingly with my secret intact. When the results came out, I had passed and was offered a place in the school.

However, my father and Caroline were very keen for me to go to the non-fee-paying school and not so keen on my going to the fee-paying school. They discussed the matter openly and spoke of how Fin would most likely go to the school I went to and therefore there would be two sets of school fees if I went to the fee-paying school and two sets saved if I went to non-fee-paying school. My father therefore made an application to non-fee-paying school to reconsider their refusal to offer me a place based on my results in primary school and recommendations from the teachers there. The school did reconsider and offered me a place which was accepted. Caroline and our father seemed much relieved at this. I was also secretly relieved, as I had been afraid that if I went to other school, all the boys would know me as the boy who wet his pants in the entrance exam. I understandably wanted to stay as far away from that school as possible.

Throughout the following six years in Templeogue College and for many years after, my father never missed an opportunity to remind me: *I got you into that school.*

Fin

From the first day Gar and I moved back into our father's house, Caroline struck me as an angry, unkind and unhappy person. She seemed to go out of her way to be mean to us and I decided early on that this was because she resented us. We seemed to make her angry by just being there.

Most days, Caroline arrived home from work visibly angry and frustrated and she appeared to use things as an excuse to vent all her frustration at us. To avoid angering her, particularly in the early days, I tried to live up the standards I thought she wanted but no matter what I did, Caroline always found different things to give out to me about. She would walk into our room and root around until she found something to use as a reason to shout and scream at us. It might be an unwashed teacup left on a desk, scribbled-on schoolbooks, a torn jumper or jacket, mucky shoes or sweet wrappers from an unknown source. We would pace around downstairs nervously waiting to see what would be the issue of each particular day. Merely not opening my bedroom window was enough for a night of ranting and screaming on one occasion.

Sometimes, since we were extremely careful to not give her any excuse to give out, she would not find anything, despite having paced around frantically in our bedroom searching for something. I would often come into my room to find it ransacked, with the presses open and clothes and books on the floor. If she was unable to find anything in the room, she would accuse us of not having done our chores up to standard. She would claim the hoovering was not done properly, or the kitchen benches or bathroom had not been properly cleaned by one of us or that her bed had not been made to perfection. This was a good result for us as we knew if she was resorting to chores then she had really nothing on us and was simply desperate for something to give out about. We could take the shouts and screams, then go off and re-do whatever it was that apparently wasn't done to the standards required, and that might just be the end of it for that evening.

Mostly I felt like I didn't deserve the punishment since I tried so very hard to please her and have my jobs done up to standard and not give her anything to give out about. When I felt I did deserve to be given out to, it wasn't as bad as I could understand why it was happening. When I put the heating on when I came home from school to warm up, I knew I was taking a risk and asking for trouble. The heating was only to be put on shortly before my father or Caroline was due home so the house would be warm enough for them. But it was not to be put on for us and Caroline would sometimes know if I had put it on for longer than I should have as there would be more hot water in the storage tank than there should have been. She would put her hand against the tank to test it. I genuinely believed I deserved to be given out to for that as I had essentially 'robbed heat' that they paid for.

I was constantly frustrated as I felt I didn't deserve the tirades of abuse she directed at me. There was one instance of her excessive shouting a few months after I moved in where I cried in frustration so much so that Caroline had mercy on me. She had been ranting at me about not performing a chore to her standards and I was sure I had done everything right. I was so frustrated that as I cried, I simply told her that I gave up. I said that I couldn't see how useless I was so the problem was worse than she even thought. I told her I had tried my very best and I simply couldn't have performed the chore any better. Since it wasn't good enough, I was clearly incapable of being a good boy in any way. I genuinely believed what I was saying too. As I stood there crying on the landing, Caroline stopped giving out and hugged me and told me I wasn't useless and that I was a good boy. I felt so emotionally relieved and happy at the time that despite all the ranting that had happened previously, I warmed to Caroline as she hugged me.

Unfortunately, things returned to normal and very soon, she was screaming at me about something else and calling me *a useless bastard* again. But I knew there was a chance she could return to be the nice person who had showed me warmth that day and I longed for it.

One thing that I was very conflicted about when it came to punishment was when I wet the bed. I just couldn't work out if I deserved it or not. I knew I couldn't help wetting the bed, but I always felt like I needed to somehow figure out how to stop. I felt Caroline was right when she said it was a *filthy* and *disgusting*. But I disagreed that I was a *lazy bastard* since I would gladly get up and relieve myself in the bathroom if only I could wake up before I soiled my bed.

I can't remember when I started wetting the bed, but I temporarily stopped when Gar and I lived with our Mam. I was quite proud of myself when I was permitted to sleep over in my friend's house on the road because I no longer wet the bed. Unfortunately, the bedwetting started again when I moved back into the house with Caroline and my father.

The bedwetting seemed to worsen with the constant chastising that followed my unsuccessful attempts to stop, which in turn resulted in further and more severe chastising. It was difficult getting hit with a horsewhip and screamed at by Caroline and my father that I was a *lazy bastard* for not getting up to go to the bathroom during the night.

Our father usually got angry if a link between bedwetting and parental break-up was ever suggested in the media. This was in line with his anger at any person or form of media that raised a point that he disagreed with or that didn't suit him. When a programme came on the television suggesting that kids were affected in any negative way by parental break-up, he would change the channel, dismissing angrily such talk simply as *a load of shite*.

So it didn't surprise me when our protestations that it wasn't our choice or wish to wet the bed were met with similar dismissal and we were called *lying bastards* for suggesting it was anything other than laziness.

Since I couldn't stop wetting the bed, I began to try and cover it up. Although this wasn't a step that I wished to resort to, it was unavoidable given the circumstances. A ritual therefore took place after every bedwetting incident whereby after I got up I would first assess the severity of the wetness and decide whether the mattress needed to be turned over. Then I would take the bed sheet off and switch the top end with the bottom end, so that the soiled area of the sheet would be further towards the bottom of the bed (I was a small child, so the soiled area was usually closer to the top of the sheet). I would hide my wet pyjamas and have a wash. If Caroline and my father were not in the house, I would have a full 'open' shower. Otherwise, if they were there, I would have a secret wash with the showerhead held in the bath so as not to arouse suspicion as to why I was having a shower. It was unusual for me to have a shower in the morning or anytime other than after playing sport. This elaborate cover-up procedure provided a Band-Aid solution for a period.

As Caroline seemed almost disappointed when it appeared I had stopped bedwetting, I felt that she didn't genuinely want the bedwetting to stop; rather she seemed to relish the excuse it provided to shout and scream at us. Noticeably, when the cover up was working, she would pace around frantically in my room, searching high and low for something else to have a go at me over.

Inevitably, Caroline discovered that I had tried to cover up the bedwetting. I had been *getting away with it* for a few weeks now and Caroline had already started rooting through my room, looking for something to give out about. As I paced around downstairs, hearing her footsteps overhead in the bedroom, I feared the worst.

Fin, get your arse up here now! She shrieked at me from upstairs.

This became a familiar refrain throughout the years living with Caroline.

These words always terrified me, because it was usually the unknown that I faced. It might be a simple thing, like that teacup left on my desk that I could apologise profusely for and fix the problem by bringing it downstairs and accepting the angry condescending words that would be directed at me. But it also might be the empty Mars bar wrapper from the Mars bar that my friend in school bought me that I would find impossible to explain. If I said my friend bought it, I was accepting charity, and this was seen as portraying them as stingy and therefore bad people.

As a result, I would have to lie and say that I found money or something along those lines, but holes could be picked in my story as the inquest grew and grew. It was this sort of thing that made for a tricky situation, one with no solution really. When there was no way of explaining something, then it was best to stop trying to explain. This led to a stand-off where I would be the bad guy until a significant time had elapsed, or until I came up with an explanation that didn't conflict with them being portrayed as terrific people.

On this occasion, I arrived at the top of the stairs and looked in to see my duvet had been torn back off my bed to reveal a stain on the sheet where it had been soiled and turned and the duvet put over it to hide it. I knew immediately that this was one of those tricky situations. Caroline shouted obscenities at me:

Filthy lazy devious, conniving, little shit!

I was surprised when she asked me angrily why I didn't simply tell her that I had wet the bed and own up to my laziness. I protested that I would be in all sorts of trouble if I had owned up so I had tried to cover it up to avoid the confrontation. This wasn't the sort of explanation that was going to end this, and so I was chastised and treated like an unruly convict for a few days.

This form of punishment was particularly frustrating. It meant not being talked to unless in an extremely derogative way or while being ordered to do something. I would also be talked about as if I wasn't there, in such a way that was designed to provoke me. I considered this to be Caroline's speciality. A good example was when we were all sat around the dinner table.

She often said things like:

Filthy little fucker slept in his own piss rather than change the sheets,

to which I would immediately want to shout back protesting that I couldn't change the sheets as I would be given ten lashes and called all sorts of names. That was the type of bait I learnt not to take and instead I just got on with it nodding and agreeing that I was all those things that she called me. She also would say these things as if I was not sitting there, right in front of her. It completely wore down my self-esteem and any sense of self-worth.

If I did shout back, which I foolishly did occasionally, she would look at our father and say something like:

Do you see the shite I have to listen to?

Then he would shout at me, saying:

How dare you!

and
after all that she does for you! This is how you repay her?

These episodes simply made me feel worthless.

One weekend during the on-going bedwetting episodes, we went to visit our Nanny and Grandad a day or two after I had wet the bed and was being given the 'unruly convict' treatment. When we arrived at our Nanny's house, my Nanny was her usual caring self and immediately picked up that I was down in the dumps. She asked me what the matter was, and I wouldn't tell her, fearing that this was one of those things that we didn't tell people outside our house for fear of giving the *wrong* appearance.

When I didn't respond, my Nanny asked our father, who told her:

Ah he's too lazy to get outta' bed at night so instead he wets the bed and sleeps in it. Disgusting.

Our Nanny looked very annoyed with our father and immediately came over and hugged me and scolded our father.

She spoke firmly. *It's the nerves causing him to wet the bed.*

If it was any other person other than his own mother who had said that, I suspect he probably would have argued back and never spoke to that person again. As it was his mother who had contradicted him, he simply ignored the comment as if she hadn't said it. But that day I felt some form of vindication, that at least someone believed me. It restored some self-worth, knowing that no matter what our father or Caroline told other people about me, my Nanny knew that I wasn't *a lazy bastard* and that there was maybe another reason for the bedwetting.

Chapter 7

Gar

As part of Caroline's disciplinary regime, we were given chores which we were to complete every day when we came home from school, including preparing the dinner. Both Caroline and our father worked, and Caroline would usually arrive home earlier than our father to make sure we had completed our chores and that the dinner was ready for our father when he got home, as he expected.

She divided up the household chores between me and Fin. One week I would clean the kitchen, the bathroom and hoover the house while Fin would clean the dining room, our parents' bedroom (including making their bed every day) and be in charge of washing, drying and folding the clothes. Every week we would switch these tasks between us. In addition, we were put to ironing and every Sunday, while they were in the pub, one of us would be responsible for ironing our father's five shirts and Caroline's nurse's uniform and cardigan for the following week. We became intimately familiar with the contours of Caroline's female nurse's uniform, her slip and her cardigan - more familiar than we ever wished to be.

Cleaning Caroline and our father's bedroom sometimes involved sweeping pubic hairs off the sheets before tucking them in and plumping up the pillows.

Our father did not clean up after himself so cleaning his and Caroline's bedroom also involved picking up his dirty socks, boxer shorts, shirts and handkerchiefs from the ground, putting them in the wash, folding, sorting and putting them into his chest of drawers. While Caroline was not as bad as our father initially, she seemed to follow his lead and soon enough we had to pick up her dirty knickers and bras and pop socks and slips from the floor to go through the same washing and drying and folding cycle. We came to learn how Caroline liked her knickers folded and which drawer in her chest of drawers each pair of knickers was to be stored.

In addition to doing our regular morning chores before school, we were tasked with the elaborate chore of making our father's breakfast before we went to school. Every morning there was a routine. We would get up before our father and have our bowl of cereal, keeping our ears pricked for the sound of him stirring upstairs. Once we heard the bedroom door open and the bathroom door close, it was time to put on the porridge or heat up the milk for his Weetabix, put on the kettle, squeeze the orange juice, set the table and have the toast in the toaster ready to go. One of us would then sit on the stairs listening intently upstairs for the sound of him to leave the bathroom and re-enter the bedroom to get dressed for work.

Once this happened, the pot of tea needed to be prepared and placed on the table, his porridge needed to be poured and his bread needed to begin toasting. When our father would take his seat for his porridge, we had to ensure that his orange juice and his tea were all on the table with his toast almost ready so that it could be served warm and the butter would melt when he buttered it. In addition to this, his shoes needed to be polished and were to be left beside his chair, so he could put them on after breakfast. Once breakfast was served to his satisfaction, one of us would hang out the clothes on the line while the other tidy the bathroom which involved rinsing our father's stubble and shaving water down the sink and tidying away our father's shaving gear, toothbrush, hairbrush and other accoutrements.

Only once all of those tasks were complete were we then permitted to go to school. The rest of the chores would be waiting for us when we returned from school and these had to be done immediately upon our arrival home.

The breakfast duties had to be completed even during Lent, when Fin and I were sent to early morning mass every morning. Caroline and our father never went to mass themselves; our father used to say that he wanted to go to mass but unfortunately, he was excommunicated as he was *living in sin.*

We got up at 6.30am and walked in the darkness to the church, attending the morning service with a generally much older crowd and walked back in near darkness to get home at 7.30am so that we could then carry on the morning ritual of making our father and Caroline's breakfast. A father of one of our friends also went to morning mass and took to giving us a lift whenever he saw us. He was a kindly widower and seemed to find it unusual that two boys would be sent to morning mass while their parents slept at home. He asked us once why our father did not go to mass with us, but we just

45

mumbled and did not give him an answer, fearing the only possible answers would not portray our father or Caroline in a good light.

Fin

Sometimes, instead of porridge, our father would have Shredded Wheat for his breakfast, which he demanded to be served to him with hot milk. When we had to heat the milk, this further complicated the process, as we had to ensure that the hot milk was served at the temperature our father demanded. The milk would take just under two minutes to heat in the microwave. Our father required that it was served at the exact same time that he sat down.

In order to gauge the exact right moment to put on my father's milk, I used to stand at the bottom of the stairs and wait until I heard the rustle of change indicating that he was putting his trousers on. That was the signal for me to run from the hall through the door into the dining room, and then take a right turn through the kitchen door and into the kitchen to press the "start" button on the microwave.

On one particular morning I was preparing the breakfast as usual, but I needed to go to the toilet. There was only one toilet in the house, in the upstairs bathroom which was occupied by my father. I dared not knock on the door and interrupt his morning shower and shave - this was strictly forbidden. There was nothing I could do but try to hold on until he was finished, and the bathroom was free.

As I fetched the teapot from the sitting room, where it had been since my father and Caroline's evening tea the night before, I heard the bathroom door open. Despite desperately needing to use the bathroom, I was behind schedule on the breakfast. I knew I needed to clean last night's tea-leaves out of the teapot, so it was ready for use. The tea needed to be served as soon as my father started eating the Shredded Wheat, at the same time as the toast was to be put on in the toaster. Our father demanded that we 'wet the teapot' by rinsing it with a splash of hot water before adding the tea leaves. We would have the tea made and sitting in the centre of the table with its tea cosy on it by the time our father sat down. This would allow it the necessary time to 'draw' and ensure it was just right for drinking when he ate his toast.

As well as all of these logistical concerns, my main worry on this occasion was the hot milk. I had yet to pour the milk into a mug to heat it up and I realised that there were no clean mugs as they were all in the dishwasher dirty. We were only permitted to put on the dishwasher every second evening. When we ran out of dishes before it was due to be put on, we were required to take the dirty dishes out of the dishwasher and wash them.

I knew time was not on my side. I took the dirty mug from the dishwasher, which was stinking, unsurprisingly as it had been sitting there in need of a wash. I used some of the boiling water from the kettle to wash the mug and I quickly opened the fridge and took out a carton of Golden Vale fat free milk. I was absolutely bursting to go to the toilet at this stage but knew I had to press on with my father's breakfast. I poured the milk into the mug but as I went to place the mug in the microwave, I could hold on no more, the floodgates opened, and I wet myself standing on the kitchen floor.

I was distressed but I was also acutely aware that this wasn't the most important thing to be concerned with at that moment. My father's breakfast remained of vital importance. I pressed 'Start' on the microwave and ran into the utility room where I found a used hand towel in the wash basket. I used this to clean up the small puddle of wee on the floor and to stop wee dripping from my pyjamas. The microwave beeped, and I quickly ran over to wash my hands before handling my father's food. However, I stopped myself and decided to not wash my hands, deliberately.

I took the mug of hot milk out of the microwave and was relieved to see no skin on top and that it hadn't overflowed in the microwave. I heard my father entering the dining room and I came out and placed the mug of hot milk in front of him, just in time. He showed no acknowledgement and poured it on his Shredded Wheat. I then ran back into the kitchen, pressed down the toaster and made the tea, which I placed in the centre of the table. I went back into the kitchen again and stood at the toaster, hidden from his view.

I reflected on the incident, inspecting my soiled pyjamas. I felt relieved that I had managed to not mess up the breakfast despite that incident. I was concerned however that Caroline would now have a reason to scream at me if she saw the wet pyjamas. She would surely accuse me of wetting the bed. I made myself feel a little bit better by bringing the toast into my father with my unwashed hands and placing it on his side plate. He was oblivious to the fact I was wearing soiled pyjamas.

I went upstairs to the bathroom and had a secret wash and got changed. I gathered the pyjamas and the towel and put them in the washing machine. I than filled the machine with the contents of the wash basket and put in the powder and the softener and twisted the switch to 'delicates'. I was in charge of the washing that week, so I figured if Caroline heard the washing machine when she woke up, she wouldn't see it as strange. I would also be home before anyone else, so I could ensure that I dried the pyjamas secretly.

I felt like I was covering up a crime that I had committed.

****

A year or two after we moved back in with our father, our Mam stopped renting the room in the house nearby and began to travel to faraway places such as Jerusalem and Gambia. We began to see her less and less. We did not know why she was travelling so much. Our father told us it was because she didn't care about us. It was very hard for us not to see some truth in what he said – if she loved us, why would she abandon us for so long on foreign holidays? But then when she was home and we did see her, she always acted lovingly towards us and seemed to miss us and really care about us.

Chapter 8

Fin

It took me quite a while to adapt to living with my father and Caroline. While Gar mostly complied with their demands and appeared to be able to adapt quite easily, I was the opposite. My inability to adapt to life without my Mam seemed to infuriate my father.

In 1989, when we were still living with our Mam, Gar went for trials for the under-eleven rugby team that would represent the local team in the community games. I went with him even though I knew I would be too young to play. I was only eight years of age and most of the players were ten. During the trials, I impressed the coaches. I was a very small child for my age, but the coaches told me that I was *more than a match for the older boys even though some of them are nearly twice the size of you.* The coach then apologised to me, saying that despite deserving a place on the squad, he didn't think it would be safe to pick me due to my size and age. I hadn't expected to be picked so I was thrilled when he stated that when I reached ten years of age, he guaranteed that he would make me the captain of the team of that year.

However, that year, when it came, was 1991. This was the same year Gar and I moved back in to live with our father. The trials for that years' community games team were on just as I was attempting to adapt to my new life. When I showed up for the trials, I was a mere shell of my former self. I couldn't bring myself to focus during a game. I spent the time on the pitch worrying about my life. My confidence was very low. My father and Caroline were in the process of breaking down any sense of self-worth I had, with their constant berating and belittling and my Mam was being pushed out of my life.

During the trials, we were put through our paces. I was awful; my head simply wasn't in it. One of the coaches asked me where the enthusiasm I used to have had gone. They seemed shocked that I had changed so much. I couldn't tell him what was wrong, knowing better than to tell an outsider that I was unhappy. I knew that if it ever got back to my father that I had told the coach I was unhappy; my father would react badly. I lived in great fear of this.

Perhaps based on the potential I had shown at the previous trials, the coach decided to name me in the squad anyway. I was relieved since my father had left me in no doubt that he wouldn't be happy if I hadn't made it.

I was also playing for a rugby club on Sundays in that year. My form with the club had also declined greatly. On the occasions that my father came to watch those matches, I would hear him shouting at me angrily on the side-line. After games when I played badly, on the drive home he would give out to me.

Stop being such a lazy bastard, he would demand angrily. *You need to be getting stuck in.*

My father showed his displeasure at my loss of form during a friendly game. He had arrived after kicking off to watch the game. I was standing on the side-line wearing my tracksuit. He came over to me and whispered in an angry tone.

Are you injured?

I shook my head.

Why aren't you playing? he asked, visibly getting angrier, but notably not wanting anybody else to hear him.

I went on the defensive, shrugging my shoulders stating that I didn't know. Thankfully he walked away, but I could tell he was furious. He didn't watch the game and instead just went back to his car. I came on for the end of the match and basically went through the motions. I was even less focused thinking of what was in store for me after the game. I heard no angry shouting from the side-line, which indicated that he had remained in his car. For whatever reason, he saved his anger for the journey home. After I got changed and I got into his car, he looked at me disgustedly.

The reason they aren't playing you, is because you're a lazy bastard, he said, *you've embarrassed me, coming out to watch you stand on the side-lines. You're like your mother, fuckin' Jo-isms. She bloody ruined you mollycoddling you all the time.*

I bowed my head and looked down at my feet nodding and saying I was sorry. I didn't fully understand why I was underperforming. I knew I was severely unhappy but, being only ten years of age, I didn't realise that my unhappiness affected everything I did. But my father seemed to be adamant to leave me in no doubt as to what he considered the problem to be: it was my all because of my Mam. He switched angrily between the mollycoddling, to me taking after my Mam and to her general bad influence as being reasons that caused me to be lazy, which in turn was why I wasn't playing well.

When we won the Dublin qualifiers, I was a sub. My father was livid with me for not making the starting team.

You don't deserve that fuckin' medal he said.

You were a sub; they should only give medals to the players who started the games.

The coach had told us we were all a team and we should all be proud of our contribution. I said to my father sheepishly that since I had played in some of the games, maybe I did deserve the medal.

He disagreed angrily:

You should be made to give that medal back, playing a few minutes of games. You're a lazy little bollix.

He was ranting furiously at me as I wept, so much so that even Caroline suggested he gave me a break.

Between myself and Gar, we had won a considerable number of medals and trophies playing rugby and they were all kept together *'on display'*. But my father wouldn't allow this medal to be included so I had to keep it hidden away in my sock press instead.

A few weeks later, our team qualified for the All Ireland finals. This time my father attended with Caroline. It was on in Mosney, which used to be called Butlins and was the place our father had met our Mam all those years ago. That fact wasn't lost on me at the time and was one of the many thoughts that swirled around in my head as I tried to get ready for our semi-final game.

I had been in and out of the team and playing in various positions, so I was unsure if I would be starting. To my disappointment, I wasn't picked. As the game started, I kept looking over at my father and Caroline trying to gauge how much trouble I would be in for not being picked. I noted that I could see all the parents of the other subs. I somehow knew that they wouldn't be in serious trouble for merely being substitutes. But I was beginning to realise that we weren't like other families.

I was completely distracted when our captain and star player, got injured and had to come off. I'm not sure if the coach noticed how distracted I was, but either way he chose another substitute to come on as his replacement. I saw my father looking over and I just looked at the ground. I wasn't even the first sub and I imagined he would soon be telling me how embarrassed he was and how I reminded him of our Mam.

I tried to keep it together. There was still hope I might be called to come on and maybe if I managed to score a heroic try, they would forget I didn't start. I was actually starting to hope that one of my team-mates would get injured, so I could come on. This made me think how my father and Caroline were possibly right about their constant assertions that I was a *selfish bastard*. But there were no further injuries and I didn't get called upon. We also lost the game narrowly.

When the final whistle blew, all the other players went over to their parents and I noticed how they were being consoled and told they did their best. As I started to walk over to Caroline and my father, fearing the worst, I burst out crying. They looked embarrassed, particularly Caroline. She was first to speak, asking me why I was crying. I told them that I knew I had embarrassed them by not being picked and how sorry I was. My father looked extremely awkward. People were turning around and looking. He gave a fake smile and told me to stop crying, saying loudly my tears were caused by the emotion of coming so close to winning. I wasn't sure at the time why I wasn't being shouted at. I was sobbing and saying I didn't care about winning but that I didn't want to be in trouble for embarrassing them. My father and Caroline just looked at me uncomfortably.

At that moment someone handed me a brand-new sports bag. I turned around to see everyone on our team had one. A team-mate's father owned a gym and kindly gave us all sports bags bearing the gym's logo. My team-mate's father told me I should cheer up and that we could still come third in Ireland if we won a playoff game. I looked at my father and Caroline and they were nodding nervously in agreement and ushering me away from them. I was very relieved, although I was also very confused. I couldn't work out why my not being picked was not a crime this time when it had been previously.

****

One evening after rugby training, my father was supposed to pick me up. It was at least a thirty-minute walk home for me from the training pitches, too far for a ten-year-old to walk, especially at night time when it was getting dark. Despite this, on several occasions my father didn't show up or showed up an hour or so late. He was never apologetic. One evening I gave up waiting for him and I just walked home. When I arrived home, he was getting out of his car and shouted at me.

Where the hell were you? I've just been up to pick you up. I've been driving around since looking for you.

I shouted back at him:

What do you expect me to do, half the time you don't show up, it was getting dark! What am I supposed to do, sit there all night?

He went ballistic. He dragged me inside to the hall and closed the door. He pushed me up against the wall, his left hand gripping the front of the top I was wearing by the collar.

How Dare You? he said angrily, raising his right hand back behind his head in a threatening manner while staring at me intensely.

Let me tell you one thing, kid, you don't want to fuck with me.

I was crying, scared out of my wits, waiting for that hand to come down and feel the sharp sting on my face.

Do you want to fuck with me? he shouted menacingly, moving his face closer to me, while maintaining his rigid stare. I could smell his bad breath in my face.

No, I sobbed, *I'm sorry.*

What did you say? he said, tilting his head as if to position it so as to hear me clearer, even though he had quite obviously heard me.

I said I'm sorry, I said hesitantly. I was struggling under the pressure to form a sentence to confirm that I didn't want to "fuck with him", but without using those same profanities, which would only worsen the situation.

Go up and have your shower he said lowering his tone in a manner that suggested he had let me away with something. He let go of me, lowering his hand to his side.

I ran up the stairs, relieved that he hadn't hit me. But he sent a clear message - to *fuck with him* meant to not argue, contradict, mock, annoy, get in the way of, distract, or just in any way burden him physically, emotionally or financially.

This message was drilled into me again and again over the years.

After another training session some weeks later, I was sitting on the grass beside the pitch, again waiting. After what seemed a long time, there was still no sign of him. All the other kids had been picked up and were gone. I sat there watching the sky get darker and darker. I stared down the road wondering if the next car might be his. The darker it got, the scarier the proposition of walking home became. But having waited as long as I could, I decided walking was the only option even though there were enough secluded areas and unlit alleyways on the journey to make it a scary enough prospect in the dark as a ten-year-old.

As I set off, I was worried that my father would show up just after I left. But if I waited and he didn't show up, I would be questioned why I didn't *just walk home*. Over the years living with Caroline and my father, I was constantly placed in these situations where I was wrong if I did and I was wrong if I didn't. As Shane used to always say, *it was a catch-22 situation.*

54

As I walked across the green, I saw a car coming down the road and it seemed to slow down as I arrived at the road. I hesitated for a moment and the car continued on into the estate.

As I continued walking, I thought about what might have happened if the car had stopped in front of me and someone had tried to coax me into the car. Some years before the separation, Philip Cairns' disappearance had caused a huge furore in our area and I thought about how worried my Mam had been around that time, constantly ensuring she knew my whereabouts when I went out to play. I considered that nobody cared about my whereabouts now as I walked home.

I wondered would my father care if I was coaxed into a car and never seen again. I doubted it, but I figured I would never know unless it happened. I then mused at the idea of making up a story of how it nearly happened and seeing his reaction. I figured it could at least divert the attention away from the fact that I had walked home and not waited on him to pick me up so when I was halfway down my road, I decided I was going to do it. I was going to tell my father and Caroline that a kidnapper tried to abduct me, and I had run away.

However, when I arrived home, the only person in the house was Shane. I looked at Shane and I considered whether to ditch the plan.

I asked him where my father and Caroline were, and Shane said that they were down in the *Delany's*. *Delany's* was the local pub and it was actually right beside the football pitches where I had been sitting on the grass waiting all that time. It made sense to me at that stage why my father hadn't come to collect me. I guessed that they probably decided on the way to go in for a drink. Then they probably decided to stay there drinking.

As they were not at home I decided to tell the story to Shane:

I was walking through the green near the school and a man pulled up in a car at the road near the school and offered me sweets, I said.

I immediately began crying. I was already worrying that this was going to backfire spectacularly.

Shane was shocked and immediately rang *Delany's* and told my father and Caroline the news. I knew it was being taken seriously when Caroline and my father came home shortly afterwards. They praised Shane for contacting them and Shane told them how he was ready to go down, find the kidnapper and *batter him*. My father was agreeing with him.

In the midst of the madness, I remember noting that this was one of the few times I had ever seen Shane praised by either my father or Caroline before. Despite the apparent awfulness of the situation, Shane was almost smiling every time our father told him he did the right thing by ringing them.

Someone then rang the Gardaí. I hadn't bargained for that and got a bit nervous.

The Gardaí called up to the house and we drove around the area with them where I was instructed to look out for the kidnapper's car. I felt bad about wasting the Gardaí's time and was sure they would realise I was making it all up. When we arrived home, I heard the Garda telling my father that there were some cars going around the area trying to pick up kids and to be careful. This corroborated my story. I thought that perhaps I wasn't the only kid who had tried this and that in reality were no *'cars going around'* at all. Before he left, the Garda turned around and smiled at me and told me to take care.

When he was gone, my father and Caroline said I had done the right thing by running away from the car. Before long, I was sitting with a glass of lemonade and a packet of crisps. My plan had worked - I had not got given out to for walking home and there was no mention of why my father had not come to pick me up. I was more relieved than happy. I couldn't actually believe I had gone through with it.

I remember when Gar was told about it. He looked at me in a way that told me that he thought that I had made the whole thing up. But he said nothing, perhaps understanding why I did it and perhaps he was grateful for an evening without conflict in the house for once. I think he knew that all I was trying to do was survive and make my life tolerable at least for a short while.

Chapter 9

Fin

I hated not living with my Mam. I hated living with my father and Caroline. I felt like I was stuck in a trap with absolutely no way out and I couldn't even let this view be known. I was perceptive enough to know at this stage if I had hinted that I still loved and missed my Mam, it would enrage our father. I wanted to tell the world how I really felt so someone might help me out. But my father had me in a position where it was impossible for me to do that.

When I went to school, I seemed to start to take out my anger on my teacher. I couldn't breathe at home without being chastised severely. School was different. I began to cause disturbances in class and while the teacher would scold me, it didn't have any effect on me. I guess it was like if you were bitten by a lion, when a Jack Russell barks at you, you're not really going to pay attention to it. Just the previous year, I had been one of the best students in the class and well-liked by my teacher. Now, I was bottom of the class and a torment to my teacher. As I was ten years of age, I wasn't consciously doing any of this for any particular reason. Still today, I don't fully understand it. I just know that I was deeply unhappy.

Unfortunately for me, schools have parent-teacher meetings. My teacher had to give feedback to my father and Caroline that my behaviour was far from satisfactory. After these bad reports, I was given the severest of punishments. There was no discussion regarding how I might be feeling about the separation or if I was missing my Mam. Instead I was confronted by my father with furious screaming and shouting about what a disgrace I was, how I was just like my mother and needed my *Jo-isms* kicked out of me and how I was *an ungrateful prick, after all he and Caroline had done for me*. I was then taken over his knee and made bare my backside as my father took the leather belt he was wearing off his Wrangler jeans and ferociously spanked me with it.

He was often angry with me and his anger was frightening. But there was something about this anger, the sheer venom, that I perceived it as being the angriest I had ever seen him. It was as if my behaviour in school was a direct attack on him. The beating stung incredibly. I was then sent to bed where I cowered gratefully. My backside was left severely bruised from the thrashing. The following Sunday, my father forbade me to use the changing rooms to change for rugby training. Instead, he insisted that I change in the car beforehand. He feared that someone would notice the bruises. I was black and blue from my backside to halfway down the back of my legs.

He advised me that I should ensure that nobody noticed the bruises. He told me that if someone saw them, that I might end up in a children's home. I considered very seriously that living in a children's home would be a positive change for me. I imagined while it wouldn't be ideal, it would certainly be a step up from the living arrangements I currently had. I felt a children's home would put me as an equal with other children there. I would have company who understood the good or bad of mine and their lives.

Although my father had previously hit me across the face and punched me in the arm and body before, this was the most painful corporal punishment up to this point that I can remember. In terms of pain, Caroline's wooden spoon punishment was fairly painful too. I was forced to put my hand out, palm up, and she whacked it with the wooden spoon. She seemed to take great pleasure in causing this pain to me. This often left me with black and blue hands and an inability to use them for long periods afterwards. I often found it difficult to write for my homework as my hand simply wouldn't grip the pen. My father's horsewhip to the hand was also painful. My father used to speak openly about how he wouldn't hit me directly in the head since a blow to the head could cause concussion or worse. He made it sound like I was supposed to be grateful.

I still look back and feel disappointed that I wasn't brave enough to just say something to someone. I knew what was happening was wrong. But I also knew my father had a way of persuading people to believe his lies. I remember thinking about ringing Child-line but being afraid. If I was caught, I imagined I would be punished severely. I also wasn't sure if our situation warranted a call to Child-line. I was acutely aware though, that if I was to call Child-line, the best time would be after my father had given me one of these physical punishments.

But in the end, I was always the most afraid after one of these episodes.

Either way, my father's punishment didn't cause me to return to the good, well-behaved child I had been prior to moving back in with our father. On one occasion, I took a box of matches from our house and went into the bathroom in my classroom with some paper and set fire to the paper. It was obviously very dangerous and foolish as I left the paper burning and left the bathroom. Within a minute the class smelt of smoke and the teacher evacuated the classroom. The teacher investigated to find the dying embers of a wad of paper in the bathroom, thankfully in time to stop the fire from spreading.

I seriously considered running away from home at this point. I was naïve as most ten-year olds are; I even considered that I could survive a few days on packets of the popular confectionary called "*Rubble Gum*". This was a relatively cheap packet of really small pieces of gum that you could chew for hours. But when I thought it through, I knew there was a danger that someone would find me and bring me home. I imagined this would lead to more trouble with our father for running away. I certainly didn't imagine a teary-eyed reunion where our father would tell me he loved me and hug me and tell me I should never feel I have to run away.

Instead, I imagined being brought home by someone, our father acting as if he was happy to see me and thanking the person and then the front door closing. Then I would face the consequences.

My behaviour in school continued in the same vein until I was eventually caught at lunchtime near a local shop with some of my classmates. We had absconded from the school playground. One of my classmate's mothers drove by and complained to the school since we were all unsupervised. The principal placed a call to all the parents of those involved and advised them to collect their children from the school that day.

To my surprise, my father's reaction to this misbehaviour in school was quite different to the last. He was clearly incensed, but unlike the last time, the belt wasn't produced. He had another more unusual punishment in store for me. The trees out the back garden had recently been cut and branches lay all over the garden, after my father had done the 'glory work' of cutting the trees the previous evening. Upon arriving home from the school, my father ordered me out to clean them up. This was a job I would have had to do anyway. I expected that the punishment was yet to come.

As I picked up the branches, I heard the John Lennon song *"Mother"*, begin to play very loudly in the conservatory. My father sat with his back to the garden with a pot of coffee in front of him, puffing on a cigar. The volume was loud enough for our neighbours to hear. Usually my father would blast music loudly on the weekend after some drinks, but it was unusual for him to do that at lunchtime on a weekday.

I toiled in the garden listening to the words emanating loudly from the back of the house: *Mother you had me, but I never had you. I wanted you, but you didn't want me, so I, I just want to tell you, goodbye, goodbye.*

It made me think of my Mam and the fact that she was gone. I welled up crying.

There were steps up to the patio on the side of the conservatory. I walked up these steps, pretending to get another black plastic bag. I knew that if I stood at the top of the steps, my father would just have to look to his left to see that I was crying and upset. I wanted him to know that his punishment had worked, and he could stop the song now and continue with whatever other punishment he had in store. I wanted this emotional punishment to end.

I looked at the conservatory. My father sat there, puffing intently on his cigar. He stared rigidly ahead, with a twisted, yet determined expression on his face. He said nothing to me and I continued on into the house.

****

A decision was made for me to change classes for my final year in primary school. I was placed in with different classmates into a class that was now thought by the same teacher who I had thrived under in fourth class. I was told this was a chance to start afresh and I remember making a conscious decision that I didn't like constantly being in trouble. I returned to being well behaved and doing well in school for the remaining year in primary school.

****

Around this time, I was beginning to come to terms with the reality that no matter how I behaved in school or at home, my future living arrangements were unlikely to change. We would never be living with our Mam again. I was becoming increasingly desperate about the situation.

While I was still in primary school, Gar was in secondary school, so he wasn't home until half four in the afternoon. Shane had recently finished school and would spend a lot of the days out, working or presumably looking for work. That meant I would come home and spend an hour or two on my own in the house before Caroline or Gar got home. My father would never really be home until later in the evening.

I would spend the hour or two doing my chores. I would listen to the radio station *Longwave Radio Atlantic 252* which gave me a form of company. It also drowned out any other noises the large empty house would make that would otherwise scare me. I was deeply sad at this time and spending time alone gave me time to reflect on my predicament.

I just kept thinking about the fact that I was trapped, and I was never escaping. If a song that was relatively sad came on the radio and I would start sobbing uncontrollably. Sometimes I would just lie down on the floor wherever I had been standing and curl up in a ball weeping.

In desperation, I started praying to God that my situation would change. I wanted God to be real as he seemed to be the only one who could possibly intervene and change the situation I was now in. I knew God was supposed to be interested in fairness and so I thought some prayers might alert him to my plight. He didn't intervene however. It was a last resort that didn't work.

I reckoned that it would be seven years, until I was eighteen, before I could move out. Seven years seemed like an absolute lifetime. I wasn't sure I could wait that long.

On one of these afternoons, I was cleaning my father and Caroline's room. I picked up my father's skid-marked boxer shorts and threw them to the corner of the room in the 'for washing' pile. I had to be careful I didn't wash clothes that weren't necessarily in need of a wash. It was a judgement call I often seemed to get wrong, since Caroline would decide purely on mood, it seemed, if I had made the right or wrong call. As I picked up one of her tops off the floor to decide if it was for the wash or not, I saw what looked like a yellow roll of sweets under the trouser press. I walked over and picked them up and realised they were just *Bisodol* indigestion tablets. I wasn't sure what indigestion was, but I had seen these lying around before. I made an impulse decision. I decided to open the packet and threw four of them in my mouth. I walked over to Caroline's dressing table and picked up a bottle of perfume and sprayed about seven or eight sprays directly into my mouth. This caused the tablets to fizz somewhat. I swallowed the mixture and stood there, waiting for a reaction. I hadn't really thought about what I was doing. I was hoping I'd pass out and that would be the end my troubles. In the end nothing happened, except leaving a chalky, putrid taste in my mouth.

This began my fascination with the idea of taking my own life and ending it all. I started looking out the window of my bedroom and contemplated whether I would die if I jumped out. I realised that the window only opened at the top, so it would be difficult to fit out, but I could manage it. I then considered that the short fall would probably not cause enough impact and I would have no more than a broken leg.

In our kitchen we had a block of knives, known as laser knives. My father always talked of how great they were since they were so sharp and didn't require sharpening. I had heard of people dying by slitting their wrists, so I decided that I would give this a go. I decided that one of these *laser knives* would accomplish this. So, I went down and took a *laser knife* out of its wooden block it was stored in. I stood by the counter in the kitchen and cut across my wrist and it started to bleed. I wondered was this the job done and started to wonder did I have any regrets. I decided I didn't and wished it was more instant.

I walked to the sink and stood over it and put the tap on to wash the blood down the sinkhole. I was still subconsciously ensuring my blood would not cause the kitchen to be in anything other than show-house condition. But nothing happened.

I tried again, I cut another line across my wrist, this time a little deeper. While I was at it, I cut a third one. Time was ticking, and I really didn't want someone coming in and finding me in the middle of this because I thought I would be in serious trouble for it. So, I gave up and went upstairs. I went into the bathroom and locked the door. I used tissue to stop the bleeding. When I went to bed I had three very noticeable slit marks on my wrists. Neither my father nor Caroline seemed to notice.

As I walked to school the next day, I decided that I wouldn't hide the marks. I thought that if any of the teachers in the school saw them, they would realise that there was something seriously wrong and they might help me out. I decided I would tell them that if they went to my father, it would force me to cut again. And so, for the whole day, I kept the sleeve up enough for a teacher to see it. I saw other kids in my class giving me funny looks when they saw. I'm not sure if they knew the significance of the cuts.

But none of the teachers seemed to notice. The cuts were already grazing over at this stage and they weren't hard to spot. The fact that it went unnoticed annoyed me further. When I arrived home from school, I went straight to the laser knives and attempted again. I tried the wrists of both arms. Thankfully, I never thought to cut vertically and evidently, I wasn't cutting deep enough so my attempts were unsuccessful. But I was still an eleven-year-old boy walking around with both wrists with fairly obvious cuts on them. Nobody noticed. This made me feel even worse about myself.

I considered ways of hanging myself from the lampshade in my room but decided that if it didn't work, it would cause damage to my room for which I would be in more trouble.

When I was inspecting the cuts on my wrists, I was so surprised that it hadn't worked. I thought that the fact that by cutting my wrists, it was impossible for me not to die. As I looked at them scabbing up, I remembered a story I heard in mass. It was about a saint called Padre Pio, who had cuts resembling crucifix marks and they healed and reappeared in a mysterious fashion.

I decided that there could only be one conclusion to why I hadn't died. It was a miracle and it could only be the work of some superhuman power preventing me from dying. It had to be God. There was no other explanation. In the end I persuaded myself that God in fact was intervening. This was God's way of telling me to keep strong and stick out the bad times and that things would change for me. I imagined God had special work for me and that this was all part of the plan.

I stopped trying to cut myself for fear I would upset God after that. In between chores and after them, I would kneel down and pray. I thought if I prayed enough, God would eventually reward me with freedom. I had full blown conversations out loud with God about my problems.

Chapter 10

Gar started keeping a diary on 1 January 1992 and maintained the diary, on and off, for three years. We have used extracts from the diaries throughout the following chapters.

The story continues in this chapter in late 1991. At this time, Fin was ten, Gar was twelve and Shane was seventeen years of age.

Fin

We had stopped believing in Santa a few years back when Shane had showed us, well before Christmas day, the bikes we were supposed to be getting 'from Santa'. I therefore found it surprising when our father, who seemed to have accepted the fact that we didn't believe in Santa anymore, suddenly started talking to us about Santa again as if he did exist after all.

Although it was a bit puzzling, there was a benefit for us in Santa's 'resurrection' in that Caroline took us out for a day leading up to Christmas to visit 'Santa', just like our Mam used to. This meant Caroline being nice to us for a day instead of shouting at us, so Gar and I were happy enough to go along with the Santa myth.

About a month before Christmas 1991, my father mysteriously started locking the door to the spare room. I worked out pretty quickly that he was hiding a Christmas present in there and I was able to see through the keyhole that it was a new computer. I was determined to investigate this further once I worked out how to get through the locked door. I told my friend next door and we decided to try a box of house keys from his house in the door. It worked perfectly as much to our joy; one of the keys unlocked the door. We started up the computer and began playing one of the computer games, a brilliant game based on the James Bond film, *"Live and Let Die"*.

I could not believe how easy it was once I had the key to the room. My father had left the computer fully set up so that he could use it whenever he wanted. I simply had to switch it on and switch it back off, locking the door behind me and hiding the key in my room.

This became a daily ritual after school. I even let Gar in on the secret and he joined in the pre-Christmas games of *"Live and Let Die"* when they were in the pub, which was often. I would laugh to myself as I would see my father *secretly* disappearing into the room in the evening and reappearing hours later and locking the door. I thought that he must have thought we were brain dead not to wonder what he was doing.

I wondered whether he was any good at *"Live and Let Die"*.

I found out the answer on Christmas morning when the computer was officially revealed as our Christmas present *'from Santa'*. Our father was amazed at the ease with which we were able to use the computer and in particular how easily we advanced through the levels in the James Bond game. He appeared to me to react jealously to the fact that we were much better at the game then he was, perhaps because he thought he had had a bit of practice already and we had not. He insisted on hogging the computer on Christmas morning to have one attempt after another to try and prove that he could get to the next level. Seeing him act like a spoiled child with no concern for the fact that we wanted to have a go of *our* Christmas present only vindicated to me my decision to play it prior to Christmas. I found his frustrations humorous.

Gar was guilt ridden though and this reduced his enjoyment of the games, which in turn led to me not enjoying them as much. I was worried that his guilt could have bad consequences for us.

Later that day, the computer mysteriously broke. Gar was sure that it was God punishing us for playing it before Christmas. I didn't tell Gar then, but I knew it wasn't an act of God. I had already cleared our actions with God and he was okay with it. God agreed that if our father cared about surprising us for Christmas with the computer, he would have hidden it properly and resisted the temptation to play with it himself. While I was well able to justify things to myself like this, Gar was not.

Gar was sure that our father would find out about us playing before Christmas and we would be in terrible trouble. As I tried to persuade him to keep calm, I began to regret ever telling him about the computer. He was already talking about just *'coming clean'* to our father, a suggestion which I strongly contested.

However, our father reacted to the computer breaking by making us sit on the stairs on Christmas evening after dinner. I'm not sure why he decided it was our fault that the computer was broken but I suppose he had to blame someone. This unexplained Christmas day punishment made even Gar feel aggrieved and this helped me to successfully persuade him not to *'come clean'*. Thankfully a short time after that, the computer came back to life.

Despite the computer supposedly being *our* present, it was returned to the spare room and the door was locked after Christmas. We were only to use it when we were given the key. Our father said we *would only end up breaking it.* I thought this was unfair, so with my neighbour's permission, I kept his key. As Caroline and our father were in work or in the pub, I could take the key out and we could play it whenever we wanted. I remember Caroline ringing from the pub one afternoon and telling us we could play the computer and where their key was hidden. I had to pause the computer game I had been playing to answer the phone and I laughed my head off at this when I finished the call to Caroline.

It was a bad idea to hide the key in my room since Caroline was always searching it and one day the inevitable happened and she found the key. In an attempt to limit the damage, I lied and said that I had only got the key *after* Christmas. I was still in serious trouble, but I knew that it was imperative that I kept pretending that Santa existed.

However, when Gar was interrogated about the key, he admitted to our father about playing the computer before Christmas. Our father's reaction to discovering what I had done is recording in Gar's diary as follows:

10 January 1992

"I never saw Dad so angry in my life. Luckily it was on Fin - not on me. He and Caroline found out about the key to the box-room so Fin was whacked. His bum is black and red - aaahh! Played the computer for about an hour and was 'forced' to eat jelly and ice-cream and chocolate cake. Went to bed at 9.55"

I remember my father grabbed me and placed me over his knee. He took his belt off and proceeded to thrash me with his belt on my bare backside. He shouted at me for pretending that I believed in Santa when I was playing the computer. I shouted back, despite the thrashing, that I had told him that I didn't believe in Santa, but he had forced me to pretend. He hit me harder when I said this. I felt a terrible mixture of physical pain and frustration.

When he finished, he threw me off his legs and before I ran off I turned around and roared at him:

I never wanted to pretend to believe in Santa!

He stared at me with fierce anger and swung the belt at me again, this time hitting me on the face and belly in that one swing. I turned and ran into my room. I hated him so much.

Unfortunately, this wasn't the end of the punishment. When they discovered that Gar had considered 'coming clean' before we had been forced to sit on the stairs on Christmas day and that I had talked him out of it, they decided that I would receive further punishment. They also wanted to further guilt trip Gar into never letting me talk him out of 'coming clean' again.

The first part of this punishment was that I had to watch him being 'rewarded'. As Gar says in the diary, his 'reward' was being "*'forced' to eat jelly and ice-cream and chocolate cake*". I was forced to stand and watch him while he ate it. Gar clearly wasn't enjoying the apparent treat he was being given.

For a period after that, I was banned from doing anything other than my chores and was given the 'standing' punishment. This meant that when my chores were completed, I was forced to stand motionless for long periods under supervision. This meant standing still, with no books or comics or anything that could entertain me. I had to just stand in silence. I remember having to stand at the sitting room door, so I couldn't see the television. Our father and Caroline were sitting watching TV and puffing on cigars. I think I stood there for four hours straight one Saturday. I remember it was extremely painful on my legs. If my father or Caroline needed a fresh cup of tea or an ashtray emptied, I could run over and do that, and it was actually a relief to move my legs. If I attempted to lean against the doorframe, my father would shout at me to *straighten up*. I remember thinking that the guards outside Buckingham Palace deserved more credit than they got.

But since they went to the pub a lot, they were not around to personally supervise my standing punishment. So, when they were out Gar was entrusted with the job of enforcing my punishment and ensuring that I stood still while they were out.

I remember one of the times when Gar was left in charge of enforcing my standing punishment and I decided I had had enough standing and sat down on the floor. Gar pleaded with me to get up.

If I let you sit down, they'll kill me! he said

I stood back up. I knew he was right that if they heard that I had sat down under his watch, he would be in serious trouble. I also knew Gar was told by our father that his problem was that I convinced him to be dishonest. After the punishments that had followed this, there was no chance he would cover up anything I did, no matter how he felt about it. I had no option but to stand on the upstairs hallway for hours watching Gar chewing his tongue vigorously trying to concentrate on his computer game with a glass of lemonade and a packet of crisps in front of him. The place I was made to stand was within view of Gar and his treats, but out of view of the computer screen. This was Caroline's doing, as she recognised that I would be entertained in a small way if I was able to observe Gar's progress in the computer game. My father instructed Gar to look around frequently to ensure that I didn't break the punishment.

Make sure he doesn't lean against the wall, my father ordered Gar. *This is all for his own good, he has to learn*, he added.

I thought the way they treated me was grossly unfair. Looking back, it appears they made great efforts to pit myself and Gar against each other but thankfully it didn't work. I reasoned that Gar didn't really have much choice in situations like this. He was hardly going to turn down the crisps and lemonade and switch off the computer and demand to be punished like me. Seeing my black and red backside wasn't going to add any desire to do this.

Furthermore, our father used to justify it to Gar by convincing him that it was the right thing to do *for Fin's sake*. I would hear him tell Gar that what he is doing was all for my benefit to rid me of my many *Jo-isms*. My father was well aware that Gar was uneasy about being the enforcer of my punishment. So, he convinced him that he would be failing to be a good big brother if he didn't. The way I saw it, was it was okay to lie sometimes to them because of the horrible situations we found ourselves in and because they constantly lied to us and to other people. I was able to justify these lies to myself without any problem.

Chapter 11

Gar

When the computer had stopped working on Christmas morning I was convinced it was God punishing us for playing the computer before Christmas. I wanted to confess to our father before he found out some other way and we were punished severely. Fin managed to convince me not to say anything, but when our father found out anyway and then gave Fin a severe thrashing, I felt that it was a lesson to me to just own up in the first place or otherwise the punishment would be severe. As my diary says: "*Luckily it was on Fin - not on me*". I knew it could just as easily be me the next time.

I regularly found myself in a bind whenever Fin and I did anything which I felt our father would disapprove of. Even small things, like spending ten pence on sweets instead of giving it back to our father as change from buying cigars for him, would fill me with guilt. Fin would make me promise not to say anything and I would promise to him that I would keep silent but once I got home the guilt would build and build. Especially as Caroline and my father would take me to one side and question me, seeming to sense that I was tormented by guilt.

On one occasion when Fin and I had taken ten pence or so for sweets, I had promised Fin I would say nothing, but the guilt got so strong that I ended up on my knees upstairs praying to God as to what I should do. I felt totally conflicted - not wanting to tell on Fin but also not wanting to be dishonest to my father and Caroline. I wanted God to tell me what to do. Ultimately, I usually ended up telling them and would be 'rewarded' with fizzy drinks or sweets but as I record in my diary above, these supposed rewards were not something I really enjoyed. I was just relieved I had survived. It was no surprise that soon Fin stopped trusting me.

****

When our parents separated in 1989, Shane was sixteen years of age and in the middle of studying for his Leaving Certificate. It seems to have been decided that it was better for him to stay in the house with our father and Caroline, apparently so as to cause minimum disruption to his studies. While Shane may not have had the disruption of moving house to contend with, he had to deal with a different kind of disruption caused by his mother and his two brothers moving out of the family home and his father's young mistress moving in.

Fin and I lived with our mother for twelve months in a rented house in a nearby estate. Besides coping with the loss of the three of us Shane also had to deal with the impact of Caroline in the house. This was difficult enough for me and Fin when we moved back in but at least for us we were young kids and Caroline was very much an adult. Shane, however was much closer in age to Caroline (she was twenty-two and he was sixteen). By way of comparison, Shane was the same age that Caroline had been when she started her relationship with our father, who was twenty-eight at that time.

When Fin and I left with our mother, we felt sorry for Shane being left in the house on his own without us. Being that bit older he was not as dependent on Fin or me as we were on each other. When the separation occurred, we were too young to really understand what was happening. Unfortunately for Shane, he was not. Shane had also spent much longer living with our mother and her loving nature then we had which must have made it extremely painful to suddenly find himself under Caroline's dictatorial regime. When we moved back in a year later, we saw for ourselves that Caroline and Shane could barely manage to cohabit. Tension was never far away.

The apparent purpose of Shane staying with our father - to cause his studies 'minimum disruption' to help him pass his Leaving Certificate – did not result in a successful outcome as Shane did not pass. It was not from a lack of intelligence that Shane failed, as evidenced by his achieving a B grade in Honours English. Shane was only sixteen years of age when he sat the Leaving Cert and turned seventeen in June 1991 just before he got his results in August of that year.

With no Leaving Certificate, he had no college prospects and minimal employment opportunities. He managed to get a job in McDonald's flipping burgers. For the couple of years that we lived in the house with Shane and Caroline, they fought like cats and dogs. It was apparent to us even as young children that the house wasn't big enough for the two of them.

Happily, whatever happened between Shane and Caroline did not interfere with my relationship with Shane which remained as close as ever. My diary records in one entry in February 1992:

<u>20 February 1992</u>

Went to town with Shane today. He got new jeans, new shoes and two new shirts. We went into Dunkin' Donuts for lunch and I got a chocolate donut covered in multi-coloured hundreds and thousands. I also got a black raspberry cream donut and a medium coke. Yum! Then we went to the chipper for a bag of chips.

In May 1992, after prolonged periods of conflict with Caroline and our father, Shane's situation came to a head. The diary entry for 21 May 1992 (six days before Caroline's twenty fifth birthday) records the usual summary of how things had gone in school and what I had for dinner. However, in a different coloured pen to the regular diary entry, I had inserted a box as follows:

STOP PRESS: Just found out that Shane's been kicked out with his gear in a bin-bag.

There was an introduction to the diary by Roald Dahl in which he described how when he kept a diary as a child, he recorded not just everyday events, but also secret hopes, fears and desires. When I read this introduction, I was determined to do the same as him. However, when it came to actually write the daily entries, knowing that Caroline or my father might come into our room and read my diary, I very often wrote only what I thought they might want to read. If I was feeling brave though, I would put the fear of them reading it to one side and write what I actually felt. In the above entry about Shane, I had finished my daily entry (which I had wrote in blue pen) and made no mention of Shane getting kicked out of the house. But after putting my diary away I felt the urging of Roald Dahl to record my secrets and re-opened my diary and inserted, in a different coloured pen this time, a STOP PRESS box with the above entry. I felt a rush of exhilaration when I had written this. I reckoned my father and Caroline would not approve but *so what, it was my diary after all.*

Shane was still only seventeen years of age when he got *kicked out.*

There is an entry from the diary from around this time which shows the perverse and confused world that we found ourselves in. The diary records:

7 March 1992

Fin went to Cork this morning so Caroline and I cleaned the house until 11 o clock. Then we went to the supermarket and then we went to Caroline's mothers. I pretended I was Dr. Owens's son. We played Super Mario Brothers one, two and three. England won the grand slam beating Wales 24-0.

Prior to this day, I had met Caroline's mother a few times before but rarely went up to her mother's house and I had not met Caroline's father or her two younger brothers. It was therefore unusual for me to be visiting her mother's house with Caroline and there was a sense of nervousness and hesitation around Caroline before the visit.

Shortly before we arrived at the house, she told me that I was going to meet her brothers and that I was to pretend to be her boss's son. She did not explain exactly why this was or why I was not allowed to be just be myself. I thought it might have something to do with the fact that she didn't talk to her father which I had gathered from overheard conversations. I was aware that it had something to do with her living with our father. None of this was explained to me, I just made my own sense of it in my own mind.

When we arrived at the house I was introduced to her brothers as her boss's son and spent the afternoon playing the Nintendo with them. Afterwards we went home as if nothing unusual had happened. Over time, I was reintroduced to her brothers as myself, her step-child, as if the other introduction had never taken place. I don't know what, if any, explanation was given to her younger brothers about this.

Chapter 12

Gar

In August 1992, a few months after Shane had been kicked out of the house, Fin and I arranged to meet our mother to take a trip into town one Friday afternoon. By this time our father was encouraging us to engage as little as possible with our mother whenever we did meet her. When we met her this particular afternoon she asked us what we wanted to do. We told her we could like to go to the cinema to see *Wayne's World*. She did not seem too happy with this suggestion. It would mean we would not be engaging with each other much at all. But I was very keen to go to the cinema as I reckoned that my father would be happy to hear we had spent the afternoon there and not sitting around talking to our mother. I told her how much we really wanted to see the film and she said *Okay, whatever you want to do*. We went to the old Carlton cinema on O' Connell Street.

The film ended at about five o'clock and our mother proposed that we go for a cup of tea and a bun in the Kylemore cafe on Mary Street. Although this was a real treat for us, I hesitated at her proposal. I had a feeling that our mother wanted us to go for tea so that we could talk with her for a while having spent the afternoon in the cinema. I was afraid that our father would not like the idea of us going for a tea and a bun with our mother and would give out to me. Fin did not appear to have any such worries though and was eager to go for this treat. I looked at my mother and my brother and thought to myself – *what's wrong with going for a cup of tea with your Mam? It's just a cup of tea.*

So, I agreed with the proposal and we happily spent another hour chatting, drinking tea and eating cake. At about six o'clock, we took the bus home and arrived home at about seven o'clock.

When we arrived home, we immediately knew that something was wrong. Our father and Caroline were not at home, which was unusual because normally after our meetings with our mother, they would be there to question us on how the meeting had gone. The fact that they were not there meant something was up. After a very worrying wait, we finally heard the key turning in the front door and our father and Caroline came into the house.

Our father was red faced and he angrily declared that they had been out looking *high and low* for us.

Where were ye? He shouted at me.

We went to the cinema, I said.

What time was that over at?

About five o'clock, I stuttered.

And what took you so long to get home then?

I thought about how I could get away with not telling him about Kylemore café but knew it was impossible, he was an expert interrogator and I was a terrible liar.

We went to Kylemore café, I said, *for a cup of tea and some cake.*

My father exploded at this.

A cup of tea?

And some cake?

He practically spat the words out.

He then nodded his head up and down vigorously, like he had made a decision.

Right, he said, *if you want to go for tea with her and spend time with her, you can. Go upstairs now the two of you and pack your bags. Youse are both going to Carlow to spend the weekend with her.*

Caroline began to say something but he interrupted her.

If that's what they want, our father shouted, *that's what they'll get. Go upstairs and pack your bags like I told you to. In fact, don't pack yet, hold on a minute.*

Our father stopped what he was saying and suddenly went into the kitchen. Fin and I looked at each other in puzzlement wondering what he was doing. Moments later, he came back from the kitchen holding a roll of black plastic bags.

He thrust the roll into my hand.

Here, he said, *if you want to live with your mother, you can live like her as well. She packs with black plastic bags and that's how you're going to pack too.*

I looked at his face and knew what he meant – he was referring to the black plastic bags of clothes our mother had given to us to take on our holiday with our father and Caroline two years before.

Fin and I ascended the stairs feeling like dead men walking. I heard our father downstairs on the phone to our mother telling her that he was going to drop us around to her in an hour and that we were going to spend the weekend with her. In ordinary circumstances, we would not have minded the prospect of spending the weekend with our mother at all. But these were not ordinary circumstances – it was made clear to us that this was punishment, the gravest form of punishment.

When we came back down the stairs, the dining room table was set and Caroline was dishing out Shepherd's Pie for dinner. Our father continued to shout at us and in particular directed his anger at me. When we sat at our usual places at the table, mine being the seat directly to my father's left, my father told me to move away from him to the end of the table, to the seat where our older brother Shane used to sit, growling that if I wanted to be a failure like him, I could sit at his seat. My father shouted at me that it was my fault in particular that we had stayed out so late, as I was the older brother and therefore was in charge.

I felt like my father was right – I knew when my mother had suggested we go for tea that he would be angry so I should have listened to myself and just went home. But I also felt sorry for myself, not matter how angry my father was. I couldn't see how our going for tea with our Mam was such a terrible crime he made it out to be. I sobbed tears of guilt and self-pity throughout dinner.

When dinner was finally over, our father ordered us and our black plastic bags into the back of the car. Caroline sat in the front passenger seat and cried throughout the journey. Our father told her to stop crying a few times but she couldn't stop for long. I looked at her from the back seat and thought to myself: *she's crying because even she knows this is wrong.* After what seemed like an age, we eventually arrived at our mother's friend's house. Our mother looked intently at the plastic bags that accompanied us.

Our father then got back in the car and he and Caroline drove off. Our mother looked at us, shaken and confused, put her arms around us and brought us into her friend's house for a cup of tea.

A dramatic couple of hours had mercifully come to an end.

****

Our mother had arranged to get a lift with a friend to Carlow and fortunately there was room for two more passengers in the car.

We drove down to Carlow in relative silence which was a welcome change from the ranting and raving that we had left behind us in Dublin. That night we did not go to our grandparents' cottage but stayed in our mother's friend's house in a suburban estate.

By evening time, we had put our earlier troubles to one side and we both danced around to *Rhythm is a Dancer* by *Snap,* the number one song on Top of the Pops that night. The next day, we went to our grandparent's cottage that our mother had been raised in along with her twelve siblings. One of those siblings was her younger sister, Geraldine. Geraldine was a kind and warm-hearted woman. When we arrived with our mother she immediately took care of us and made sure we were having a good time. She asked us if we would like to go to town with her and we said we would.

Geraldine drove me and Fin into Carlow town. She asked us if we wanted ice cream and we said we did. She brought us to the freezer in the shop and told us that we could have whatever ice cream we wanted. Caroline sometimes bought us ice-pop only if we were in the company of other people buying ice-pops and it was made abundantly clear to us that when this happened we should always choose a cheap ice-pop, no matter what the other kids were getting. So, when Geraldine asked us to choose an ice-pop, we told her that we wanted *Sparklers*, the cheapest ice-pop in the freezer. But she seemed to sense that we didn't actually want them and insisted that we choose whatever ice cream we really wanted. We cautiously told her that we would really like to try the most expensive ice creams on sale, *Magnums*. She said that it was absolutely no problem. To our delight, she bought them and gave them to us and we gobbled them up joyously.

After we had ice cream she asked us why we didn't seem to want to spend time with our mother or to hug her or take presents from her anymore. I recall feeling ashamed and looking at Fin who was also feeling sheepish but neither of us told her the truth, which was that we were doing what our father told us to do.

Geraldine, being a kind and sensitive woman, did not push the issue as it was causing us discomfort. She simply said that our mother might be a bit scatter-brained and a bit mad for the religion but that she loved us very much and she wanted us to know that. We did not disagree with her but only hung our heads even lower than before.

Once this was said, Geraldine changed the subject and asked us if we might be interested in watching some movies with her that night? She said that she was babysitting in a neighbour's house and that they had a huge TV. If we wanted, we could pick out some videos from the local 'Xtra-Vision' and watch them with her that evening.

We were very keen on this plan and quickly agreed that *Batman* would be one of the movies we were going to watch. The other two movies we chose, after much discussion, were the unlikely pairing of Fin's choice, the *Little Mermaid* and my choice, *Dances with Wolves*, much to Geraldine's amusement. She asked us if we were sure about *Dances with Wolves* in particular as she thought it might be more of a film for adults. However, I had read a very positive review in the newspaper and was insistent that we got this movie. I had also loved Kevin Costner in *Robin Hood, Prince of Thieves*. Geraldine laughed and said *whatever ye want* and rented the three films.

We drove back to the cottage in high spirits. We had dinner with our mother who then took us up to the village bar to play a few games of pool and drink red lemonade before we were due to go with Geraldine to watch the movies.

It was when we were in the bar that I saw a public phone and I immediately thought I should call our father. I had already called him on the Friday night but had unsuccessfully tried to call him on Saturday and felt that if I did not call him today I would be in trouble. I saw how he had reacted to us going for a scone with our mother so could only imagine how he could react if he thought we were down in Carlow 'enjoying ourselves' with our mother, even though this was actually the case. It was therefore important that unless I wanted to feel his anger again that I should call him. I told Fin that I wanted to call our father and he said he didn't think that was a good idea. He suggested we call our father in the morning.

However, I insisted, as the older brother, that we should call home. I got a twenty pence piece and we went out to the hall. I dialled the number and stood nervously in the hallway of the bar as I held the receiver to my ear waiting for someone to answer. After a few rings, our father answered and in an unusually friendly tone asked me how we were. I hesitated before I told him we were fine and that we were playing pool and drinking red lemonade. My father's tone changed, he was not happy with the positive status. He asked me why we had not called sooner and there was a threatening tone in his voice. I thought to myself that I had to be very careful with what I said next. I told him that I had tried to call but there was no phone in the cottage, as he knew, and this was the first chance I had got to use a public phone.

He slowly digested this and then asked, in a tone that did not countenance a negative response, whether *we would like him to come and collect us and take us home.*

Fin who had heard this question and who was staring at me shook his head vigorously from side to side to indicate what he thought the answer should be. I hesitated; the wonderful prospect of movie night in front of the big TV with our Auntie Geraldine was receding fast. Our father, sensing my hesitation, demanded angrily:

Do you want us to come down and collect you or not?

The tone in his voice demanded only one answer, which I duly gave him.

Eh, yes, I said, *we do, we do.*

Fin's face fell at my response, knowing as I did that the movie night was no more and instead a long car journey back to Dublin with our father and Caroline awaited us.

Good, he said, *see you at the junction at the end of the road.*

Great, great I said, *see you then.*

When I hung up the phone I felt acute disappointment that our evening's activities would have to be cancelled. I also felt a kind of guilt that we would have to ruin Geraldine's plans and let her down. I knew that she had been extra nice to us and it was not right for us to throw her kindness back in her face and tell her we were going back to Dublin because our father had decided as much.

When we went back in and told Geraldine and our mother that our father was coming down to collect us, they both were disappointed. I told Geraldine I was sorry that she had rented the movies but now we would not be able to watch them with her. When we left, we said goodbye to our mother. Similarly, we said goodbye to Geraldine and to Carlow.

It was the last time we would talk to our mother in person for eighteen years.

Our father collected us wearing his stern-but-smug face. The drive home to Dublin was torturous for me as the guilt hung heavy in the hurt-locker car for the entire journey.

****

Although that weekend in Carlow was the last time I spoke to my mother in person for eighteen years, there were a few phone conversations with her over the next few months before my father put his foot down and brought this means of communication to an end as well.

On the night the phone rang for that final phone call with my mother, my father and Caroline were in a different room in the house to me when I answered the phone.

I heard the voice of my mother on the end of the line. She sounded upset. She asked me how I was and I told her that I was doing well. She asked me how Fin was and then she told me how she missed me and Fin. Midway through telling me this, her voice broke and she started to cry. When I heard her cry, I cried too. I told her I missed her and we both cried together for a while. I remember then getting this guilty feeling that I shouldn't be having this conversation with her and so I told her that I had to go and finish my homework. She said she was glad to hear my voice again and we said goodbye and hung up.

After she hung up, I wiped the tears from my face and sat in the chair for a few moments. Suddenly the door to the room opened and my father came in and stood over me, glowering. I had that terrible feeling that I had done something very wrong and that I had made him angry.

Who were you talking to on the phone? he said.

I sensed immediately that he must have been listening to the conversation on the phone in the other room. I had heard a click during the conversation which I knew from experience was the sound of the other phone having been picked up. Fin and I were both used to our father and Caroline listening in on our calls.

It was Mam I answered,

And what did you say to her? he said.

I sensed that I needed to be very careful what I said, but I could only answer him honestly.

She said she misses us, I told him, *and she was crying.*

My father shook his head from side to side.

Crocodile tears, he said. *That's what they were.*

I didn't really understand what he meant and I looked at him with puzzlement.

Crocodile tears, he shouted this time. *She doesn't love you. If she did love you why would she have spent all her money travelling around the world instead of buying a house so you could visit her? She doesn't care about you or Fin or Shane. She rings you now when it suits her after not seeing you for months. Don't buy into her tears.*

She sounded sad, I said.

Well don't mind her, my father said. *The next time she rings just hang up the phone and don't talk to her. Okay?*

Okay I said, *okay.*

Fin

The day we went to see Wayne's World with our Mam was one of the best days of my childhood, until we arrived back in our father's house to his anger. An amazing film with popcorn and coke was already an almighty treat for us. To follow that with tea and cake in Kylemore Café afterwards was wonderful. The three of us could not have been happier as me and Gar scoffed our cake and our Mam laughed at how we couldn't stop repeating lines from the film. How I wish that day had ended there.

I actually let myself believe that our forced trip to Carlow was the start of another twist in the tale of our lives. I believed our father had had enough of us already. I was surprised at the circumstances of him wanting us to leave but I had always expected he would eventually get sick of us or even just me at some stage. I certainly had hoped he would. But I thought it would have to be something serious, like if I broke his 'Pioneer' Hi-fi or his guitar or something. I didn't even know what he was angry about and I was quite sure Gar didn't either.

My father had surpassed all previous manners of meanness as far as I was concerned. I had never seen him so angry and I couldn't see what we had done wrong. I was genuinely confused at his aggressive and disproportionate reaction. He had also gone to town on Gar much more than me. Seeing that I was always the one who seemed to disappoint him, this was very unusual. There also seemed no apparent reason for it. But when you are punished as a child, you tend to assume you did something wrong. I thought that maybe at eleven years of age, I was too stupid or naïve to know what we had done wrong. Gar, being the older responsible thirteen-year-old, should have known. That appeared to me to be the message.

And as much as I had never seen my father as angry, I had never seen Gar as upset. When he was moved from sitting beside my father to the other end of the table, the tears and snots were literally dripping into his shepherd's pie. I was upset too, but I was secretly praying that my father wasn't going to move me to Gar's previous spot on his immediate left at the table. I wanted to be as far away from this ogre as possible.

So naturally, once we were in the house with our Mam I was delighted. I even went into the front room of the house and looked out the window to make sure my father had driven off and he was definitely gone. With this confirmed, I was relieved. Gar seemed relieved too but I remember him saying that this visit was only for the weekend. After that the three of us went to Carlow, getting a lift with our Mam's friend.

When we arrived in Carlow, I was secretly hoping that my father would contact our Mam to tell her that we were too much trouble and she could have us back. I didn't want to say it to Gar though, mainly because I didn't want to be convinced otherwise. I also wondered if it was possible that Gar might be coming around to my way of thinking after my father's explosive and erratic behaviour. I thought this episode might have convinced him how much better it was to live with our Mam.

Unfortunately, I found out soon enough that this was not the case. Our Mam gave us money to buy an ice cream - I think that Gar asked our Mam could we have money to go and buy an ice-cream. As soon as we left the house and were down the driveway, Gar was insisting that we had to find a payphone. I groaned and asked *why?* Gar said we had to find a phone to ring my father. I insisted that we didn't, that our father had been mean and angry for no reason. I reasoned that if he wanted to talk to us he wouldn't have kicked us down to Carlow. I was bewildered as to why Gar wanted to talk to him and seemingly patch things up. As far as I was concerned, our father could stay angry with us forever and never see us again. Our Mam could look after us and we would all live happily ever after.

But Gar insisted. He said that it was our own fault that our father had been so angry and he just had to figure out why. He turned to me in what seemed to be for him a Eureka moment. He said that he thought sending us to Carlow was a test. I continued arguing and Gar obviously realised that I could not be convinced that easily, so he tactfully found a different way to get me to go along with his plan.

I have the money, he said, *so if we find a phone, we can get ice-cream. Until then, we can't get ice-cream.*

Gar knew me well. As any normal boy of my age, ice cream was definitely one of my weaknesses. I had noted that our Mam had given us enough money to get a Tangle Twister each and I was picturing it in my mind.

Right than, let's go, I said determined to help him find the payphone so I could get the ice cream.

Off we went and Gar took another detour, this time successfully finding a payphone. Gar stepped into the payphone nervously and I stood outside. As I watched him speak on the phone, his face seemed to light up as the conversation progressed. Looking back, it was as if he had settled a terrible dispute with a good friend. It appeared to me that that's what my father made Gar believe he was to him; a good friend, with Gar's best interests at heart.

When he exited the phone box, I asked him what he had said. He said our father didn't seem mad anymore and that he had talked to Caroline as well. He seemed quite pleased, like he had just done well in a test, which I suppose in many ways, he thought he had done.

I remember asking Gar was I mentioned in the phone conversation and he said I wasn't.

We had been gone over five minutes now and we didn't know exactly where the shop was. Gar called it straight away:

Come on, let's go back. We can just say we didn't find the shop.

I couldn't believe he had passed up an ice cream, just so he could talk to 'them'. This was not the brother I had grown up with.

But Gar was at ease for the time being and we really enjoyed ourselves, particularly with our Aunt Geraldine. Our father had instilled in us a hatred for 'the country' and the belief that all people from the country were not to be liked or trusted. He had a special hatred for Carlow, our

Mam J home county, which he used to call *the kip of the country*. Although I disliked our father, I was at an impressionable age. This is why I was always so surprised at how nice and *cool* our Aunt Geraldine was. Her music cassette collection left a lot to be desired, with *Bananarama* and *Michael Jackson* featuring strongly in it. But her willingness to play any games with us, and her generosity more than made up for it. She was just one of those adults who was a really fun person to be around as a child. We loved spending time with her.

The next day when we were back in the small village where our Mam parents' cottage was, Gar insisted that we walk up to the crossroads where there was an old payphone. Again, I was annoyed at being made to leave the fun we were having with Geraldine. When we arrived and the phone was broken, Gar seemed distraught. Even though it blatantly didn't work, Gar fiddled with the receiver and tapped on it, trying desperately to make it work. I was at my wit's end with him. He wouldn't listen to reason and started talking about walking further to find another phone. We were pretty much in the middle of nowhere. I had had enough. I insisted that I was walking back alone to the cottage if I had to. He would have had to drag me kicking and screaming if he wanted to keep looking for a phone. Gar considered this option but thankfully chose against it.

The next day, when we were playing pool in the bar with Geraldine and my Mam and sipping on red lemonade, I was as happy as can be. We were playing doubles and until we started playing, Gar was as happy as me. But out of nowhere, Gar seemed to get distracted. We had to remind him that it was his go. He kept looking at where the payphone was and in the hall of the bar and when I noticed this, I knew exactly what he was thinking. I couldn't for the life of me understand why, but I knew he wanted to call our father.

Him and his stupid test, I was thinking.

I tried to distract him without mentioning that I knew what he was thinking. That wouldn't be tactful, as it would bring it to the fore.

Come on Gar, your turn, I called out to him, trying to divert his attention back to the pool game.

I can't wait to watch those videos later Gar. I added, rather over enthusiastically.

86

I couldn't wait though; this was going to be a day that was going to continue to be good day right up until we went to bed, unlike the day of Wayne's World. I was determined to go to bed happy that night. I felt I had a great opportunity where I wouldn't have to worry about my father or Caroline until I woke up the next morning.

But Gar kept staring at the phone. The more he looked at it, the more distracted and agitated he was. He seemed to be spellbound by it. Unable to control his urge any more, he said what I knew he was going to say.

Mam, I just want to make a phone call, he said.

I tried to talk him out of it. I pleaded with him not to. I knew this was a bad idea to phone our father. Geraldine backed me up and I remember noting the fact that this was unusual that people were saying I was right and Gar was wrong for a change. I was just getting used to being constantly told to be more like Gar and that Gar was a good boy (and I was not). This made it unusual to hear someone saying:

Gar, Fin's right.

Gar was hesitant at first, but the guilt trip that my father had put him on had worked its magic. He insisted.

When I heard the news after he got off the phone that we were leaving Carlow that evening, I was upset. Again, Gar had that look as if he had done well in an exam, but he didn't look entirely happy. Why would he be? I knew he wanted as much as I did to spend the night in Carlow too but he just did what he felt he had to do. He did what our father had convinced him was the *'right'* thing to do.

Gar, the videos are already paid for, I argued, *we can't go back to the house tonight.*

But our father was already on his way down to Carlow to pick us up. I was devastated. I spent the next hour or two in the sitting room of the house we were supposed to be watching the films in, waiting on our lift to arrive. I persuaded Geraldine to put on the Little Mermaid and watched some of it. I was thinking of 'what could have been' that evening if Gar hadn't made the phone call.

Chapter 13

Fin

Although I didn't realise it at the time, that was the last time I would speak to my Mam for eighteen years. On the journey home from Carlow, my father was playing the Beatles album, *Abbey Road*, in the car. Caroline was being quite nice to us. Our father was too, he seemed quite happy with the situation. There was some discussion about Shane possibly calling to our house just as the song "She came in through the bathroom window" came on. I pointed out that since he had no keys that Shane would likely climb in the bathroom window. Everyone in the car laughed.

Music was one thing Gar and I had in common with our father. He had a good taste in music and introduced us to some great bands, including *the Beatles*. I saw music as our common interest and that's why at a younger age, I was so disappointed when he didn't seem to encourage my interest in learning guitar.

By this stage, our father must have known how much music meant to us. Gar and I both loved to sing along to songs with our father. I was very taken by one particular album our father had by Rory Gallagher's band, *Taste*, called *On the Boards*. Gar was also a big fan of it and the two of us used to put the album on and sing along even when our father wasn't there.

A week or two after our weekend with our Mam in Carlow, Rory Gallagher played a free gig in Dublin City Centre on 15th August 1992 as part of the Temple Bar Blues festival. He was quite ill at the time and this turned out to be his last Irish gig. We didn't know any of this when our father told us he was bringing us to the gig. We were delighted.

We attended the gig with our father and his friend Dermot. Rory played mostly his own tunes from his solo albums and I couldn't understand why he wouldn't play a few tunes from the *Taste* album. I said this to my father carefully as I didn't want to get into trouble. He was actually quite nice about it and said he hoped Rory would play some of the songs I was hoping for too. My father and Dermot got very excited when Rory started playing a song called "Bullfrog Blues" and he offered to take me up on his shoulders. I was delighted and gladly accepted his offer to see Rory on the stage. It was a great feeling looking out over the crowd although I was surprised that nobody in the crowd or on the stage jumped up and down pretending to be a bullfrog during the Bullfrog Blues. It seemed to me that it would have been the thing to do.

I was also fond of our father's friend Dermot, not just because he accompanied us on this particular day. He always seemed to me to be trying to make everything okay for me and Gar. On other occasions, I sometimes wished he was my father. But this day had been a very nice day spent with our father. It made me think he wasn't so bad, for a while at least.

****

As we no longer saw our Mam, the postcards and greeting cards we received from her during this period were simply a reminder to me that she existed but was notably missing from our lives.

We were instructed by our father and Caroline to leave the cards on the dining room table with the rest of the post. My father would look at them and air his disgust about her *off gallivanting* wherever she was at the time.

I realised at this stage that there was very little hope that we were ever going to be living with our Mam again. I used to look at the postcards and wonder why she wasn't standing at the door instead. Our father and Caroline would drive this point home.

If she loves you, why isn't she at the door looking for you, instead of swanning off on holidays?

I was certainly starting to come around to thinking that my father had at least one thing right. She was off on holidays and we were not. It was starting to seem very much like he had a point when he said that she didn't care about us.

Another point my father had made played on my mind. She was enjoying what appeared to be the longest and most exotic holiday she had ever had, yet she had never taken us on a foreign holiday of any sort. Gar and I only started going on holidays abroad when our father and Caroline took us to France.

Bearing all this in mind and having tried various methods to impress my father and earn his praise, I discovered an easy way how to please him and obtain praise quite by accident.

I was home alone and the post had just arrived. As part of my daily routine, I had to separate my father and Caroline's post into separate piles and leave them on the dining room table. As I flicked through it, I was left holding a postcard addressed to me and Gar. I knew immediately it was from our Mam. I read the message, which included the sentiment that she *missed us*. It hurt to read it. Here I was stuck living a nightmare and the one person who I felt had the power to save me was, as it seemed to me, on holidays in the Middle East.

The next time a postcard arrived I decided not to leave this postcard on the table. I was sick of listening to my father's rants about *'Jo-ism'* and the whole situation. In some way to bring closure to any ideas of my Mam coming back to get me, I tore the postcard in two and threw it in the bin.

When Caroline arrived home and used the bin, she saw the torn postcard in it. She didn't say anything to me at the time but when our father came home, she told him, within earshot of me, that our Mam had sent a postcard and that I had thrown the postcard in the bin rather than put it on the table as per the instructions that had been given to me. She looked at me, smiling wryly as she said it, seemingly relishing the thought that I would be in some trouble with my father for this act of disobedience.

My father called me over coolly. He had the postcard in his hand. He didn't seem angry. Instead he seemed quizzical. He asked me why I threw it in the bin.

I'm sick of reading about her massive holidays, I said.

My father's reaction was unprecedented. He looked at me as his face lit up with delight. He was beaming from ear-to-ear.

Did you hear that Caroline? he shouted happily, *Did you hear what Fin said?*

I heard him hun', she responded, in her fake happy tone but with clear awkward surprise.

My father then praised me, calling me *a great kid*.

That evening, I didn't go hiding in my room but stayed downstairs in the sitting room with my father and Caroline. My father was constantly looking over at me, smiling, seemingly proud. For a few days, I remained 'in the good books'. I soon realised that my moment of frustration at my Mam had gained me all this praise and welcome attention from my father.

From then on, I was delighted if I saw the post first when a post-card from our Mam came. I would rip it in two and put it in the bin and await the praise and recognition. On one occasion, the postcard wasn't noticed by the time it got buried under more rubbish and so I dug it out from under the rubbish and placed it on top of the rubbish so that it would be seen. It worked and our father saw the postcard.

Did she send another postcard? he asked knowingly.

Yeah, another one about her off gallivanting in exotic countries, I responded, robbing the very line from him that he had often said to me.

He was delighted again. He enjoyed hearing this as much as I enjoyed the praise. He was bouncing around after it like a man who had just won on a scratch card.

In some ways, this was a rather devious plan by me to gain an evening or two where I was not subjected to Caroline or our father's rants. But I justified my behaviour by convincing myself, based mainly on my father's assertions, that my Mam had abandoned us in favour of a long expensive holiday. There was a feeling that I was betraying her but my options were limited. The truth was secondary to survival. Maintaining this act meant gaining the praise of our father and having conversations with him as if he liked me. Caroline's rants were reduced and there was a happier atmosphere in the house.

But in the back of my mind, it still bothered me. I knew that our Mam had tried to maintain visits, only for our father to scupper them. She had tried to maintain phone calls only for our father to prohibit them.

Deep down, I wanted to keep the post-cards and dig deeper into why my Mam had really gone to these places. I knew she was, even in my youthful opinion, overly religious and God was some part of this.

Until this point, I believed that my father was ultimately responsible for my Mam not being there and I think that my father knew this. My father seemed to suspect that I still yearned for my Mam and he was correct in his suspicion. He would make remarks alluding to my suspected yearning and attempting to persuade me to accept that our Mam was a terrible person. He would say that the *mollycoddling* that my Mam had given me had almost ruined me. He would tell me that the sooner I stopped any thoughts of my mother, the better, *for my own good.*

The reason that tactic hadn't worked to this point was that I knew it wasn't *for my own good.* I knew it was for his good. I didn't even understand why or how it helped him financially or otherwise. I knew it was good for him because it was what he wanted. This seemed obvious to me. The very fact that I knew he was lying about it being *'for my own good'* made me think that all of this was his fault even more. Why would he try to be so persuasive otherwise? If our Mam was so terrible, then surely, we could come to that realisation ourselves in our own time.

However, even though I knew this, I learnt that by carrying out simple acts that appeared to show loyalty to our father, I could temper his suspicions about me. It didn't matter anymore what I thought or whose fault it was or was not. The simple fact was that, if I acted as if I thought my Mam had in fact *abandoned us* and that our father was due gratitude for *saving us from her,* life was a bit more bearable living under the same roof as him and Caroline. Once I realised how I could do these small acts to make my life easier, I maintained the act.

Chapter 14

Gar

In September 1992, one month after seeing our mother for the last time, our father and Caroline went to Florida and to Puerto Rico for three weeks. Our father and Caroline had gone to Puerto Rico to get married abroad as they could not do so in Ireland in those pre-divorce days as our father was already married, although separated. They were then to spend a few weeks in Florida on a honeymoon. The three-week period which they spent away was a period of great relief for me and Fin.

The downside was we were split up for the three weeks; I stayed with my friend in his mother's house nearby and Fin stayed with our Uncle who lived in Clondalkin. We both enjoyed this time immensely and swapped stories about what a great life my friend and our cousins had - they could have a second bowl of breakfast cereal if they wanted and as many slices of bread as they wanted until their hunger was satisfied. It was all so different to how things were for us at home and we revelled in it. From then on, we always took every opportunity we could to spend time away from our home having seen how the rest of the world lived.

We saw each other once over this period. Our father's friend Dermot, who had attended the Rory Gallagher concert with us, had arranged for Fin and me to meet up so that we would not spend the entire three weeks apart. He brought us to the cinema and the three of us had a great day. We both thought Dermot was a very decent man and we used to spend a lot of time with him and his family.

When our father and Caroline returned home from the wedding/honeymoon, they threw a 'wedding party' in a nearby venue. This is recorded in the diary as follows:

26 September 1992

Today was the party. At 5.30 we arrived. We had soup, beef, fruit salad and cake for dinner. Then everyone came. We danced and got up and sang. Everyone said we were good! Yaaahhh! We all went home at 1.30 and they had a big party. When we got up they were still up. I cut my finger on glass so I put it under the tap and I went white and nearly fainted! We went to the Open Day and I got a bronze in the 200 and I bet a 15 year old and got a bronze in the 600.

Fin and I were important guests at this party and our father even encouraged us to get up and sing with the band. As attention-seeking kids who loved singing, he eventually had to tell us to stop as we were taking over the stage. I do not remember Shane being at the wedding party, whether he was not invited or whether he chose not to attend. He had been kicked out of the house by our father earlier that year on 21 May, four months prior to the party, but had called up to the house a number of times since.

In relation to my cutting my finger, that incident occurred the morning after the wedding party, when Fin and I had got up in the morning to find Caroline and our father still up drinking and looking the worse for wear. Caroline was in the conservatory, sprawled drunkenly across the couch grinning from ear-to-ear as she counted the cheques and cash that they had received as wedding presents. After re-counting the cheques a few times, Caroline became convinced that one cheque had gone missing and ordered me to immediately trawl through the black plastic rubbish bins to see if I could find the missing cheque. The bin bags contained empty bottles and cans from the party and it was while I was rummaging through one of these bags for the cheque that I cut my finger on broken glass and my finger bled badly. I put it under the tap which just made it bleed more and seeing the water turn red caused me to start losing consciousness and nearly collapse on the kitchen floor. I recovered shortly afterwards, wrapped my finger in a bandage and resumed helping Fin clean up after the party while they had a few more drinks in the conservatory before they eventually went to bed later that morning.

Fin

While I enjoyed the time spent away from our father and Caroline in my Uncle and Auntie's house in Clondalkin, I was reminded of my father and Caroline when surprisingly I got a postcard from them from Florida. The postcard, dated 3 September 1992, says:

"Hi Fin
Having a great time, just relaxing at the pool now.
Tell you all about it when we get home.
Love Mum and Dad."

I read it and didn't know what to make of it. It was strange to see a reference to "Mum". I reasoned that it must be a reference to Caroline even though she was not my "Mum". Who else could he mean?

I saw from the handwriting that the postcard had been written by my father. Caroline usually wrote any greeting cards that our father and Caroline sent so I was surprised that my father had taken time out of his holiday to personally write me this postcard. I read it a few times and tried to see if he was trying to tell me something secretly. I remember reading *"tell you all about it when we get home"* and thinking that this might be a threat with a hidden meaning. I couldn't understand it at all.

Upon further examination I noticed that Caroline had written the address even though the message and the all-important *"Mum and Dad"* was written by my father. It seemed strange to me to have two authors on a postcard. It was the *Mum* reference that really confused me though, especially coming as it did only a month or so after our father had sent us down to Carlow with our Mam as punishment.

Chapter 15

Gar

By 1992, our father was successful in forcing us to call our mother by her first name only (Jo), and we were not allowed call her Mam. This is evidenced by my diary from 1992, in which I reference my mother only once and I refer to her as Jo and not Mam. The following entry is from 13 April, my father's birthday, five days after my thirteenth birthday which was on 8 April.

13 April 1992

I got a card (and badge, note) from Jo. She's in Gambia (where next?). Do you want good news or bad news? Good is that I got 71% in Science and 78% in History. Mr. Walsh gave me forty nine percent. I've forgotten all my vocabulary since 6th class.

Once we had stopped calling our mother *Mam*, our father took me and Fin to one side and asked us:

So how do you like living with Caroline?

Fin and I looked at each other. We both knew there could be only one answer to this question. We looked back at our father and said:

Eh, well, it's grand.

That's good, our father said, *so you like Caroline?*

We looked at each other again; as if to verify with each other that our father expected a positive answer.

Eh, yeah, sure, we said awkwardly.

That's good, our father said again, and then he paused momentarily, before continuing:

If you like her, maybe you can start calling her your Mam, if you like?

We were both taken aback by this, knowing again that a negative response was not an option. We looked at each other again and nodded our heads.

Eh, maybe, we said, *maybe.*

Good, our father said, and he smiled and walked off.

When Fin and I had some privacy later on that day, we discussed our father's proposal and agreed that calling Caroline our Mam did not make much sense. We already had a Mam - it was not like she had died or anything. And Caroline was Caroline so it made sense to keep calling her Caroline.

This continued for a little while before our father took us to one side again but this time with a sterner tone in his voice, the kind of tone that turns a request into an order.

I see you haven't started calling Caroline your Mam yet.

Eh, no, we replied, *it just feels a bit.... weird.*

Our father shook his head disapprovingly.

Well, he said, *I think it would be good for her and for you if you started to call her Mam. It upsets her that youse haven't started calling her Mam yet after all she's done for you.*

Okay, we said, looking at each other again, *we will then, we will.*

Good boys, our father said.

And so, the charade began.

I felt it was best, given the threatening tone our father employed, to try to do as he wished and to try to call Caroline our Mam as much as possible. For a while, every sentence from my mouth addressed to Caroline would begin with:

Caroline, I mean, Mam...

My brain was not able to simply switch from calling her Caroline to calling her Mam, even though my father had ordered me to. Matters worsened when our father took me to one side again and told me that while it was good that I was trying to address Caroline properly, I should be addressing her as 'Mum' and not 'Mam'. He did not explain why this was but I guessed it was linked to the fact that we called our mother 'Mam'.

So, I then went through a period of addressing Caroline with:

Caroline, I mean Mam, I mean Mum…

It was all very confusing.

Eventually, through practice and under my father's gimlet eye, I got used to addressing Caroline as my Mum and my father began introducing her to people as our *mother* and referring to her in conversation with us as *your mother.*

Throughout the diary entries in 1992, I refer to Caroline by her name, 'Caroline', even referring to her as Caroline on her birthday on 27th May 1992. However, by January 1993 I am referring to her as 'Mum' as the following entry shows:

13 January 1993

Mum saw the zip on my jacket and went mad. Ah well, better sew it up. Had Shepherd's Pie for dinner.

The diary shows the changes that took place as a result of our father's actions in the space of about eight months:

- May 1992 – We are still calling Caroline by her name
- August 1992 – Our father cut us off from our mother
- September 1992 - Our father 'married' Caroline
- January 1993 – We are by then calling Caroline our "Mum"

Fin

When our father originally *suggested* addressing Caroline as our mother, I was abhorred by the idea. It actually made me feel physically sick at the thought of it. I tried not to allow our father to know my true feelings.

As it transpired, I had no choice in the matter - the word "Mum" would not leave my mouth when addressing Caroline even if I wanted it to. It was just too unnatural.

After a few verbal attempts by our father to persuade us, it appeared that Gar was getting the message. Our father told us that it upset Caroline that we didn't call her Mum. The truth was that I didn't care if I upset her or not. Despite being constantly told that I owed Caroline for all she did for us, I didn't believe I owed Caroline anything. In my view, she had done nothing for us and I would have happily seen her walk out of our lives at that point. I felt it was her who owed us for all the work we did for her.

I found the whole thing even more frustrating that despite our father insisting that Caroline desperately wanted us to call her our mother, Caroline herself didn't ever request this of us personally. I was already of the opinion that she didn't want us to be living in the house with her, so it seemed completely bizarre to me that she would want to be our mother and for us to call her our mother. I was sure my father was wrong in his assertions that she wanted this. I desperately wanted to challenge my father's insistence, but I was too fearful of his reaction.

Since Caroline appeared to be indifferent about the issue, I realised that when my father wasn't there, I could get away with not calling her "Mum". I could simply address her as Caroline. If my father was there and I wanted to get her attention, I found another way of doing it, without having to actually call her "Mum". My usual method was to loudly say:

Ehhhhhhhhhhh, for as long as necessary.

Then when Caroline looked around and I had her attention, I could say whatever it was that I needed to say

Should I put the potatoes on now?

I would also get her attention while blatantly avoiding calling her Mum by walking over to her in the same room and tapping her on the shoulder to ask her a question. I would do anything rather than call her *Mum*. This worked for a while but it was only a matter of time before my father put a stop to it. One morning, I was in the kitchen and our father ordered me to ask Caroline (who was upstairs) about something or other. I walked out to the hallway and heard the hairdryer on so I knew that Caroline was in the landing at the top of the stairs drying her hair.

Caroline, I said in a hushed tone so my father wouldn't hear it from the kitchen.

Having got no response and hearing the hairdryer still whirring, I glanced into the dining room and checked to ensure that our father was still in the kitchen and out of hearing distance.

Caroline, I shouted a bit louder this time.

Suddenly, my father came storming out of the dining room, his face red with anger.

What are you still doing calling her Caroline, he said, seemingly careful not to let Caroline hear him saying it. He grabbed my arm and twisted it and dragged me into the dining room. The hairdryer continued to whirr upstairs.

Well? he demanded, pushing me.

Would it not be easier to just do as you were told? he added, pushing me again and slapping me across the side of my face.

S-ssorry, I said, starting to cry, *I'll do it in future*

Do what? he said menacingly, even though we both knew what *it* was.

I'll….I'll call her Mum, I said hesitantly, finding it hard even under duress to say that I was going to do it.

Do it now, he said *Go on* and he motioned me towards the stairs.

And stop your whinging first! he insisted

I instinctively knew this meant he wanted me to call up to Caroline, addressing her as *Mum* as if I was doing it voluntarily. He stood towering over me, staring at me threateningly.

Mum, I called up, my voice wavering as I pretended to be happy.

Yes, Fin, she called down in a more pleasant voice than usual. The hairdryer had stopped whirring a few minutes before so I knew that she had heard at least the tail end of my argument with my father. The fake niceness really annoyed me - I was eleven years of age and they seemed to think that meant I was stupid.

I asked her whatever it was I needed to ask her and she answered, again in a fake happy way that she did sometimes when she talked to people on the phone.

There, my father said sternly, *that wasn't hard was it,* he sneered.

Isn't it easier to just do as you are told? He remarked as he walked off.

From then on, I addressed Caroline as *Mum.*

****

The charade that we had to play out extended much further than calling Caroline our "Mum" and agreeing with denigrating comments our father made about our real mother. We had to pretend to like Caroline all the time, despite her temper and obvious dislike for us. In public, we had to pretend to like her even more. Many frosty conversations took place in our father's car on the way home from a relative's house because Gar or I had said the wrong thing or acted in a way that didn't make us look like two happy boys with their happy parents.

The charade also extended to strange things that we were forced to play along with that made no sense to us at the time. In October of 1992, I was in sixth class in school and feeling quite senior. My father told me that I was to be dressed up for Halloween to go trick-or-treating. I told my father and Caroline that I didn't want to dress up since none of my friends were doing it anymore as we considered ourselves too old to do it. Despite this, I was told I had no choice. I didn't understand why and I watched in dismay as Caroline proceeded to make a 'tree' costume with black bags, Sellotape and leaves. Photographs were taken and I was sent out to call from house to house showing off my costume. I remember a friend a year younger than me laughed at me as I walked out onto the road. I was honest and laughed and said shaking my head:

I know it's ridiculous, I don't have a choice, my parents are making me do it.

This made my friend laugh even more and the two of us stood there chuckling. Kids a few years' younger stared at me as they walked past, making accusations that I was going to take sweets from houses that were meant for them. It was all very bizarre and I decided to look on the bright side that I would have a bag of treats at the end of it.

In December 1992, despite the *computer-locked-in-the-spare-room* episode of the previous Christmas, Santa was once again resurrected. This time I knew to completely play along with the fiction and our father managed to hide a decent sized snooker table away from our prying eyes until we woke up on Christmas morning. When we came down on Christmas morning, we found half chewed carrots on the tiled floor in the kitchen. I knew that this was supposed to show us that Rudolph had been in the kitchen. So, I played along. I told Caroline, under my father's watchful eye, that *Rudolph had eaten the carrots*. She looked like she believed what she wanted to hear too and we had a nice, if a little strange, Christmas.

I remember trying to convince my father and Caroline that I believed in Santa so much that I wrote a letter to Santa and placed it in the fireplace. Of course, I knew this was all another charade but after the previous year I duly played along, as did Gar. We even went to visit Santa with Caroline as if the whole computer-room key episode had never happened.

A day or two before my birthday in 1993, Caroline had taken off a pair of shoes when she arrived home from the pub and left them lying in the hallway. As I tidied up the day before my birthday, I took the shoes and put them in the small storage room under the stairs. This was a room where the Hoover was stored with space on the floor for putting your shoes when you came in the front door. As it transpired, this particular pair of shoes (a pair of high heels) was what Caroline deemed to be one of her 'good pair of shoes'.

Caroline was not impressed that I had put these shoes in the downstairs storage room instead of bringing them upstairs to her bedroom and lost the head screaming at me that they could have been damaged with the Hoover being put on top of them.

I received the 'unruly convict' treatment as punishment. Then on the day of my birthday in January, the 'unruly convict' treatment was lifted and Caroline was as nice as pie to me. I had a very pleasant day with birthday cake and smiles. I was allowed to wear my good clothes and we had cake and crisps and lemonade after dinner - a proper party. My father produced his Pentax camera and tripod and we all smiled for a *"family"* photo. This was the norm on these supposedly happy occasions and could take twenty or thirty minutes to set up and get the photograph 'just right'. The tripod was used to ensure that we were all in the camera together. Without it, our father wouldn't be in the picture. There was a running "joke" when our father said he was getting the camera that he took too long to get what he considered to be a *good* picture and killed the mood. Caroline always seemed uneasy as the camera was set up but smiled all the same. But messing with cameras aside, I went to bed happy after a good day.

On 8th January, I awoke to find that since my birthday was over, it was back to normal - the 'unruly convict' treatment was back as if my birthday hadn't happened. It amazed me how Caroline could pretend to be nice and act like she liked me on this one day of the year and then switch back to "normal service resumed" the very next day. She was also able to affect this temporary personality change when certain visitors were in the house or if we were visiting others. She would suddenly and temporarily become that person she was when I had first met her, an apparently very pleasant person. The real Caroline would reappear as soon as the visit or the birthday was over and her ill treatment of me would return.

Chapter 16

Fin

In and around this time in early 1993, the topic of our father and Mam's impending separation proceedings in court became a regular discussion around the dinner table. We were asked by our father what would we say in certain situations and what I understood to be a test was carried out. I would be asked in varying ways by our father about how I felt about my Mam and I was expected to answer in a way that showed that I disliked her and that she was a bad mother. He told me that someone may ask me these questions (there was talk of meeting with a child counsellor before the court case) and if I didn't answer them correctly, *I would be put in a home.* I remember hoping a child counsellor would ask me these questions because I really wanted to be put in a home and taken out of my father's house.

So, in order to try and get put in a home, I would answer my father's questions in a vague way, refusing to say what I knew my father wanted me to say. My father and Caroline would discuss my responses intently with each other in front of me. I realised that it was a going to take a lot for me to get put in a home. I actually suspected at the time that my father knew I was secretly hoping to be put in a home because he stopped using the home as a threat after a while. Caroline continued to use it though and would shout things at me like:

You'll end up in a fuckin' home and you won't like it or

You think you have it tough now? Ha!

My father seemed to be edgy about my nonplussed reaction to Caroline's words.

But most of the time, I knew what they wanted me to say and so I said it. If my father said to me:

Did you like living with your mother?

I would say *No.*

This was a blatant lie but it was what I knew my father wanted to hear.

After these discussions, I would retire to my room and lie on my bed and cry and think about why this was happening and work out ways that I could answer in such a way that would get me into a home without consequences from my father. I thought at the time that he would always be there when the questions were asked. I pictured him staring intently as a stranger tried to get the right answer from me. I could never give any answer other than the one my father wanted in that situation. I was too afraid of him.

I cried out of frustration but not that I felt sorry for myself. I actually thought that the situation was my own fault. The fact that I wanted to be in a home or wanted to live with my Mam meant that I was a bad person. That is how it was portrayed to me by my father and Caroline so I started to believe it. As much as I disliked them, they were still adults with power over me, so I figured they were right.

****

Our father got us involved in helping him win his case against our Mam in a number of different ways, including collating documents for court as described in the following entry from Gar's diary:

2 February 1993

Jo sent a letter this morning so Dad was writing one to his solicitor. This certain document was missing so we had to look for it. We didn't find it, of course.

There were certain standard places where you would look for "documents" misplaced by our father: the writing desk in the dining room, his bedside locker and certain presses in the kitchen. We all had access to these places to the extent that I found my father's affidavit for his separation case against our Mam and read through it. There were other documents that were more carefully guarded however. The photographs from Christmas, Halloween, family holidays etc. were stored in a brown suitcase upstairs in the so-called *guest room* (although there were rarely any guests). The suitcase had a coded lock and it was spoken about by our father and Caroline as if it was a treasure chest. Neither Gar nor I understood the

106

significance of this when we were younger, but as Gar innocently points out in his diary, the photographs within that case were very significant for something:

19 April 1993

Sorted out all the photographs with Mum for the solicitor. I hope we win (with a little help from God) night! It's 1040.

The "we" that Gar refers to is, of course, "Team Dad": us, Caroline and our father together. Strange as it sounds, I also hoped "we" won. I understood that winning meant our father and Caroline (or "us" as it was presented to me and Gar) would not have to give our Mam any money and losing meant "us" having to give her money. There wasn't a chance that losing could mean Gar and I would live with our Mam. So, selfishly or otherwise, I knew the consequences of us losing would lead to my father and Caroline being even angrier than usual. I also figured I would somehow get the blame if we lost, especially as Shane was gone out of the house at this stage.

I worried about my Mam. I thought that if she had no money she might have no food or shelter but I tried to forget that. Perhaps my father realised this as he said disdainfully on numerous occasions:

Don't worry about her; she's well able to look after herself, she always fuckin' has been.

Worrying about my Mam conflicted with me rooting for "us" winning so I tried to believe my father to ease my own conscience. But he was so detestable that it was difficult so I usually justified it in my own way. I decided my Mam had let me down. She had let my father take me even though he was clearly mean. So, I decided it was her fault for not stopping that. I still felt terrible but I felt it justified me being up for "Team Dad".

Gar

As the above entries show, our father and Caroline took steps to ensure we helped them with the preparation of our father's court case against our mother, whether it was finding documents, sorting out photographs or just listening to our father's views on our mother's case or her Legal Aid solicitor. We always knew when a letter came

107

from our mother's solicitor as our father would loudly make his feelings known about the contents of the letter and our mother's solicitor:

That fucking stupid prick, Mc Nulty!

Fucking Legal Aid!

She's never worked a fucking day in her life. I'm rearing ye, she's off swanning around and she wants fucking maintenance? She can fuck off.

The day after I had helped Caroline sort out the photographs for my father's solicitor in advance of the court hearing, Fin and I met with our father's solicitor to talk about our mother which is recorded in my diary as follows:

<u>20 April 1993</u>

The solicitor said that it's okay to meet her [our mother] if it has no effect on us. Well, one, it reminds us of all the bad things that happened and she keeps telling us she forgives us even though we did nothing (we were only about eight or nine). Two, she asks questions but isn't interested in the answer. Often I had to repeat myself before she said "Oh, that's nice". Three, it makes us feel depressed. Well! Night! It's 9.10.

Before I met with my father's solicitor, my father had a number of conversations with me to nail down the supposed reasons why I didn't want to see my mother. These reasons did not naturally occur to me but were what I made up to try and give my father the answers I thought he wanted to hear. When he asked me what we spoke about with our mother, I told him that she had said she 'didn't blame us' for not wanting to take presents off her or giving her hugs. He was triumphant when he heard this and by the time he was finished interrogating me had twisted this into our mother *"saying she forgives us even though we did nothing wrong"*. He told me to make sure I told that to his solicitor when I met him, as well as the other things he had said.

When I did meet his solicitor, I got the impression the solicitor was sceptical about my claim that I did not want to see my mother. He specifically told me it was *okay to meet my mother*. When he said this,

108

I wanted to tell him that I did want to see my mother but I was very conscious that I needed to stick to the script I had went through with my father so I recited the three reasons above to him as my father had coached me to do. When I finished my recitation, he seemed to me to be even more sceptical.

The diary records that we went to see the solicitor again the next week:

29 April 1993

We went to the solicitor today so I think everything's grand (please be to God).

What I meant by 'grand' was that my father seemed happy with me that I had said what I needed to say to his solicitor. I was still very anxious though of the upcoming court case. I was afraid that I would say 'the wrong thing' either to my father's solicitor or to the court and my father would be angry with me. My diary records a few days later:

2 May 1993

But first comes the court which I hope we win and never have to see Jo again (please be to God). Night! It's 930.

I wrote the above entry as if my father and Caroline were standing behind me, reading it over my shoulder. By this stage I desperately wanted the outcome to be what my father wanted so that he would not be angry with me. I did not actually hope that I would never see my mother again.

Two days later, the day of the court case is recorded as follows:

4 May 1993

So we went to court today. It was adjourned! But what that means is that it won't be on for a year or two so I'll be 16 and Fin will be 14 so it's the best result we could have got! We had biccies and Coke paid for very nicely by the solicitor. We got home and went to running. Then we went to Nanny's. She looks really well. Had a lovely chicken curry. Night! It's 9.30.

Our father was very happy that the court case had been adjourned and he had pushed off the day of reckoning for a year or two at least. He explained to me why this was a good thing; by the time the court case was eventually heard, I would be a few years older and therefore, as he explained it, I would make a more credible witness in court against my mother. Although I was not happy at the prospect of having to give evidence against my mother, I was relieved that at least I had got through the current process without making my father angry.

As it transpired, the court case was never heard.

****

With our mother having been out of our lives since the previous year, our father increasingly portrayed Shane as the example to us of a useless family member. We were told that Shane had followed in his mother's footsteps and anytime we stepped out of line, we were behaving like Shane, our *'loser brother'*. Comparisons to Shane replaced the *Jo-ism* comparison our father had previously used. Our father's attitude to Shane is reflected in my diary entry less than ten days after the court case when I record how I lost the key to my school locker but was afraid to ask my father or Caroline for the money to replace it:

13 May 1993

I don't want to ask Mum for money and start hassling her (she's enough on her plate) and Dad would only start comparing me to how Shane was (which, although true, I don't want to be told).

Usually when we asked Caroline for money for anything, regardless of the amount, it was met with a tirade of abuse. Then our father would tell us that we shouldn't have hassled her, stating the common phrase that *she has enough on her plate*. So, we soon learnt that any way of avoiding asking for anything from Caroline was usually the best option, hence my desire not *to hassle her*.

The entry also records my certainly that my father would compare me to Shane because I had done something wrong. Shane is still only eighteen at this stage having been kicked out of the house a year before. The locker key saga plays out over the next few days:

110

I ran the mile really fast today. Skinner [a teacher] wants the locker keys on Friday. I'm bricking it. Please please God I get £1.50 somewhere. I don't want to ask them. I'm praying, please Mary and Auntie Anne as well. Night! It's 10.50.

20 May 1993

I got £1.20 off Bod [my best friend] for the key. I'll use my 30p. Night! It's 930.

The saga was finally over and I was relieved that I didn't have to ask my father or Caroline for anything. Fin's travails continued though. As the below entry records, we were in trouble if we just went to a friend's house to play the computer:

22 May 1993

Fin went into Bob's and played the computer so he's in trouble. Anyway. Night!

The diary records a few days later, on Caroline's birthday, the toll that everything was taking on Shane:

27 May 1993

Mum's birthday today. We bought her a bunch of flowers and a card. We had a party. Real bad news, diary, Shane has had a nervous breakdown and is in a private hospital. He's moving back in with us. I hope he gets better quickly and has a brilliant and prosperous and long life (please God, please Mary and please Auntie Anne). It's 930. Night!

In my naivety I do not seem to have seen any significance that Shane's breakdown occurred on the same day as Caroline's birthday.

Fin

After Shane's breakdown, I heard Shane try to explain what had happened to our father. Shane said that he had been down in Carlow visiting our Mam and our other relatives. On the day of his breakdown, the same day as Caroline's birthday, he was in the house our Mam had grown up in, when, according to Shane:

I just saw red.

He said that he ran out the door into a field and started screaming at the top of his voice. He fell to his knees, still screaming.

My father's reaction to Shane's explanation that he had "*just saw red*" was typically unsympathetic:

What the fuck do you mean, you just saw red? he said sneering.

By what he said and the tone of his voice, I felt that my father thought that Shane was making it all up.

Chapter 17

Gar

A few days after Shane's breakdown, the diary records:

1 June 1993

Dad is in visiting Shane.

Shane was diagnosed with paranoid schizophrenia and for a few months he stayed in St Patrick's Institute, a private psychiatric hospital. Here, Shane had his own room and television and constant care as it was a private facility. Shane recalls St Patrick's as the land of milk and honey compared to St James's public psychiatric ward which he later came to know so well.

Our father told us that he knew Shane better than the doctors and regularly proclaimed that Shane was not schizophrenic and that *it was all an act*. He visited Shane regularly in St Patrick's which was surprising to us as our father had never seemed interested in Shane at all before this. It was clear to us from conversations our father had with Caroline at the time that the visits to Shane did not involve the two of them sitting around eating grapes. From what I gathered, the visits instead involved our father variously telling Shane to *get his act together*.

The whole schizophrenia thing was, in the words of our father, *a cod*.

After a few months in St. Patrick's, Shane's condition had stabilised to the extent that he was discharged from hospital. Both myself and Fin were pleasantly surprised to hear that he was moving temporarily back into the house.

However, a diary entry from a year after Shane's breakdown shows that it wasn't long before he was back in hospital:

26 April 1994

Broke Shane's light bulb and put a new one in his room. Shane is back in hospital. He needed it I think.

For the next decade or so, Shane was never far from another spell *"back in hospital"*.

Fin

Throughout this time, our father and Caroline spoke incessantly about what a failure Shane was and how our own bad behaviour could result in us ending up like him. We were told that they had given Shane so many chances but he had failed to take them.

Shane occasionally called up to the house but his moods and behaviour were erratic. We were told by our father and Caroline that this was because he was using drugs. Some of his behaviour seemed to tally with this. On one occasion, Shane had been in the sitting room with us drinking tea and had said he was going to the toilet. A few minutes later, he hadn't returned. We checked the hall and saw that the front door was wide open. It turned out that Shane had taken our ghetto blaster from the kitchen and ran off up the road with it.

I was particularly annoyed by this episode as I had recorded all of my favourite songs on a cassette tape that was in in the ghetto blaster at the time. As a result, it wasn't difficult to convince me at that stage that Shane was indeed a bad person. He had crossed the line this time by stealing from the house. Shane was now a pariah.

He didn't call up for a while after that episode and the message that he was a very bad son was forced upon us time and again. Shane's confirmation portrait that hung in the hall was taken down by our father or Caroline and put up in the attic. The portraits of Gar and I still hung there beside a faded patch of wallpaper where Shane's used to be. Every time I looked at that patch, it was a sinister reminder that nobody was safe from exclusion from our father and Caroline's world. I knew that if I didn't toe the line, my confirmation picture could be the next one taken down and I could be cut out of the family.

Over dinner one evening, we were instructed that Shane should be avoided. If we saw him while we were out, we were to ignore him. If he called to the door, under no circumstances was the door to be opened to him.

Our father ordered us that if the doorbell rang, we were to check who was there by looking through the glass on the front door. If it was Shane, we were not to open the door. I remember one occasion where I looked through the glass and Shane was standing looking the opposite way to the door. I was aware that if Shane had looked at the glass, he would see me, so I dropped to the floor. I hid at the bottom of the door where it was likely Shane wouldn't see me. Shane rang the bell twice more. I crouched uncomfortably, conflicted between hoping I wasn't seen and wanting to answer the door to my brother and see how he was. Eventually Shane left and I squirmed out of my hiding place, feeling immensely guilty.

I told our father how difficult it was operationally to pretend to Shane that no-body was in the house. Shortly after this, our father had a CCTV camera installed at the front door that beamed through to the television in a room at the back of the house. At first it was passed off as being installed to fend off any potential burglars, sales people etc. but I thought it was primarily to allow us to see if it was Shane at the door. Now, when the doorbell rang, I could check who was at the door by changing to channel zero on the TV in the back room and I could watch whoever it was at the door pace up and down and maybe pick their nose and get frustrated and walk away.

Now we had no excuse to answer the door to Shane. There was one hitch with this plan, however. Shane was more persistent than our father gave him credit for.

On an occasion with this new installation, Shane rang the doorbell when I was in the back room watching television. I flicked to channel zero to see Shane standing there. I muted the volume and sat watching my brother looking around in a mildly agitated state. He rang the doorbell three more times and stood there. I was hopeful that he would turn around and walk away. I closed my eyes, consumed by guilt, and hoped the doorbell would not ring again. It did not. I opened my eyes to see that Shane was no longer on the television screen. I assumed he had gone and considered whether I should ring Caroline to tell her that Shane had called. I figured it might quell my guilt if I got reassurance from her that not answering was what I should have done. But before I even got to the phone, I heard what sounded like footsteps on the roof above me. This backroom that I sat in was a one-story extension and it was quite obvious from the stomping noise above that Shane was on its roof. I sensed immediately that Shane was climbing over into the back garden and very soon, he would look through the back window and see me sitting there. So, I raced around into the hallway into an area that was completely out of sight of any window in the house. It wasn't that I was afraid of Shane. I was afraid that I would have to answer his inevitable question:

Why didn't you answer the door?

I reasoned that I could not say it was because our father told me not to. This would surely cause Shane to wonder why this was. It would obviously hurt Shane. I could not say it was because I did not want to, since this was simply not true. I figured I had no excuse to make. I felt so guilty sitting there on the floor. Eventually I heard Shane attempt to open the back door with no success since it was locked. I heard the thuds of Shane climbing back over the extension to the front of the house. I sat in the secluded area of the hallway for a further few minutes to be sure that Shane had gone. Eventually I got up and peered out through the glass of the front door, then double-checked the back garden before I was eventually convinced that Shane had gone.

I relayed the story to my father and Caroline later that evening. The story only further entrenched my father and Caroline's belief that Shane shouldn't be allowed in the house.

I was actually praised for outwitting a determined Shane.

Gar

Despite outwardly obeying my father's orders in relation to my mother, inwardly I did not fully abide by his rules and allowed myself one small act of rebellion. I used to say my prayers every night in bed before I went to sleep. This was something I learned from my mother who encouraged us to say nightly prayers.

I used the same format every night for my prayers. I always began with the gratitude:

Thank you God for all the good things you have given me. I would insert examples of good things – Ireland beating England in the rugby, nice food we had, fun that Fin and I had playing the computer.

116

Once the gratitude was out of the way, I felt it was okay to launch into the requests. The first request was always to keep my family safe from harm. Before my father's replacement of our Mam with Caroline, it went as follows:

*Please God, keep my family safe from harm - Dad, **Mam**, Fin, Shane, all my friends and relatives, all my cousins, Aunties and Uncles and a special prayer for my Nanny and Grandad.*

After our father's substitution of Caroline in our mother's place, I changed this part of the prayer:

*Please God, keep my family safe from harm - Dad, **Caroline,** Fin, Shane, all my friends and relatives, all my cousins, Aunties and Uncles and a special prayer for my Nanny and Grandad.*

After my father ordered me to call Caroline our "Mum", I changed it again:

*Please God, keep my family safe from harm - Dad, **Mum**, Fin, Shane, all my friends and relatives, all my cousins, Aunties and Uncles and a special prayer for my Nanny and Grandad.*

But that was not the end of the prayers - there was one person left to pray for. Even though I knew that my father would not approve of it, I always included my mother in my prayers and so I would also add:

And please God, a special prayer for Mam, please keep her safe from harm.

Over time I changed the Mam reference to "Jo" as I did not want to be *totally* disobedient to my father, even in my prayers.

I maintained this secret prayer for my mother - my silent, solitary act of rebellion.

Chapter 18

Gar

Many of our childhood memories involve rugby and these rugby memories begin from around the time Caroline was introduced to us. Our father's relationship with rugby was an unusual one. He was from Crumlin, an area not renowned for its rugby. He never played the game (although we sometimes overheard him claim that he had during some bar-talk in the rugby club) but around the time of his separation from our mother in 1989 he enrolled me and Fin in mini-rugby and Shane in the under-15s team. Rugby on a Sunday morning became part of our relationship with Caroline as she would attend with our father at our matches and at the socialising that took place afterwards.

Our father and Caroline seemed to enjoy the social side of the rugby club. When I went to London for a weekend rugby trip to London Irish, Caroline and my father came with us with many of the other parents.

After a few years, in and around the time of the adjournment of the court case between our mother and father in May 1993, their love affair with the rugby club abruptly came to an end and with it their support for us and our lift to rugby every Sunday morning. We continued to attend training and matches sporadically as we received lifts from the parents of other kids for a while. With the increasing awkwardness of mooching lifts while our father and Caroline slept off their hangovers, we gave it up. At around this time we were now both in secondary school and we could play rugby there instead of up in the club.

My father and Caroline showed no interest in watching or supporting us playing for the school, where there was no social side for them.

When I had started out in secondary school in September 1991, I was reasonably popular kid with a lot of friends. Some of my primary school friends had also moved to the same secondary school and were in my class. Because of my experience playing mini rugby with a club team, I was immediately installed as captain of the first year "A's" rugby team.

However, despite starting out with a lot of friends from my old school and being the captain of the rugby team, my popularity declined quickly throughout first year. There was one episode in particular which had a negative effect on my self-confidence and popularity with my classmates. I had a group of friends that I used to spend lunchtime with and we used to play chasing in the fields and waste-ground behind the school. One day a group of second year students came upon us and chased as shouting and yelling, but without any particular malice. Unfortunately, in my rush to escape, I slipped on a muck hill and my trousers were covered with muck from belt to toe. I was immediately very worried that Caroline would kill me when she saw my trousers and spent a futile hour trying to clean them in the bathrooms. If anything, the water only seemed to make the muck stains worse. As I walked through the corridor, the Dean of my year, a friendly priest, stopped me and asked me what had happened to my pants.

I hesitated before I answered him. *I could just tell him I fell*, I thought, but then, *what would Dad and Caroline say?*

As this thought flashed through my mind I thought that if the Dean got involved then I could tell Caroline that I was a victim of these boys and it was so serious that the Dean had been forced to get involved. The Dean's intervention could save me from being given out to by Caroline. Although a part of me felt it was wrong to tell on the other boys, I reasoned that it must be okay to do that sometimes as Caroline and my father had always encouraged me to tell on Fin and Shane and not to *be a fuckin' liar*. My mind was made up.

I fell at lunchtime, I told the Dean, *when I was chased by some older boys.*

The Dean's face became serious. *What older boys?* He asked.

One of the boys had a very distinctive Morrissey type quiff and pair of crepe shoes and it was not long before the Dean recognised who I was talking about. He told me to wait and went down the corridor and reappeared with the boy in tow.

I began to regret my decision now. I was going to have to rat on this boy to his face. That had not been part of the plan.
Is this him?

The boy stared at me, mouth open, incredulous.

Yes, I said, *that's him.*

The Dean nodded and told me to go to my class and he would deal with the offender. I found out shortly afterwards that the boy had been suspended. I went home and explained everything to Caroline and I was not blamed for what had happened; Caroline said it was the older boy's fault. A few days later, the boy confronted me in the corridor. I remember he didn't seem angry; he just seemed to be unable to believe why I would do such a thing.

Why did you do it? He said. *Why did you rat on me?*

I stuttered some reply about *not wanting to get in trouble.*

He shook his head at me, *Rat,* he said.

For the next few days I watched as the boy pointed me out to his friends. Soon everyone knew me as a Rat.

As a result of episodes like this, my former friends started to drift away and I lost self-confidence. I started to get bullied. This started out as verbal bullying, in the corridors and in the classroom, with insults and accusations of homosexuality:

Shut up Murphy you queer

Murphy you fag

Gaylord!

The strange thing was, while the abuse upset me, I had become almost used to this sort of verbal abuse from living at home with Caroline. An entry from the diary from 1993 (when I was in second year), gives a good example of this:

In training it snowed. It didn't stick though, got home had a lovely lunch and rang Bod........ His mom asked me did I want to stay for dinner so there was a big rigmarole and Mum ended up calling me 'queer' and said I acted like a gaybo.

Caroline calling me a 'queer' and a 'gaybo' made me more afraid of her then ever. Not only was she being mean to me, she now seemed to know the names that the bullies in school used.

The verbal bullying in school moved onto physical bullying as I got older. There were two episodes with one bully in particular that stood out.

On the first occasion, I was walking with my friend Bod near the local church when the bully approached me. A group of girls stood nearby looking on giggling. I was not afraid when I saw the bully as he was somebody who had been friendly towards me in school and who occasionally walked home with me from school.

So, when he started a conversation with me, I talked back to him as normal although I did begin to get a bit nervous as he kept looking back to the group of girls and grinning. After a few minutes of this, he suddenly drew back his fist and punched me in the face. I was stunned by this. I put my hand up to my nose and asked him what did he think he was doing? He challenged me to punch him back and I told him I would not do that and I turned around. As I walked off I could hear him laughing as he went back to join the gang of girls that were watching. It later became apparent that this episode had merely been a test to see if it was true that I did not fight back and the proper beating was yet to come.

Although I felt humiliated and embarrassed walking home, I felt that I had done the right thing by not fighting back. I remembered being told in school about Jesus 'turning the other cheek' and my mother used to quote this to us when we were younger too. I thought it was the right thing to do. So, no matter how bad the provocation, I always tried to turn the other cheek and ignore it.

The proper beating took place on a sunny Sunday afternoon on 18 June 1995, the day that Jonah Lomu almost single-handedly overpowered the English rugby team in the semi-final of the Rugby World Cup in South Africa. I was sixteen years old and had watched the match with my father and Caroline in the bar of a local GAA club. When the game was over I left while they stayed drinking in the bar and on my way home I went into the newsagents to pick up a bottle of Coke. Back then, the supermarket itself was closed as it was Sunday so the car park and surrounding area was empty with the exception of a small number of people popping into the newsagents and a gang of teenagers around my age who used to hang around outside. The gang was a mixture of guys and girls as you would expect at that age.

As I walked across the car park that afternoon, I saw the gang sitting outside the newsagent. My self-preservation antenna began to tingle – I recognised the bully as being among the gang - but at this stage they had seen me and there was no turning back. Nothing was said as I entered the shop but as I walked out and away from the gang towards home through the deserted car park, I heard one of them say:

He doesn't know what's coming to him.

The hair stood up on the back of my neck in fear and trepidation. I had a strong feeling that I knew exactly what was coming to me.

Just keep walking, I told myself.

Halfway across the car park I heard the sound of tyres screeching and a car shrieked to a halt in front of me. The bully got out of the passenger seat and walked towards me menacingly. The gang from outside the shop had now assembled closer to the action and were looking on in anticipation and laughing. The bully was a short stocky muscular lad with spiky hair. He was wearing a white vest to show off his muscles which he flexed a few times towards the gang before he suddenly turned back towards me and punched me in the stomach. He pulled back his fist and then punched me in the face.

I raised my hands to protect myself but did not punch him back. The bully laughed over at the gang. He looked at me again –

Punch me back, he said, *why won't you punch me back?*

At this stage I was very sure that if I so much as a raised a finger in anger the fight would have ended with me in a bloody pulp lying on the ground. He wanted me to fight back because he wanted to impress the girls with his fighting skills. My refusing to engage was lowering not just the entertainment value but also the value he could claim as a lean, mean fighting machine. He didn't let this stop him punching me a few more times but when it became clear I would not reply he stopped and stood there looking at me.

I was angered by the sheer injustice of it all.

Is that it? I shouted at him, *are you finished now?*

No, he said, and hit me a few more times.

Eventually he got bored of this and turned around with his hands raised in the air like a champion boxer. He walked back across to the gang to receive his adulation. They cheered him and jeered me, the girls in particular, as I stumbled on across the car park and onto the road towards home.

It is a curious thing that in all the episodes of physical bullying I endured, I never cried at the physical pain until it was all over. Perhaps it was because I had played rugby since I was nine years of age and was well used to receiving knocks to the head and body. I sported with pride a black eye in both my communion and my confirmation photos. I also suspect it was sheer pride and bloody-mindedness that I would not give the bully the pleasure of seeing me cry. However, that did not stop me from crying once the episode was over and the bully was out of sight.

On this occasion, as soon as I was away from the car park and walking along the main road, I felt my nose and realised it was bleeding heavily. I then looked down at my top and saw that it was covered in blood. This upset me not just because of the blood but also because the jersey was an Australia rugby jersey which I had just bought for myself from my earnings over the summer. I had hoped this top would be admired by my peers and lend me some much-needed respectability in the cool stakes in school.

Looking down at it now, covered in blood on its first wearing, it seemed to make a mockery of my attempts to beat the bullies. As the shock and injustice sank in I broke down on the pavement and bawled my eyes out.

As I bawled, a car pulled over beside me and a kind looking, middle-aged woman opened the window and asked me *if I was all right*. When she saw the blood on my jersey she saw that I clearly was not. I blubbered to her about what had happened and she offered to give me a lift home which I accepted gratefully. When we got to the house she asked me if my parents were there. I told her they were not but they would be home soon. She asked me did I know where they were so that we could call them.

Even though I knew exactly where they were, I hesitated. I knew my father and Caroline would not want me telling strangers that they were in the pub on a Sunday afternoon. Especially as I was covered in blood - it would look bad for them. So, I told her I did not know where they were but reassured her they would be home soon.

I thanked her for all her help and went into the house and turned off the house alarm.

I stood in the hall, feeling very sorry for myself, and started to cry again. I felt completely alone and just wanted to disappear. My hopes of being accepted again by my peers and ending the bullying had been dashed in spectacular fashion. I could not seek comfort from my father or Caroline who were in the pub. I decided that despite it being only five or six pm, I wanted to just go to bed and get away from everything. I took off my blood-stained clothes, drew the curtains, climbed into the top bunk and closed my eyes.

A few hours later I was awoken by the sound of my father and Caroline returning from the pub. After a few minutes, Caroline opened the door of the bedroom and asked me what I was doing in bed so early. I told them, half ashamed, what had happened. My father's immediate reaction was to propose rounding up some friends and a van to take the perpetrator up to the Dublin Mountains to administer retribution. I am not sure if he was serious but he didn't go ahead with the plan.

He asked me:

Did you fight back when the bully attacked?

No, I said *I didn't.*

Why not, he said *why didn't you?*

Because if I had, it would have been much worse, I mumbled.

My father was disappointed by my answer. He shook his head slowly from side to side and said to me:

You know what your problem is? You're just not streetwise.

He said this in such a sad and disappointed tone that I felt ashamed and cowardly that I had not fought back.

It made me feel as if the whole episode was my own fault because *I was not streetwise.* I felt that I was a failure in his eyes.

Chapter 19

Fin

One night after Caroline had given out to me for something and I was upset she said mockingly to me:

Don't worry Fin, maybe you will get another postcard.

I knew that Caroline suspected that I was still thinking about my Mam and that she was trying to provoke a reaction from me. At that time, I was trying to convince my father that I 'believed' my Mam was a bad person so I figured that this comment was a trick on Caroline's part to get me to say something to show that this was not the case. But I did not rise to Caroline's provocation and said nothing.

Such was the constant fear and feeling of necessity to cover everything up, that when she spoke those words, I wasn't outraged. Instead I was worried that she was close to uncovering my secret that my tearing up the postcards was indeed, as she apparently suspected, all an 'act'.

Caroline made a few more 'honest' remarks to me after that. One morning when I was cleaning up the sitting room after one of their boozy mid-week nights, I realised that I didn't have time to finish the job and make it to school on time. Around this time, Gar and I often left at around the same time as one of our neighbours who would usually offer us a lift. Gar had gone already and taken the lift so having missed it, I knew I needed thirty minutes to make it to school on time by foot.

In order to avoid being late for school, I suggested to Caroline that I would finish cleaning up their mess from the previous night when I arrived home from school later that day. Caroline looked at me as if she couldn't believe my suggestion. She smiled maliciously and said:

I couldn't give a fuck if you're late for school.

Then she let out a little laugh as if to scoff further at my suggestion.

I was angered at her remark. I never seriously believed she was the loving mother our father wanted us to believe she was, but I felt she could at least pretend.

I decided I was right to be angry. I realised quickly that she wouldn't be comfortable telling our father what she had said since it went against the whole pretence. I also saw no point in continuing pretending myself since she wasn't willing to so I shouted back at her.

Go fuck yourself

and told her that she was:

a schizo bitch.

I added for good measure that

I hope you crash your car on the way to work.

Instead of cleaning up the mess, I threw a small coffee table over, which landed on its side and I headed off to school.

My heart was racing as I walked up the road to school. I kept thinking that this was a big moment. The lie was no more. The truth was out. She didn't care about me, she had said so herself and I had told her where to go.

I was gutted at the realisation that nobody else had heard it. I'm sure Caroline was aware of this when she said it. I knew my father wasn't going to believe me over her and I was sure Gar wouldn't believe me either.

I thought about what would happen if Caroline told my father about my reaction and I was afraid that he would kill me. As I walked to school and thought about it, I turned to see Caroline's car driving by me slowly. She must have left the house shortly after me. With her window rolled down, she smiled out and simply said:

Bye, Fin, have a nice day at school.

I couldn't work out if it was a threat or had she realised what she said was wrong and this was her way of apologising. She drove on, waving out the window as she disappeared into the distance.

****

While I spoke back to Caroline occasionally, I was still petrified to talk back to my father. I didn't want to be in an argument with him over anything, I feared him greatly still.

Late into the summer of 1994, my father invited me along on a trip to buy some wood and things he needed at a DIY store. I was surprised at his invite and welcomed it as a nice gesture. Our father always picked the music to listen to in the car and we weren't allowed change it unless instructed to do so.

On this particular journey with my father, he was acting quite friendly towards me. We stopped at a garage and I was left alone in the car. Buoyed by my father's pleasant mood, I changed the station to a pirate radio station called Pulse FM. As my father got back into the car to the beats of some dance music, I waited to be told to switch it off. But he didn't tell me to turn it off and started the car and drove on. I was delighted. He did comment, jovially, that it was *repetitive shite* but he appeared to be considerate to the fact that I was enjoying it. We chatted some more and I was thinking that I could get along with him after all.

As the journey continued, a silence developed as we seemed to run out of things to say. I tried to say something but I got no response. I stole a glance at my father and saw that he had a pensive look on his face. He almost looked nervous. I looked away and as I turned to look out the window, he spoke again:

What would you do if you were to meet Jo now? (by 'Jo', he was referring to my Mam).

The usual uncomfortable feelings I felt when I was around him flushed through my body. I knew if I said the wrong thing he would shout at me and the whole trip would be ruined. I hesitated for a good few seconds, took a deep breath, before I responded with great gusto:

I'd walk past her in the street if I saw here, she abandoned us!

I said it with as much conviction as I could muster but feared that I had made it obvious that I didn't mean it by waiting so long to say it. My fears were allayed immediately as my father thumped the steering wheel and laughed jubilantly.

Ha, I knew it, Fin. Do you know what, some people used to say to me, they said that blood is thicker than water and all that shite. They were all wrong! he bellowed triumphantly.

He was even happier than when I'd torn up the postcards my Mam had sent us.

When I looked at him smiling victoriously, I felt a bit sick. I realised that I wanted some kind of father-son bonding so I could convince myself that I had a normal father-son relationship with him. He had let me play my music and been nice to me building up to this, but once he asked the question, I felt like that had all been a swizz and I had been set up. I looked at him again, with his triumphant, almost gloating grin. *How could I ever like this guy?* I thought.

Gar

When we were in our early teens, our father and Caroline took up horse riding and started spending most of their weekends in Kilkenny.

When they started this hobby, we were deemed to be too young to be left home alone so we were sent to stay with our Nanny and Grandad in Crumlin. We absolutely loved these weekends and wanted them to last forever. A typical entry from my diary (when our father and Caroline went to Scotland for the rugby weekend in January 1993) records one day spent with our Nanny and Grandad:

17 January 1993

Grandad got up and burnt four slices of toast. Then he burnt another four slices. It was so funny! Nanny copped on but she didn't say anything. We watched Cannonball Run II. Grandad loved it. Then we watched Romancing the Stone which was gas as well.

Nanny and Grandad thought it was deadly. I had ham and potatoes and beans for dinner. It was lovely.

The reaction of my Nanny to my Grandad burning the toast was in stark contrast to the drama that would surround burnt toast in our house. If Fin or I burnt even one slice of toast, we would be screamed at for wasting a slice of bread that Caroline had to pay for. The way that my Nanny pretends not to notice what my Grandad had done made a big impression on me. I marvelled at how she could have *given out* to my Grandad but she decided not to. Instead of a drama, the whole episode ends up being a big funny joke.

The first few weekends that our father and Caroline went to Kilkenny we stayed with our grandparents for one night, Saturday. After a while that became two nights on Friday and Saturday night and after another while our father and Caroline started staying down in Kilkenny on Sunday night too and driving home early Monday morning. They would usually decide to stay on the Sunday night last minute and place a call to our Nanny or Grandad on Sunday afternoon. Fin and I spent Sunday morning fervently hoping and praying that the phone would ring with the instruction for us to stay another night. There was absolute joy for us when this phone call came in. Just being away from them for another night was reason for celebration.

Throughout our teenage years, Fin and I manufactured every excuse we could to spend as much time as possible away from our father and Caroline and they seemed happy enough for us to do this, once it suited them.

In around 1995, a friend of mine moved from our road to the north side of the city. As it was such a long journey to visit him, I persuaded Caroline and my father that it was necessary for me to stay overnight in his house whenever I did visit, provided I had all my chores in the house completed before I left. The relief I felt when I walked out of our house knowing that I had 24 hours without worrying about being given out to was palpable. When I got on the first of the two buses required to get to my friend's house I did so with a spring in my step.

By this time, Fin had spent so much time with our grandparents that he made good friends in Crumlin and would visit our grandparents regularly to meet these friends and escape our house.

Unfortunately, the flipside of any time away from the house was that when we returned home Caroline would invariably find something to give out to us about to bring us back to reality. This led to Fin and me becoming experts at identifying whether or not they were at home by looking at external signs visible from the road as we walked back towards home.

The first sign we would look for as we walked down our road towards our house was whether the upstairs windows were open or closed. If the windows were open this meant our father and Caroline were almost certainly at home and the hope would be replaced with disappointment and the stomach churning fear of what punishment awaited us. If the windows were closed, then excitement would build that they were not at home. This would have to be confirmed as we got nearer to the house by the ultimate sign – was the car in the driveway or not? If the car was gone we would know we were in the clear and know that we would have peace when we went inside, at least until they came home.

Once we entered the house we would try and suss out where they gone so that we could answer the most important question – when are they likely to come back? Clues would be gathered to paint the fullest picture: Has the shower been recently used? What shoes are missing? Was the horse-riding gear gone? Did Caroline bring her hand-bag? Did our father wear his good jacket? Was the kettle still warm?

We could also check for signs of what we might face whenever they arrived home. Did our room look like it had been searched? Was anything missing if it was?

These weekends and nights spent with our grandparents or our friends showed us how normal people lived. It was always remarkable to us when we visited our friend's houses that they seemed to be able to simply help themselves to food from the press. There was no rationing of biscuits or chocolates, let alone bread and Weetabix.

The cloud of fear that hung menacingly in the air in our house did not seem to exist in our friends' houses.

Our father and Caroline took up horse-riding in and around 1995, when I was sixteen and Fin was fourteen. For the remaining years that I lived with them, they went down to Kilkenny almost every weekend for two or three nights. That meant that Fin and I spent a huge proportion of our weekends for many years either staying with our friends or grandparents or, when we were considered old enough (when I was eighteen or so), staying in the house without them.

These arrangements suited us just fine.

Chapter 20

Fin

I found it interesting when my father and Caroline took up horse riding which required them to travel down the country to Kilkenny, a neighbouring county to Carlow and socialise with people from the area. I remember my father having a particular dislike for people from rural Ireland - *culchies* as he called them derogatively. He appeared to have had a change of heart.

This new hobby was great news for Gar and me. After a couple of years, I was sometimes staying with my Grandad from Friday to Tuesday. The longer I could stay away from my father and Caroline, the better.

The feeling I got when I left the house on a Friday morning for school, with my sports bag packed to go straight to my Grandad's house after school, was one of pure delight. If you can think of the feeling you get when you leave your house to go on holiday, without the underlying fear that you have forgotten something; that is the feeling I got walking up my road on these fine Friday mornings.

My Nanny and Grandad were both lovely people. They were very welcoming and clearly loved seeing me and Gar. I remember staying there for a weekend in 1994. Gar and I were watching the Eurovision with them on a Saturday night. We drank red lemonade and munched on crisps. We were all excited that Ireland might win, which in the end they did. My Grandad chuckled away to Terry Wogan's cynical commentary. Even though he was clearly enjoying the spectacle, our Grandad jokingly gave out about us watching the show as if he wasn't interested in it. Nanny scolded him, knowing that he wanted to watch it as much as the rest of us. He laughed guiltily. Nanny was laughing too at his boyish antics. There was such a happy atmosphere in the house. As I watched them, I considered how great my life would be if I lived there permanently.

Having witnessed the relationships between my father and my Mam and then my father and Caroline, it was beautiful to see a real honest relationship of love that my Nanny and Grandad clearly had. I remember one simple moment where my Nanny was sitting on the couch and my Grandad came in from the kitchen and started singing to her. Then he grabbed her hands and she stood up and they danced a little in the sitting room and kissed. It was so spontaneous and wonderful.

This is love, is what I thought. It was like a revelation.

My father and Caroline's relationship always seemed phoney by comparison. When my father would go on his *business trips,* they would kiss goodbye with a tongue kiss in the hall. Gar and I would usually be standing in the hall also as we were required to stand on ceremony and wave our father off. It was so awkward, I would look at the floor and try to remain upbeat at the fact that Caroline would be relying on our company and might be nice to us for the time he was away.

Even the apparently phoney love was often on the verge of collapse. They constantly rowed – usually away from the public eye. My father would often make solo trips to the pub after work for which Caroline would flip out at. Caroline rarely seemed happy to me. She would regularly pack up her gear and threaten that she was *moving back to her mother's.*

Our father sometimes said nothing as if he was disgusted with her and was just ignoring her. Sometimes he'd just get in his car and drive off without saying where he was going. This drove Caroline even wilder. Other times he argued back. One argument that sticks in my mind was him telling Caroline that he didn't care if she left because *there would be a queue of women lining up to take her place.*

In the end, despite repeated threats, she never actually did move back in with her mother.

Living in the midst of this kind of relationship only highlighted to me the special relationship our Nanny and Grandad had with each other. My Nanny and Grandad appeared to be in love with each other more than they were in love with either material goods or their own selves. They did selfless acts for their partner to make their partner happy, without expecting anything in return. I decided that when I was older and had a relationship, I wanted it to be just like my Nanny and Grandads' and nothing like my father and Caroline's. I wanted to grow old with someone and love them as much as I could see that my Nanny and Grandad loved each other.

Unfortunately, by the time of that Eurovision weekend in 1994, the whole family had noticed changes in our Nanny. Although she maintained her generous and loving manner, she was forgetful of names and of time and other things. Sadly, she was diagnosed with Alzheimer's disease. Despite her illness, she never lost her kindness. Every time Gar and I visited she would always give us an apple or an orange to take with us when we were leaving. She would usually smuggle these into our hands wrapped in kitchen paper so our father wouldn't see her 'mollycoddling' us. Once when she was in the throes of Alzheimer's, Gar and I were surprised and a little disappointed when we got outside and opened up the kitchen paper to see she had given us an onion each. Her heart was always in the right place though, no matter what stage her mind was at. After some time, it was decided that she would see out her days in St. Brigid's Nursing home in Blessington, otherwise known as Crooksling, where she could be cared for adequately.

Since it was said that our Grandad couldn't boil an egg, it was going to be a bit of a task for him to fend for himself. It seemed to suit everyone at the time that Gar and I would spend a lot of weekends with him, since we were well able to cook a dinner and keep his house clean (for which we received gratitude from our Grandad - in stark contrast to at home). So much so that instead of our Grandad doing our father a favour by minding us while they enjoyed their horse riding in Kilkenny, our father turned it on its head and presented it so that he was sending us down to mind our Grandad and thus my father was doing our Grandad (and everyone else in the family) a big favour. It didn't bother us either way, Gar and I were delighted to spend time away from home and Grandad seemed to enjoy the banter with us.

Even though our Grandad was our father's father, it was interesting how different they were. Our Grandad's nickname was *Spud*, which our father and practically the whole family called him. I don't think our Grandad was too fussed about being an authoritative type of parent (as opposed to my father, who demanded respect); he was more of a friendly type of man. I can't pretend to know what kind of a father he had been to my own father when he was younger, but certainly in my relationship with him; I found him to be quite easy going and loving. I held him up as a role model for me and decided he was the type of person I would like to be as an adult. He was sociable and everybody seemed to know him and stop to talk to him. He was also extremely kind and great fun. He always had entertaining stories to tell and loved to joke and slag.

As my Grandad and I both wanted to extend my visits beyond the weekend, we both sought ways to make that happen. In the beginning, I used to ring Caroline to ask her could I stay with my Grandad on the Monday night, having spent the weekend there already. This was usually unsuccessful and Caroline would tell me that my jobs at home needed to be done and that I was to *get my arse home to do them*. So, then my Grandad offered to make the weekly phone call to Caroline on my behalf, which was effective for a period, although there was usually a backlash for me when I eventually went home but I always felt it was worth it. However, after a while Caroline began to ask my Grandad to put me on the phone and would give me the usual instruction; *to get your arse home to do your jobs*. My Grandad was quite cunning though and he suggested that if I went upstairs when he made the call, he could tell Caroline I wasn't in the room to be put on the phone. As I was upstairs, he was telling the truth and he usually managed to persuade Caroline to let me stay another night this way.

After one of these particular phone calls, my Grandad called me down the stairs. He said that we were all set for another night but seemed a little perturbed, saying that Caroline was *annoyed on the phone for some reason*.

Then he blurted out:

I don't think they can understand that I love you and you love me and the two of us enjoy spending our time together.

I was touched by his comment and although I didn't think that was why Caroline was annoyed, I nodded saying that I thought he was right. I felt loved and it felt great. I had never felt loved by my father or Caroline.

****

By this stage I was spending at least every other weekend in Crumlin with my Grandad. This meant that with school Monday to Friday and the weekends spent with Grandad, I just had to survive the weekday evenings living with my father and Caroline so I took to spending as much time as possible in my room 'studying'. Like so many others in the world, I would be counting down the time for it to be Friday again.

When the summer arrived, Gar was working in the local supermarket at the weekends and could no longer go to Crumlin. However, I continued to go regardless. Grandad was always happy to see me and I was always delighted to visit him. I started to settle in Crumlin. I made friends with some of the other teenagers who lived there.

After many happy weekends spent in Crumlin, my Auntie, who was a very regular visitor and carer for my Grandad began to stay over in my Grandad's house a lot more, including on the same nights that I was staying over. For a while, I slept on the couch downstairs as there was only one spare bedroom. That worked for a while but as my Auntie began to stay more and more frequently, it became clear that the arrangement could not continue. I also sensed that there was a general feeling that the supposed reason for my visits, *to mind my Grandad,* had been reduced since my Auntie was now there to look after him.

One evening, my Grandad and I were watching TV when he lowered the volume down and told me that he thought I should be off chasing girls and having fun. He said that it would probably be better for me to not come down every weekend anymore. He said there were so many other people coming down that he didn't want to see me wasting my teenage years. He said if I came down and visited him for a few hours, he would be happy enough. I was a bit torn when he said this because I enjoyed spending the weekends with him, I had made lots of friends in Crumlin and I was not looking forward to spending any additional time back with Caroline and my father again. However, as my Grandad pointed out, they were in Kilkenny every weekend now. Neither of us stated why this was important but I sensed that my Grandad had a fair idea at this stage why that was.

My Grandad then took out a box with some memorabilia that he said he wanted me to have. He proceeded to talk me through its contents. Among the items in the box was a poster seeking people's support when he successfully ran for Mayor of Crumlin back in 60's or 70's. He had held the poster up outside the local church after mass, years before, when he was campaigning for election. It did not say which year it was but suffice to say it was when he was in his heyday.

Also, in the box was a roll of bus tickets from when Pope John Paul II had visited Dublin in 1979, with the back of the tickets advertising the event. There were some other things as well but these two mementos stood out to me as defining Grandad. He had worked all his life as a bus conductor and it seemed that in his spare time he had given back to the community he lived in. I was glad of the gesture my Grandad made and I remember thinking that these items were more valuable than money as these were items that seemed to mean something to my Grandad.

As upset as I was by the prospect of ending my weekends with my Grandad in Crumlin, when he had said that I should be out chasing girls, I had blushed a bit, because as he perhaps suspected, I actually was out chasing girls already. As was typical of him, he pointed out my blushing to lighten the mood but I was too shy and embarrassed to tell him that the reason was because he had hit on the truth.

Chapter 21

Gar

Throughout our teenage years, our father constantly reinforced the myth that Caroline was our mother. Our real mother was never mentioned, except occasionally by unwitting neighbours or relatives who would quickly be quietened by a dark look from our father. All photos of us with our mother were destroyed or hidden in the attic.

Over the years, my father and Caroline developed few friendships that lasted more than a couple of years. It was very common for our father and Caroline to become 'great friends' with a couple from the rugby club, or a couple from the pub, or a couple from our father's youth, or a couple from the horse riding club and for us to spend time with their children and for us all to spend time on holidays together.

Then one day, inexplicably, the friendship would be over and we would never see the family again. Although no official explanation would be given to us, usually a few harsh words would slip out of our father and Caroline after a few drinks giving us an indication as to why we were no longer spending time with the couple and family in question. Generally, it seemed that somebody had had the audacity to question our father's opinion on something important to him or to offer a view of the world that was at odds with his and that potentially was even critical of him. It seemed that people who expressed such opinions were not the kind of people our father wanted to spend time with.

Occasionally, somebody, a neighbour or a cousin or someone who knew our mother, would innocently ask us – in front of our father - how our mother was. The person's enquiry would usually go unanswered and our father would change the subject or we would mumble something apologetically and change the subject ourselves.

Sometimes our father would have to use stern words to *remind us who our mother was* [i.e. Caroline].

When I was sixteen I went away with my class on a trip to the Gaeltacht in Donegal for the weekend. The Sunday of this particular weekend was Mother's Day which was a day I generally did not enjoy as it brought up memories of my mother and made me wonder where she was and how she was doing. I would have much preferred to just skip Mother's Day but that was not possible in our house as our father made sure Mother's Day was commemorated fully every year from the first year Caroline moved into the house with us.

Every year we had to buy Caroline a card and a gift for Mother's Day. Every year we performed the awkward ritual of presenting the gift and card to Caroline in front of our father. Caroline herself even seemed to feel awkward about the whole charade but we all partook in it because our father demanded it.

It was therefore with some relief that this particular year, 1995, I realised I was in Donegal for Mother's Day so that I would not have to go through this annual ordeal. On the Monday after Mother's Day, I found a payphone in the middle of the Donegal Gaeltacht and called home as I was expected to check in. My father answered the phone and before I could say anything, he asked me menacingly:

Why didn't you call your mother yesterday?

I was a bit thrown by this and replied nervously:

My mother? Caroline?

'Caroline' was clearly not the right thing to say and my father lost the plot on the other end of the line.

Your mother! he said, *your mother! It was Mother's Day; why didn't you call her to wish her Happy Mother's Day?*

I apologised and lied and said I had tried to call her but I couldn't find a phone the day before as we were in the middle of the Gaeltacht. My father eventually calmed down but gave me very clear instructions to make sure I had a card and a bunch of flowers for *"my mother"* when I got home from Donegal that night. After the call I then spent the next six hours on the bus fretting about what awaited me when I got home and hoping that if I got a card and a bunch of flowers everything would be okay. As it was, I managed to get a card and flowers. They were accepted with due ceremony that evening by Caroline full of fake smiles and my father scowling over proceedings.

****

On another occasion around this time I was in Religion class and our teacher was leading a discussion on marriage and divorce which was a hot topic at that time in Ireland as there was a Divorce Referendum in November of that year. I was feeling even more sensitive than usual that day so when the teacher opined that *there was never a situation whereby a child should not see one or other of his parents* I interjected to disagree with him. He was a good teacher who tried to engage in adult discussions with us so he asked me *when I thought such a situation might arise.*

I told him, as I burst into tears, that it was ok:

Not to see your mother when she's abandoned you because she doesn't care about you.

As I balled crying the teacher tried to console me and admitted that maybe there were times when it was ok. I eventually regained my composure but by that stage more damage had been done in terms of lowering my self-esteem and the esteem my class mates held me in.

****

Throughout this time, despite disappearing for months on end, Shane always reappeared and continued to call to up our house, usually when our father and Caroline were not there. When he rang the doorbell, we generally obeyed our father by not answering the door and cowering out of Shane's line of vision as he stood outside trying to see in the window.

One night, Fin and I were awoken by the simultaneous sounds of shattering glass and a car alarm blaring. We were in our bedroom at the back of the house and could hear our father and Caroline moving around in their bedroom across the hall at the front of the house. We got out of our bunk-beds to investigate. Caroline opened their bedroom door, invited us in and told us to keep quiet.
Shane is outside the house, she said

It was pitch-black outside. Caroline motioned us towards the window and we pulled the curtains gingerly to one side so we could see what was happening. My eyes took in the scene of Shane walking in circles around my father's BMW with what appeared to be a metal pipe in his hands. The front windscreen was already smashed and as we watched he raised the pipe in the air and smashed down on the rear windscreen of the car. He then slowly and methodically smashed the remaining windows of the car before he dropped the pipe, turned on his heel, and strode purposefully up the road.

We were shaking and upset by what we had seen. It was very unusual to see Shane acting so aggressively. Our father seemed pensive but did not show much emotion at what was happening. Caroline's reaction was strange as she had seemed to invite us to observe the spectacle as if she wanted us to see what was happening. When Shane disappeared up the road, Caroline told us to go back to bed.

The next morning, we were told that the hospital had been on to say that Shane had checked himself into St. James's in the early hours and he was now in the psychiatric ward. We did not talk about this incident much directly afterwards. We did not discuss why Shane might have behaved the way he had. It seemed to me that Shane's choice of our father's BMW as the object of his aggression represented Shane's desire to make a statement against our father. Shane would have been aware that our father was very proud of his BMW, symbolic as it was of his perceived achievements in upward mobility.

However, as always, I kept these thoughts to myself. Over time, our father repeated his belief that Shane's behaviour was simply the behaviour of a drug addled maniac. The incident was spoken about as further evidence of why we should never allow Shane access to the house and as proof that the decision to banish him in the first place was the right decision. Our father and Caroline acted almost smug at how right they had been.

Fin

With my Auntie looking after my Grandad in Crumlin, I spent most of my weekends at home with Gar when our father and Caroline went show jumping in Kilkenny.

Over the space of the previous four or five years, Gar and I had drifted apart from each other. We did not spend time together like we used to when we were younger and there was deep mistrust between us, something which our father and Caroline seemed to foster. However, when we found ourselves as teenagers having a "free gaf" practically every weekend, we found that we needed to trust each other more so that we could take full advantage of our situation.

In the early days, we would innocently play Super Nintendo and watch movies when they were away. After a while Gar and his friends would hang out in the conservatory listening to the Smiths and the Stone Roses while my friends and I would be in the sitting room with MTV blasting The Wu-Tang Clan and Tupac out of the television.

After a few more weekends, Gar and I both witnessed some interesting things in our unsupervised house. I witnessed one of Gar's friends spraying an aerosol can into a plastic bag and then putting it over his head. Gar was with him out our back garden and it looked as though he might be even willing to have a go too. I quickly realised that Gar was no longer the rule-complying Daddy's boy any more. But I was taken aback by what they were doing. Given that I considered myself as a bit of a risk taker, I knew that if I thought that something was a step too far, it most certainly was. With our father and Caroline out of picture though, we were both prepared to take some risks.

On another aerosol related occasion, Gar came home to find one of my friends in the sitting room spraying a can of aerosol with a lighter in front of it to make a dangerous fireball. Rather than telling the person to stop, I sat watching. Now it was Gar's turn to be worried. Neither of us were too impressed with either of our friends' antics and I think there was a realisation that we had to set some limits to the behaviour that was to be allowed in the house. In turn, if we agreed on what we would allow in the house, we could be a lot more open with each other about what we were up to. The problem was that we were still a bit cagey around each other. In order to implement agreed rules that would work, we needed to be more honest with each other. We needed to accept that both of us would know a lot about the forbidden things that both of us could get up to. I still wasn't sure if I trusted Gar, fearing that he might divulge anything he knew about me to my father or Caroline, like the old days.

As it turned out, it was smoking cigarettes that allayed that fear. It was pretty much common knowledge that I smoked since I had been caught with cigarettes before. But I was pleasantly surprised when I heard from a friend in school that Gar was smoking too. Although I found it hard to believe, the guy who told me was very trustworthy and I failed to see what he had to gain by telling me that Gar smoked if it were untrue.

I still needed to see it with my own eyes though to believe it. One morning after one of our Saturday night house parties (and having just finished our top to bottom house sterilisation in anticipation of Caroline's return) Gar invited me out the back garden for a cigarette. We both knew that it was the start of a new era. As I had already been caught smoking, Gar sharing his secret with me was a bit more of a risk for him. In turn, he probably realised that me trusting him was a risk too as I was entitled to be more dubious of him.

When I saw Gar smoking that cigarette, I realised that he was very confident that he would not be crumbling under any interrogation any time soon. We had a chat about it and Gar said to me that he realised why I felt the desire to start smoking to fit in and that he had done it for the same reason. We agreed that we should be able to talk to each other and be more trusting with each other.

As much as I hate cigarettes now and the damages of smoking, lighting that cigarette rekindled the friendship and some of the trust that Gar and I once had when we were younger kids.

The result of this was that we were happy to let each other enjoy the freedom that came with my father and Caroline being away, provided there was no lunacy involved such as the aerosol incidents. We both worked together to ensure every Sunday that the house was in pristine condition for when they came home.

As a result of this teamwork and trust, we started hanging out more together. I no longer sat in the sitting room with my friends; instead, both sets of friends would sit in the conservatory together, all of us listening to the Stone Roses and the Wu-Tang Clan. Some people would be drinking and smoking and as long as it was somewhat controlled, neither of us complained. Gar went from being deemed by me as somewhat of an annoying rat to be a trustworthy older brother that I could confide in and that I respected.

When our father and Caroline returned on Sunday or Monday night, they never really asked what we did when they were away. Caroline would inspect the house when she got back to check that everything was in order and we would always ensure that it was in tip-top condition. But it was evident that their only concern when they went to Kilkenny was that the house and its contents were kept in that condition when they arrived home. I wondered at the time why somebody who was usually so hell-bent on finding things to rant about never seemed to take the opportunities that presented themselves when they came back from Kilkenny. I used to wait for questioning about what we did at the weekend but it never came. I gradually came to feel that they seemed to be only worried that their capital asset remained intact. After that, we seemed to have free reign to do whatever we wanted, provided it didn't impact on them in any way.

Chapter 22

Fin

One day, I was walking home from the shop after getting my father and Caroline cigars, when a woman who lived nearby stopped me on the street. I recognised her and I was aware that she was deaf and dumb. Despite her impairment, she was very comprehensible and she began to inform me that Shane was sleeping in a shed in his friend's back garden. I was disturbed by the news but because I didn't trust this woman enough to tell her what I really thought, I said a line that I thought my father would approve of:

He brought it on himself, I said

The lady asked me to repeat it, which I did. She was disgusted and stormed off. It wasn't my true feelings on the matter but I dared not let a neighbour know that, lest it get back to my father.

When I went home, I told my father about the conversation and he seemed more concerned that people knew that Shane was living in a shed than the fact that his son was apparently living in a shed. My father told me I should have told to the neighbour to:

Fuck off and mind her own business.

I was a little taken aback by his aggressive suggestion, especially as the woman was, in my opinion, a harmless neighbour. It all became clear however, when I heard him repeating the story to Caroline. As I listened in, he informed Caroline that my Mam had been friendly with the woman and the woman had in some way aired her opinions about my Mam being kicked out of the family home at that time. I felt appreciative of the woman upon hearing that. As I walked out of the room, my father stated that if the woman ever spoke to me again, I was to ignore her or better still, tell her to *fuck off*. I nodded that I understood.

I actually found the idea of Shane living in a shed somewhat amusing and somewhat reassuring. I was glad that he appeared to be living nearby and given that someone was willing to let him stay in their shed, I figured he was in an okay condition. After he smashed the windows of our father's BMW, we were aware he had checked in to

St. James' hospital for a period but went off the radar after that. As always when he went off the radar, there was a nagging threat that the next phone call we got about Shane could be to say that something very bad had happened to him. So, it was reassuring to hear that he was alive and living nearby, albeit in a shed.

I started to see Shane a bit more frequently around the area or on the bus and would stop and have a chat and a smoke with him and reassure myself that he was OK. He said he was staying in a friend's house until he sorted out accommodation for himself. He seemed in good form. After a while Gar and I went so far as to invite Shane up to a house party when our father and Caroline were away. He came up and seemed to have a pretty good time hanging out with our friends.

Without telling Caroline or my father, I sometimes met up with Shane away from the house. On one occasion, I met him for a pint in the Harp Bar on Westmoreland Street. I was underage but they didn't seem to mind serving me with Shane. Afterwards, he took me back to his new digs in the Oliver Bond off James's Street. I was a little fearful walking into the complex but relaxed when Shane started shouting back and forth with a few of the residents in a jocular fashion. I laughed as they referred to him as *Spud*, like my Grandad. Once inside his decrepit flat, I was greeted by the sound of snoring. Given it was mid-afternoon; I was a bit surprised to see this man lying on the couch who seemed fast asleep. We sat down and opened a can of beer and the man woke up and introduced himself. Then he mumbled something about *"needing a fix"* and left the flat. I looked at Shane worryingly and he just said *"Don't worry, I wouldn't go near that shit"* as he shook his head convincingly.

I enjoyed spending these times with Shane, edgy as they were. However, they often left me feeling more worried about his wellbeing.

Gar

In 1996 when I was seventeen, and earning money from part time work, I arranged to go with Shane (who was twenty-two) to Cork to see Oasis and the Prodigy in Páirc Uí Chaoimh. I was not a big Oasis fan but Shane was and we both loved the Prodigy. I had recently enjoyed my first weekend away with my friends when I saw

Radiohead in Galway and was keen go on another trip, this time to Cork. We had a great laugh on the bus down with Shane pointing out what he claimed were undercover Gardaí wearing light blue *Definitely Maybe* t-shirts. Shane told me he *was wide to them*.

Unfortunately, when we got down to Cork, Shane began to feel unwell (possibly relating to prescribed and non-prescribed medication) and decided he was going to sit out the gig in the stand. There was no way I was sitting down for the Prodigy so luckily I met some lads I knew in the standing area and enjoyed the gig anyway. I recall that when I met Shane afterwards he was a bit sheepish but we had a good laugh about it.

From what Shane told us, his existence at this time seemed to contain endless unpredictable episodes but yet would always follow a vaguely predictable cyclical pattern of peaks and troughs. The nadir would take the form of an incident or a breakdown which would convince Shane to seek help and check himself in to the psychiatric ward in St. James's Hospital. There would then follow a period of recuperation when Shane would listen to the doctors and take his medication and generally get better.

Upon getting better, Shane would then check himself out of the hospital and move back into some flat in the Oliver Bond or some other place, continuing to take his medication and generally leading something close to a normal life. After a period of time at this, the zenith of the cycle, Shane would proclaim himself cured and stop taking or dramatically reduce his intake of medication. This would inevitably send Shane back towards some incident or altercation with authority that would convince him to go back into care to get better again and restart the cycle.

According to Shane, at various stages he lived in less salubrious parts of Dublin such as the aforementioned Oliver Bond flats and the St Michael's Estate flats in Inchicore (since demolished). For a period, Shane was homeless, living in the Simon Community hostel on the Quays and getting his meals at the Mendicity Institute (or the "Mendo" as Shane called it) near Usher's Island.

Having Shane as our older brother was never boring.
On one occasion, desperate for cigarettes, Shane had walked into a newsagent in Rathmines and handed the man behind the till a piece

of cardboard upon which he had written *please give me 40 John Player Blue and I have a gun.* The shop assistant pretended to look for the cigarettes and while doing so gave the security guard the nod whereby the security guard immediately manhandled Shane to the ground. Shane started laughing at this and it quickly became clear to the security guard and to the shop assistant that Shane did not have a gun and was not in fact a physical threat to anyone. However, the Gardaí were called and Shane's behaviour was noted.

On another occasion, Shane decided to repeat the trick except this time at the Bank of Ireland in Rathmines. Rather than use a note, Shane decided he would stick something under his jacket that would look like a gun so that this time he would be taken seriously. For reasons unclear, but possibly because it was the nearest thing to hand when he had this brainwave, Shane chose a capo from a guitar as the pretend gun which he stuck under his jacket. In the middle of the afternoon, Shane walked in to the bank with no attempt to disguise himself with a capo sticking out from under his jacket which he brandished in front of him declaring that he had a gun and demanding cash.

This time, there was no need for a nod from the clerk as the security guard had already sized Shane up and grappled him onto the floor before he had a chance to use his capo in anger.

Later that day I answered the house phone and a Garda introduced himself and said they had arrested a man who refused to answer any questions except with laughter and they were trying to identify him. He said he had no ID in his wallet but the phone number was written on a piece of paper. I told the Garda that the man was probably our brother Shane and asked him did he know that he was a psychiatric patient? The Garda said he did not but was not surprised by this and asked me which hospital was he connected with. I told him to contact St. James's psychiatric ward. Shane was checked in later that day and we received a phone call from the nurse in the hospital to let us know. Our father and Caroline's reaction to such phone calls was usually met with annoyance, as if it was a hassle they could do without. The way it was relayed to us was that Shane had been *up to no good again* and ended up back in the hospital as a consequence.

Chapter 23

Fin

We were still expected to serve breakfast to our father and Caroline during our summer holidays from school. Since I was up early, I always tried to complete my chores in the morning time when most of my friends would still be in bed or having breakfast. This left the rest of the day free to be enjoyed until late afternoon when Gar or I would have to start preparing the dinner. As I had a free house, I invited friends in to listen to music or watch TV or simply have a chat, provided that I ensured that they were gone by the time Caroline got home, that the house was back in pristine condition and the dinner preparations were as she instructed. By 1997, I started to feel like I had a normal life like that of my friends and I actually woke up looking forward to each day.

There was also another reason for my new-found happiness. Following an initial meeting on the green with a girl I fancied, whose name was Fiona, we had spoken more and got to know each other better. I became friendly with her and some of her friends. Before long, I was hanging around with the group that she hung around with. Much to my dismay, she was going out with another boy in the group. However, after what seemed like a long time, she and that boy eventually broke up.

In April 1998, during our Easter holidays from school, I was watching MTV in my house with a good friend of mine. Fiona and her sister called at the door and I invited them in. My friend liked Fiona's sister and so he asked her could he talk to her and took her out of the room. This left Fiona and me alone in the room. I decided to take my chance and I asked her did she want to play 'spin the bottle'. Since there were only two of us there, it was clearly a cheeky attempt by me to steal a kiss. I was delighted when she agreed to play. It wasn't long after that day that we declared ourselves boyfriend and girlfriend.

Most of my relationships and my friend's relationships at that age hardly lasted a few weeks. But there was something about my relationship with Fiona that made me realise very early on in it that it was special. I remember after a couple of months professing to Fiona that I loved her. I started joking and telling her that I thought I might even love her more than ice cream and chocolate. As I was saying it, I realised that I truly loved her not only more than these things, but maybe more than any other person in the world. It was a revelation to me and to her and when I said it to her; she was a bit taken aback.

She told me that I should at least love my parents more than her and that although she was flattered, what I was saying wasn't exactly normal. She rather honestly told me that she loved her parents more than she loved me. I tried to backtrack by saying I loved my brothers and my Grandad just as much but I could tell my comment was something that she found very strange. All I could say was that love wasn't something that I could decide to feel for a person; I felt love for her and I didn't for my parents.

I think back now that until I had met Fiona, I hadn't really felt any meaningful affection for a long time. I had had some short relationships with girls but they never really developed into genuine love. Fiona would hold my hand or hug me or even just look at me in a way that showed me that she cared about me. I realise now that I hadn't had any affection that made me feel cared for, since when my Mam used to *mollycoddle* me many years before.

Caroline took a strange view of my relationship with Fiona. She used to ask me in a childish mocking way:

So, are you meeting your girlfriend today? with sneering emphasis on the word *girlfriend*.

Or sometimes she referred to Fiona as:

Your girlfriend, if that's what you're calling her, with similar sneers.

I'm not sure why she reacted like this.

On one occasion around this time, I was cleaning the kitchen and happily singing along to a song when Caroline came in. She looked at me and asked me *what I was looking so happy about*. I told her it was because it was mine and Fiona's six-month anniversary. She blurted out condescendingly:

Sure youse don't even know what love is.

I knew that a lot of teenage relationships didn't last forever but I couldn't understand why she wanted to constantly put down my relationship with Fiona. Her attitude reminded me of a bizarre comment she had made when I was about eleven years old and me and Gar had first moved in with her and our father. I was acting up in school and Caroline questioned how I was planning on living when I was older, given that I wasn't too concerned about my schoolwork. She stated that unless I was going to marry a rich woman, I would live a very poor existence as an adult. She then went on to say that she couldn't see that happen since no rich woman would marry me.

She went on to tell me that she found it hard to see *any woman* marrying me.

I thought of this episode and her current behaviour and thought to myself that Caroline had a very strange view on relationships. However, I wasn't going to let her behaviour get in the way of my happiness if I could help it.

****

It was around the time that Fiona and I got together when my father's attitude changed to being somewhat friendlier towards me.

As it happened I was re-evaluating my relationship with him anyway. One of the reasons for this was Fiona's reaction to me telling her I loved her more than my parents. Fiona had been the first person I had ever said it to and her concerned response made me realise my feelings were not normal

During this re-evaluation period, I reflected on an incident that had occurred a few years back when I was only ten or eleven. A friend of mine suffered an awful tragedy of his father dying. I remember seeing my friend crying at the funeral and feeling very sad for him. But I also remember feeling awkward at a thought that popped into my head at the time: that if it was my father that had died I wouldn't be able to cry. I then started worrying that if he died people would probably think I was heartless. I imagined people pointing at me in disgust because I didn't cry at my father's death.

Six years on, I still felt like I wouldn't cry if my father died and that bothered me.

I also had a general feeling of wanting to appear normal. I figured the best way to really portray normality would be to try to love my parents, or my father and my fake parent, as it was in my case. I ignored my previous assertion that love wasn't something I could just feel. Instead, I decided that I would attempt to force myself to at least make it seem to the world like I loved them. This meant a lot of trying to delude myself that actions my father had taken against my Mam, Shane and anybody else were done with some degree of good reason. I didn't feel I had to agree with his actions but I considered that perhaps my Mam or Shane had done something really terrible to him that I didn't know about or that he was keeping secret. I tried to tell myself anything to try and justify why he had done what he had done and I could tell myself that maybe he wasn't so bad.

****

In 1998, by the time I was seventeen, I felt that everyone living in the house was getting on as well as we had ever gotten on together. Gar was now in college and had plans to go away for the summer with his friends and all of the freedom that entailed. I was in the latter stages of my penultimate year in school so would soon be of an age where I could taste freedom too if I wanted.

I was already considering moving out of the house after school. I reckoned that I wouldn't have a hard time relying on just myself to survive. I had been cooking, cleaning, ironing and everything else in between on a daily basis for the last six or seven years so I considered myself very self-sufficient.

I wasn't worried about the financial aspect either. From the beginning of fourth year, when I was fifteen, Caroline insisted that I would fund my own schooling entirely from then on. I bought the books, the uniforms and stationery with money earned from my part time job. I also had to hand up a third of my earnings to Caroline, as did Gar.

I had grown up thinking basics like bread and milk were outrageously expensive given the way Caroline counted and rationed them. I was pleasantly surprised to find that this was not the case. I figured I would be quite satisfied with dinners of beans on toast if I was stuck for money when I moved out. I got a strong sense that Caroline wanted me to move out. It seemed to be what she expected of me.

I also considered that I would probably get on a lot better with her if I didn't live in the house with her. Caroline had treated Shane with similar condemnation to me when he lived in the house. But there was a period immediately after Shane had moved out when he used to call up to visit us. During these initial visits, it appeared to me like he was treated like a human being. He was welcomed and tea would be made for him and biscuits produced. He was treated like other visitors. It was all a very fake niceness but it was a huge step up from how he had been treated when he actually lived in the house. So I figured when I moved out, I would call up for dinners and visits and I would be treated with dignity like Shane had been for that period. The way I viewed it was so long as I didn't have a mental breakdown or stop towing the line as Shane had, it could continue indefinitely like that.

Despite all her mistreatment of me, I longed for the day when Caroline would treat me like a human being. Although I never bought my father's *mother/son* charade, Caroline was still a person in authority. Deep down I still wanted her to see that I wasn't the *useless lazy little fucker* that she constantly told me I was.

I'm not sure what caused that yearning and it pains me to admit that it existed. All we seemed to do was row with each other but if Caroline had turned around at any time and said she didn't want to row anymore and that we should be friends, I would have immediately stopped rowing and been happy that she had finally accepted me. The only realistic way I saw that happening was if I moved out.

Weighing everything up, I figured that if I moved out and I also maintained my new friendly relationship with my father, the ultimate goal would be achieved. I would have a happy relationship with my parents (my father and Caroline) in a similar way that my friends did.

Chapter 24

Fin

Fiona and I were almost inseparable during that summer of 1998. My house was usually free so we would hang out there listening to music and chatting. We were madly in love, which turned out to be just as well.

One day late in 1998, Fiona called up and told me that she needed to tell me something. I actually feared she would say something like her parents thought we were too close at such a young age and we should break up. It wasn't something her parents were likely to say, but I just feared the worst in situations like that.

Instead, she told me she was pregnant. I remember I was quite calm considering the news. I just walked over to her and put my arms around her. I told her everything would be okay. She was sixteen and I was seventeen. I figured it wasn't such a long ago when most couples had their first child at this age or even at an earlier age. I knew we were in love and I only ever saw our relationship continuing forever, even though other people thought that was naive. But there were some obvious worries.

The main worry was money. I wasn't sure how her parents would react and I was used to my father and Caroline's unwillingness to spend money on me so I was concerned. I reasoned, however, that there must be a system in place that allowed people who didn't have much money to successfully give birth to a child. I concluded that we would find a way to get through this.

Fiona was also worried that she would be expelled from her school for being pregnant. Nuns ran her school and the rumour was that strict Catholic rules were applied and a pregnant student would be expelled. I tried to reassure her that this sounded too unfair to be true but she was genuinely concerned.

Fiona was also obviously worried how her parents would react. We agreed to wait a while before we would tell both sets of parents. I was just glad that she had a twin sister who she could talk to when I wasn't around.

As much as my relationship with my father seemed to be improving, I didn't really expect anything from him. I was well aware he became a father to Shane when he was very young too so I couldn't see how he could react in an angry way. However, he could also be a hypocrite so I did not feel that I could go to my father to look for advice. I decided that I needed a responsible adult I could trust to discuss the situation with privately and in the end, I decided that the guidance councillor in our school was the most qualified to give me advice. This turned out to be a wise decision.

The guidance councillor agreed to meet me once a week and these weekly meetings were very beneficial to me. Although I had told some of my close friends, I realised that hearing them tell me that my life was over was not going to help, so I chose to ignore them. I remember one friend advising me to move to South America and start a new life. That helped in that I got a great laugh out of it and so did Fiona when I relayed that piece of advice I had received to her. But the only sensible conversation I had on the subject with somebody other than Fiona was with the guidance councillor.

During our conversations I tried to explain to him that my parents wouldn't be much help. I was vague about the reasons as I was still afraid to tell the truth. But the guidance councillor was obviously interested to know why I didn't think my father would be any help to me. I distinctly remember walking out of one meeting worrying that I may have said too much. I worried that he might figure out that something was not right with my parental situation. I worried he would explore it further on his own and possibly contact my father which could have dire consequences for me.

In our subsequent meetings, I steered any conversations away from my parents or Caroline. But the longer I went without telling them, the more the guidance councillor would press me on the issue. I figured he suspected that all was not well and I was convinced he was going to tell them what was going on. I decided that I had better tell them first before he did.

One Sunday night as I lay in bed thinking, I heard my father and Caroline coming home from the pub. I reckoned that the booze would most likely improve their moods, it usually did. If I waited until the next day, their moods would be worse since it was a Monday and they would be hung-over. I heard laughter downstairs and I decided that this was definitely a good time to break the news to them.

Gar was also in bed in the room we shared. We had been getting on well in recent times but I decided it was in both our interests to not tell him up to this point. It was such big news that I knew it would be a very hard secret to keep. It wasn't like the old days, I trusted him now to not say anything but I knew that if the shoe was on the other foot, I would rather not be burdened with that secret.

But since I was now on my way downstairs to tell my father and Caroline, I decided to tell Gar that I was going to tell them some news. Gar was concerned and asked me what the news was. I told him that Fiona was pregnant. He sat up, looking startled. He seemed lost for words before he finally said:

Will I still be able to go on my J1?

It is telling that Gar was looking forward to his freedom so much that this was the first thing he thought of. He then asked me if I was sure I wanted to tell them now, with them just home from the pub? I told him I was.

It felt good to have gotten if off my chest and tell somebody else the news first. Telling Gar was like a test run. I went down the stairs quite quickly, knowing that if I slowed up at all, I would most likely end up turning around and going back to my bedroom. I got to the bottom of the stairs and went through the dining room and into the kitchen. I paused for a moment. The door leading into the TV room was closed. I could hear the television volume was turned up loud. I took a deep breath and walked towards the door.

When I opened the door, my father and Caroline turned around a little startled. They obviously hadn't heard me coming. I told them I needed to speak to them. My father lowered the volume on the television and asked me to continue.

I blurted it out:

Fiona's pregnant,

The reaction was rather bizarre. Caroline started crying and put her head in her hands. My father started smiling, even laughing a little and said:

Well, you'll know all about it now.

He patted me on the back as if I had made him proud. It felt like approval and it was strange but awkward, particularly since Caroline was crying. She didn't look at me as she cried; she looked down and kept covering her face with her hands. My father looked at me, still smiling:

Look, he said pointing at Caroline

Your Mother is so upset because she thinks you've ruined your life, give her a hug and tell her everything will be alright.

I felt a little bit sick. I thought I had fair idea why she was crying, and it wasn't for the reason claimed by my father.

For many years before this, Caroline herself had tried to conceive without success. Over the previous years I had seen all sorts of hormonal pills and prescriptions in the house. I also heard many discussions about fertility and doctors between Caroline and her mother on the phone.

It therefore did not surprise me that she was upset at my news.

But my father seemed to want me to believe that these were the tears of a disappointed mother. He was actually beaming and poured himself another glass of wine as if in celebration.

Although it was awkward, it was certainly a better reaction than I expected, so despite my reservations, I did as he told me. I had already concluded that this recent news meant that I wouldn't be in a position to move out anytime soon, so I needed to be on their good side. I was also relying on them to not make any phone calls to Fiona's parents so I felt it was certainly best to keep my father sweet.

I went over to give Caroline a hug as was requested by my father. She was still crying and as I awkwardly put my arm around her she remained motionless and looking down at the ground. It was like hugging a statue that was crying. It did nothing to change my view on why she was in tears.

****

Fiona broke the news to her parents soon after I had told my father and Caroline. Fiona's parents' reaction was certainly more constructive. They invited me and my father and Caroline to meet in their house to discuss our plans. Secretly Fiona and I wanted to move in together but it was so impractical at the time.

The two of us got engaged without telling anyone and talked about potentially just getting married in a registry office and then telling people when it was done.

My father, Caroline and I attended the meeting with Fiona and her parents. Fiona's parents stated that Fiona and I should still be afforded the opportunity to go to college. Fiona's Mam spoke of how if we wanted to go to college, she and Fiona's Dad would do everything they could to help us with our new baby. As she spoke, my father and Caroline just sat there listening. I think they were nodding and agreeing but without actually offering to help. I considered Fiona's parents' words to be very kind and reassuring.

Over the next few months, I had two things to think about, the upcoming birth of my child and my Leaving Certificate exams. I realised that I was being offered a chance that other people in my situation might not have. I could go to college instead of rushing into the first job I could get once I finished school. A part of me wanted to just try and find a job because I knew a job provided the opportunity to move out to my own place. I was aware that student digs on a part time job were no longer a viable option as I needed a baby-friendly place to live.

This made me realise that I was completely dependent on my father and Caroline for a roof over my head and a place to bring up my new baby. I wanted to make sure I acted as nicely to them as possible to ensure that they wouldn't kick me out like they did with Shane. When I was younger Caroline had told me on many occasions that when I turned eighteen, I would *be out that door with my bags packed.* At the time I hadn't been worried, I wanted to be gone out the door. However, now I was going to have a baby, things were different.

So I constantly smiled and *plámásed* them. I picked up the art of *plámásing* from watching Caroline with visitors and many other people. The two of them lapped it all up happily.

This led to my relationship with both of them improving. They were talking about buying a house in Kilkenny which meant that they would be spending even less time at home. All of this was good news for me and I was able to convince myself that my living arrangements weren't so bad.

****

I was in work on the 6th July 1999, a few days before Fiona was due to give birth. At lunchtime, I went into the Cherrytree pub and used the payphone to ring Fiona to see how she was. It transpired that the baby was in breach position and the doctors had decided that the baby would be born via a C-Section. Reality began to kick in when Fiona told me that the doctors wanted to perform the procedure the very next day.

I remember Fiona being wheeled into the operating theatre in Mount Carmel Hospital. Fiona's parents and I waited outside in the waiting area. A nurse came out and told us that Fiona *wanted her Mammy*.

I felt strange when I heard this request; I didn't understand why she called for her mother and not for me. I didn't understand it because I simply didn't understand parents. I was considering that it was best that we hadn't acted on our idealistic plan of somehow moving in together. It was clear that Fiona still needed her parents very much. Unlike my relationship with my parents, Fiona's relationship with hers was far more than just a roof over her head.

She needed her parents and relied on them for support. It perplexed me. As I sat there, it dawned on me that the insincerity of how I acted towards my father and Caroline was not normal. I felt a little ashamed that I didn't love my parents the way Fiona loved hers. I wasn't being nice to them because they were my parents and I loved them, I was basically spoofing them so they would allow me to stay in the house. I felt guilty.

The fact that they weren't present on the day my son was born didn't make me feel any better. I justified their non-attendance by thinking that they were right not to come and support me. It was the least I deserved, considering that I was essentially using them for a place to live. I thought of all the times they had called me a *selfish* or *greedy bastard* and how that felt true to me now. My father's assertions that I owed them *after all they had done for me* had not fallen on deaf ears and I was now considering this to be a fair point.

I kept these thoughts to myself and tried to focus on the bigger issue. I could see that Fiona's father looked quite nervous. I was so naïve at the time; I couldn't understand why he was nervous. It was my opinion that doctors and surgeons were simply infallible. I genuinely was sure that nothing could possibly go wrong. I had never heard of a surgical procedure going wrong so I presumed that it never happened. When they eventually came out to say that the procedure was a success, I wasn't surprised. I expected nothing less. This led me to think that perhaps I was abnormally underwhelmed. I was so used to twisting and suppressing emotions in order to remain happy and pleasant with my father and Caroline, that I thought I may have done some damage to the emotional department of my body. I knew I should feel something strong at this point and I didn't seem to be feeling it.

Eventually, the nurse told us the operation was a success and we could go and see the new baby boy, who was in an incubator. I was delighted it was a boy as I felt I knew how to keep a boy happy. Never once at that stage did I consider that he mightn't like sports, computer games or music. As I walked down the corridor of the hospital with all these thoughts flying in my head, I started to consider that it was a great moment in my life. I prided myself on remaining calm in situations and I was considering that I was keeping it together in this situation quite well. My only worry was if I was too calm. I hurried up a bit in my walking. I really wanted to meet my son.

As I was starting to walk quite fast, Fiona's parents indicated to me that they didn't mind if I went ahead to see the baby first. I almost broke into a run to where the incubator was. I can't remember the surroundings, as I was so transfixed on the beautiful baby inside the incubator.

His eyes were wide open, seemingly staring right at me. Every part of him was so tiny, his fingers, his toes, and his little face. To say I was bowled over is an understatement. He was just so perfect. Suddenly I was completely overwhelmed. My calmness and lack of emotions had been turned on its head.

As he looked up at me, I was blissfully unaware of any vision impairments that new-borns have and considered that he already knew his Daddy. He let out a little sneeze and my heart skipped a beat. He seemed to be unmoved by the sneeze and he continued to gaze up in my direction. I studied his face, still in absolute awe at this incredible creation. I couldn't get over the silliest things, such as the fact that he had two ears, just like me. His fingers had fingernails and wrinkles at the joint, just like mine. He was clearly a full human being, albeit an extremely tiny and vulnerable one. I immediately felt like a Dad. This tiny boy was going to require all the assistance and love he could get to flourish and grow in this world. I felt very determined that I would provide that for him. I felt honoured to be able to do that. I felt grateful to him that he was giving me this incredible feeling of joy by just being in my presence. I knew at the time that those few minutes were the happiest moments of my life because until then, I had never even believed I could feel such happiness.

Chapter 25

Gar

When James was born, I was in New Jersey for the summer on my J1 working in Seaside Heights and enjoying my independence. I called home in early July and spoke to Fin who told me James had been born and I felt a wave of emotion wash over me. When I got off the phone I cried, partly out of happiness that everything had gone well and partly because I missed Fin and felt that I should have been there to support him because I knew my father and Caroline were not likely to be very supportive.

That summer was my second summer away and those summers abroad helped me see that there was a world outside of our house and that, more importantly, I was able to survive independently in that world.

When I arrived home in August, one of the first things I did was take my bed out of the shared room I had with Fin and put it one of the two unused "guest" rooms. I did this without asking Caroline and my father (I had a feeling they would disapprove) so Caroline asked me *what did I think I was doing* as I carried my mattress into the other room. I told her I was nineteen years of age and too old to be sharing a room, especially when there were two other spare rooms in the house. Once the bed was moved it became a fait accompli and nothing more was said. It was one of the first times I had ever done something I knew they would not approve of, right under their noses. It felt good to assert myself.

Although I was standing up for myself a bit more and gaining independence, throughout my college years I still believed my father's story - that he was a great father who had saved us from our lazy, selfish, greedy mother. I still believed him when he said how grateful I should be to Caroline who had *put manners on us* after our mother had *ruined us* with her pathetic so-called-mothering for ten years or so. I never stopped to question these beliefs. I never asked myself - do you believe what he is saying?

I believed unquestioningly because I had to believe. Otherwise, if I did start questioning, and it turned out not be true, where would that leave me? The world as I knew it would have fallen apart. I was living in a Potemkin village of my father's making and I had no desire to look behind the façade.

Fin

Over the next few months, I spent most of my time in Fiona's parents' house with Fiona and our new baby, James.

I arrived one day at Fiona's house to hear that Shane had called up to see James when I wasn't there. As usual, Shane's wellbeing was up and down at the time and I didn't know what to say to Fiona's parents, knowing that Shane was liable to have said anything to them. I was therefore relieved when Fiona's Mam and Dad told me that he had been polite, despite seeming a little off. I was worried they would think less of me having seen my 'mad brother' but it turned out that they were concerned for his health and enquired about him. I was relieved but not really surprised. I knew that regardless of Shane's state of mind, his state of heart was as good as usual and I was delighted that he had dropped me in a CD he had burnt with a collection of songs we both liked and with a cover he had designed himself with the title "Spud".

On the inlay card, he had written,

To Fin, Fiona and baby James, love Uncle Shane,

Every night, when James was asleep, Fiona and I would sit in the TV room downstairs together. We would watch episodes of *Friends* and *Ally McBeal* and other programmes with the monitor on to hear if James woke up. At about half ten or eleven I would go back to my father's house to sleep. I would leave the house the next morning and go to work or college and go back to Fiona's house as soon as I could and spend the rest of the day or evening there with James and Fiona. On weekends, we would often pack up everything we needed for James and head off for the day on the bus or on the Dart.

I thought about suggesting to Caroline and my father that I might take James to stay with me in our house overnight but fearing Caroline and my father's reaction to any extra "hassle" in their life, I decided not to even mention the idea lest I rock the boat.

164

I felt a bit sad not having James at night-time and I imagined James maybe waking up and looking for me and being sad that I wasn't around.

At this stage though, I was sometimes fearful enough just bringing James up to the house in the evening (even without him staying the night). I wanted it to seem to everybody that my father and Caroline wanted to see James too. So I would put James in his buggy and walk up to my house and have dinner and do my chores. At first I would try to time it when my father and Caroline were elsewhere. I wouldn't tell Fiona or her parents when I went back that they weren't there.

It therefore came as a surprise to me when my father suggested that I bring James up some evenings to the house when they were at home. I was even more surprised when he said that Caroline really wanted to see more of James. I was very dubious of this but I wanted to believe it was true and evidence that they were decent people and good grandparents.

When I did bring James up, they were nice to him, played with him and smiled at him. It became a weekly routine. I did notice a lot of the time that Caroline seemed agitated, although she tried to hide it.

However, one afternoon, having spent a few hours in my house with James, I was getting ready to go back to Fiona's house with him. I was deliberately leaving the house before Caroline got home. With all of James's paraphernalia packed up, I strapped him into his buggy. He was about one-year-old at the time. Realising I had left the windows open upstairs, I ran upstairs to close them. When I was upstairs, I heard Caroline arriving home and my heart raced as she immediately starting screaming:

Fin, where are ya? What the fuck is he doing here? I'm only in the fuckin' door!

Realising that my one-year-old son was downstairs with this shrieking witch; I raced down downstairs to find him crying in his buggy, cowering, while she was standing over him screaming.
I lost it.

What the fuck are you doing? I demanded.

She redirected her screams to me.

I don't need to be coming home from work to this. Youse aren't due here today, for fuck sake, I work hard all day…

I was in shock. All I could think to shout back was along the lines of:

Shut the fuck up you stupid bitch, you're shouting at a baby, what is fucking wrong with you?

I grabbed the buggy and wheeled it outside and slammed the door.

Poor James was still crying in his buggy so I tried to calm him down. I picked him out of the buggy and gave him a hug and a tried to tell him everything was all right. He was wearing a red puffy jacket and I remember his cheeks were the colour of the jacket because he was crying so much. He stared at me and at the direction from which we had come from. I felt bad because I had also shouted and cursed. I should have just run out the door with him and shouted at Caroline later. But all I could do now was to hug him and wipe the tears and snots away. I couldn't explain to him what had happened.

As I held him in one arm and pushed the buggy with the other, I decided that I needed to ensure that I spent as little time in that house as possible, for James' sake.

I realised that I should move out of that house altogether but it wasn't as simple as packing my bags and heading off. When I saw how unaffordable the rent was in any of the places that matched my criteria, I realised I was going to have to leave college if I wanted to move out of the house. I was attending a four-year degree course but it was possible to complete two years and get a certificate and complete the other two years at a later date. I decided to finish my second year, get my certificate and get a full-time job and move out. The degree could wait.

At the time I was getting on relatively well with my father. I decided since I was a Dad now, I had to be responsible and take some action. I decided to have a talk with him about the episode with Caroline and how I couldn't risk it ever happening again. When I told him, he tried to be very diplomatic about the incident. I spoke honestly and he responded in an understanding tone. He said that Caroline was stressed out and that I just needed to be sensitive to this.

She has a lot on her plate, he said

This was a familiar line I had been told about Caroline since we had first met her. On the rare occasions that our father actually acknowledged that something she did was wrong, this was his response. I took it he meant that she was still a wonderful mother and her mean or selfish acts were purely caused by her supposed overloaded plate. I disagreed.

I maintained that it was outrageous behaviour but he managed to convince me that it was behaviour that could have been avoided if I had left the house earlier. Effectively it was my fault. I didn't exactly agree but he persuaded me that in future that I should just ensure I wasn't there with James when she came home, unless it was one of our planned visits. If I did this, then it would never happen again. So I agreed to do just that. In the back of my mind, I considered that my father would most likely speak to Caroline privately about her behaviour and she wouldn't do it again.

He seemed to genuinely want to help and so I decided to tell him how I felt that I didn't have the option for James to be able to stay overnight with me in the house and how I felt it was important for him and for me. Again, he responded in an understanding tone, although he looked a bit uncomfortable at the idea. He took the advantage it gave him to undermine the significance of Caroline's behaviour towards James by saying;

So this is the real reason you wanted to talk, that thing with your Mum was just a lead in to soften me up.

He grinned after saying it, waiting for my agreement. I duly obliged. As if as a reward for agreeing with him, he said that he would talk to Caroline about it and he would let me know. I walked away from the conversation feeling much better. It made me think again that I was lucky to have a father like him. I chose to forget all the past issues and was delighted to embrace what I saw as a nice moment solving problems together.

I was excited about taking James over, mainly because I usually missed a lot of morning times with him. But as happy with the idea as I was, I knew the awkward part was going to be telling Caroline.

As it turned out, my father brought it up at the dinner table when I was present. He intimated to Caroline that I had something to say. So I came out with it and asked her how she would feel if James was to stay over a few nights a week. She wasn't pleased at all and she couldn't hide it.

She started talking about how she worked hard every day and shouldn't have *to come home to more hassle*. I told her I would play with James up in my room most of the time and she wouldn't even know he was there. She threw her eyes to heaven and repeated that line as a question as if to ridicule the statement

I won't even know he's here? she said and then answered herself:

Yeah – fuckin' right.

Luckily, the decision appeared to have already been made by my father and I was allowed to bring James over.

****

Caroline seemed unhappy with the situation and seemed to deliberately make it as hard as possible for me. At night when James slept in my room, I couldn't sit in my room too or I would keep him awake. But I was told in no uncertain terms that I wasn't welcome to watch television with them in the television room either. I couldn't go out, as I had to listen to the monitor in case James woke up. I remember on one occasion, I invited a friend in and we sat in the conservatory and chatted. Upon hearing I had company; Caroline came out from the television room and screamed at me and my friend that I wasn't allowed have friends over either. My friend left, embarrassed.

****

In 2001, when I finished my two years in college, I began working full time for a bookmaker. I saw it as a good stop-gap place to work.

168

I knew, based on her comments to me around that time, that Caroline was still unhappy with the arrangement of James staying overnight in the house. My father, on the other hand seemed fine with James staying over. However, the more I argued with Caroline, the more I worried she might convince my father that it was time for me to be *kicked out of the house*. I considered the possibility that she was responsible for Shane being kicked out when he was seventeen. I was slightly fearful that I could be *kicked out* at any stage on a similar basis because I was constantly arguing with her. I worried that if I was *kicked out*, that I would struggle to get a place where I could live and also have James stay over with me.

But I reckoned that my father had the final say in what happened so once I kept on his side, I stood a good chance of keeping my room in the house.

For his sake, my father seemed to be experiencing some form of satisfaction from our apparent relationship as a happy father and son. He began to regularly offer me titbits of advice. It seemed to me that he now considered himself to be a great parent, since he was passing on his 'fatherly advice' to his son. Some of the advice would be quite trivial but some of his advice could be more sinister.

I knew by the delivery of some of that advice that he considered it to be both valuable and unique, as if he was disclosing a secret family recipe. I was starting to feel like his trusted confidante. I was still dependant on him so I usually reacted by acting as appreciative as possible. One night he imparted to me what he seemed to consider his greatest secret formula to succeed in life.

I had arrived home relatively late one evening and my father was still up on his own watching television having a beer. Having exchanged pleasantries with him, he stood up and went upstairs. I got a pint glass and filled it with water under the tap. My father came down and rather oddly, he checked that the doors and even the windows were closed and there was nobody around. His apparent paranoia was slightly disconcerting. He turned to me and said very seriously:

I'll tell you one thing to always remember.

OK, I responded.

Make sure you always look after number one, he stated, emphasising the word *always.*

He looked at me intently, allowing it to register. At the time, I just considered it another thing I had to humour him about and didn't even really think about it.

I know what you mean I replied, nodding. *I'll take care of myself don't worry,* I added for good effect. I took a sip of my water.

My father kept staring at me, almost incredulous at the lack of conviction in my response. I was a bit fearful that he was aware that I wasn't taking on board what he was trying to say.

Awkwardly I edged towards the door and made up an excuse why I needed to go to bed. I said goodnight and left. I dismissed the episode and thought about my plans for the next day and drifted off to sleep.

A few months later, after quite a few repeats of these *'always look after number one'* moments, my father's imparting of his great advice escalated. One morning, we were in his car stuck in traffic and I was telling him some story about something to do with James. I thought he would be somewhat interested; James was, after all, his only grandchild. But as I spoke, I noticed that I was getting no reaction from my father. I glanced over to see him staring ahead. He appeared to be thinking hard. I peered ahead to see whether there was some obstruction that he was trying to look at that had captured his entire concentration. His stare was so intense he seemed to almost be in pain.

Let me tell you something, he said. He reached down and muted the radio.

He looked at me and then he looked ahead again, as if to examine the traffic ahead.

James is your kid and all but you have to remember that you're Number One, he said.

I shifted awkwardly in my seat. I thought to myself: *Is he saying what I think he is saying?*

Hmm? I murmured, thinking I must have heard him wrong or simply misunderstood him. He decided to expand further.

You have your own life, you have to look out for yourself first and foremost, he insisted.

Your life is the most important; your kids comes next.

I hesitated as I was flummoxed by this.

I thought about James and how small and vulnerable and dependant he was. It seemed unnatural to even think of not making him priority number one in life. This wasn't just bad advice; it was far worse than that.

I looked at him. He was still staring ahead intently. He had a serious but knowing look on his face. He knew I was looking at him. His face wore a look of regret. *Did he expect me to nod and agree again?* I thought to myself. I couldn't bring myself to do that so I just remained silently aghast. He quickly turned the radio back up and banged the steering wheel.

Fuckin' poxy traffic he proclaimed loudly, *I really hope you're not late now,* he declared in a false worried tone.

You would have been quicker walking; he said and started to laugh, again falsely. He looked at me. Feeling his stare and not knowing how to react, I chose my default reaction, which was to humour him. I let out a fake laugh and responded,

Quicker crawling even.

I saw him in the corner of my eye look at me again. I looked ahead trying to appear unmoved. That uncomfortable feeling I often felt around him was stronger than ever and I wanted to just open the door and exit the vehicle. After a short period of awkwardness, I think even he was glad when I told him I might *actually* be quicker walking and we both agreed I should do just that. I was relieved to get out of his car and out of his company.

I spent the rest of the day wrestling with the advice my father had dished out and I realised that I could no longer just humour him and ignore my inability to live comfortably in the house with Caroline and my father.

Working in the bookmakers, I had actively been trying to find a steady job with some form of career path since I left college. I decided that the search had become more urgent.

Chapter 26

Fin

I had told my father my plans to get a new job and he was supportive of the idea. One day, he rang me and invited me to his office in town after I finished work to discuss how my job hunting was going. I thought this was a nice gesture and I agreed to meet him. When I met him, I told him that I intended on applying for a few jobs, including one in the civil service. He said he thought it was a great idea and fully backed the plan. He had been working in the civil service for a while now and he recommended that job in particular.

I applied and happily got the job. In November 2001, I began working in a new full-time job as a civil servant. It was agreed that I would hand up €400 a month to Caroline since I was on a consistent wage. I agreed but stated my intentions to move out when I found the right place.

I noticed that Caroline's attitude changed after this. She seemed to be nicer to me than she ever had been before. She also talked about the bills I would have to pay when I moved out as being far too high for me to pay on my wages. In many ways I agreed. It became clear to me that she was encouraging me *not* to leave the house. I was very surprised.

I contemplated her change of heart and couldn't really pinpoint the reason for it. At the time, I reasoned that perhaps the reality of the situation kicked in since I was now in a realistic position to move out, having enough money and a steady job. I didn't consider it was because she actually wanted me around so I found the whole thing intriguing. I was making the dinner on one of the days around the time and I mused that perhaps she realised that since I did a lot of chores in the house that I was quite useful. I reasoned that since our father rarely did any chores that Caroline would be left to do them all herself.

When I turned twenty-one years old in January 2002, I was given a present from Caroline and my father of a new television and video for my bedroom. The gesture of spending money on me for a television for my room seemed so unlike them. I took it as meaning that they really liked me living there and for the first time under their roof, I felt welcome.

There was an even bigger surprise a few months later when in the spring of 2002; Caroline announced that she was pregnant. She was understandably delighted; it was the first time she seemed to me to be truly happy with life. We were all delighted.

For a while, we all seemed to get on, it was as if we *were* a big happy family. Even when I thought of my Mam, I was able to convince myself somewhat that I shouldn't feel guilty about not knowing where she was. My father helped to quell the guilt, saying things like:

Imagine how you'd have turned out if you stayed living with her?

He would say similar things about Shane. One of the local lads that Shane used to hang around with was a chronic addict and we were sad but not surprised when we heard that this lad had died of a heroin overdose in the *Abrakebabra* on Baggot Street. This made Gar and me worry even more about Shane, to the point that we half expected every phone call to the house might be somebody calling to deliver some bad news.

Again, my father would help me deal with this guilt, saying that if Shane didn't smoke hash when he was younger, he would have never turned out the way he did. He sounded quite genuine sometimes and he usually followed that up, seemingly regretfully, that if Caroline had only gotten to Shane on time, he wouldn't have been such a 'failure'. I didn't always agree, but I wasn't sure if he was right or wrong. I found when I openly agreed, I felt less guilty about things. I could persuade myself to give my father and Caroline the benefit of that doubt, at least for the time being. It was the preferred option for me and it was the option that kept everyone just about getting along.

Chapter 27

Gar

When I was studying for exams in around 2001, Shane called up to the house. I was the only person at home. Despite our father's prohibition, I invited him in for a cup of tea and we sat out the back having a smoke and a chat. Although I knew technically I was disobeying my father's instructions, I thought that maybe with all the time that had passed that it might be okay to just invite him in for a cup of tea.

That evening, I foolishly mentioned at dinner that Shane had called and that he was in good spirits. I specifically mentioned that he was in good form as I thought this was good news that would be welcomed. I was wrong. As soon as I finished the sentence, my father turned to me and said in a fierce tone:

Shane is not to set foot in this house again, do you hear me?

Caroline nodded beside him in agreement.

I was quite upset by this. I thought at the time how easy it was for Caroline in particular to tell us to ignore somebody who she wasn't related to, but to us, he had always been our big brother. Refusing him a cup of tea and a chat seemed totally unnatural.

However, we were bound by our father's orders, as he liked to constantly remind us –

While you live under this roof, you live by my rules.

****

One night over St. Patrick's weekend in March 2002, Shane called up to the house but there was nobody at home. Fin and I were out and our father and Caroline were in Kilkenny horse-riding. This episode occurred when I was about twenty-three and still living at home (I moved out later that year). The St. Patrick's Sky-fest fireworks festival was taking place in Dublin. I was in my girlfriend's house on the other side of the city when her house phone rang. It turned out it was a Garda on the line asking to speak to me (to this day I do not

175

know how the Gardaí knew where I was or got my girlfriend's number).

The Garda asked me if I was Shane's brother and I confirmed that I was. He said I needed to come home as soon as possible as Shane was at the house and he was in a bad way. He asked whether there was anyone else around and I told him my parents were away that weekend but Fin was nearby and I would contact him. When I talked to Fin he said he would go straight up to the house to see what was happening.

I then undertook the journey from one side of the city to the other by DART and bus. I was obviously anxious to get back as soon as I could but traffic was at a complete standstill because of the fireworks display. By the time I arrived at the house it was about 10pm, Shane was gone and it appeared the commotion was over. I noticed that the front window of the sitting room was boarded up. Fin was there and explained to me what had happened.

Fin

I had also received a call from the Gardaí while I was with Fiona and James in her house. Being close by, I raced up to the house. As I came down our road I was stopped by our next-door neighbours' dad and a Garda. The Garda advised me that Shane was still in the house and that he was in a bad way. He told me that it would probably be better if Shane didn't see me and to stay out of sight.

Confused and upset, I heeded the Garda's advice and walked down the neighbour's driveway where I could stand out of Shane's view. I explained to the Garda that Shane had schizophrenia and that he was not actually a threat. I reasoned that if he saw me, he might co-operate better. But the Garda insisted that I should not go out to him.

I watched as Shane was escorted up our driveway. He was bloodied and babbling about a fire that did not exist. I wasn't sure what to think. Noticing that the Gardaí were being pleasant and humouring Shane, I made to walk up the neighbour's driveway and out to Shane. I wanted to tell him that everything was alright and try to figure out what was upsetting him. Another Garda stopped me however and apologetically stated that it would be better for everybody if I didn't go out. He reasoned that it would be for the best if Shane didn't see me. The neighbour agreed and comforted me. I wondered was this the same angry Shane I had seen smashing up my father's BMW with a pipe.

The neighbour was being nice and he tried to downplay the incident in an attempt to make me feel better. He stated that he had problems with his own son and sometimes these things just happen. Despite the madness, I was very well trained to recognise that playing down the incident was what my father would want. They were in Kilkenny and I feared that if I didn't play it down and they were forced to come home from their horse-riding early, that I would be in trouble. I nodded and pretended that it was indeed 'no big deal'. Inside my stomach was sick. Hearing my brother's voice and not being allowed to go out and just give him a hug and tell him everything was okay was a wrench. I tried again to tell the Garda that Shane would never hurt me but he insisted that I wasn't to go out to him.

The Gardaí established that Shane needed to go back to the psychiatric ward and arranged for an ambulance to come and take him there. After Shane left, I was relieved when one of the Gardaí told me that there was no malice in what Shane had done. He said that Shane had mistakenly thought there was a fire in the house and that we were all inside the house. He said that he broke the window and tried to get in in an effort to save us. This seemed a perfectly good reason for why Shane had done what he had done.

One of the neighbours who used to hang around with Shane kindly helped me board up the broken window to protect the room from the elements. I then called our father on the phone and told him what had happened. He stated that they would stick to their plan to come back from horse riding the next day. He seemed to be dispassionate about the event. He noted almost jokingly that it must have been very difficult for Shane to break through the double-glazed windows with a rock. He said it as if Shane had accomplished what a lot of people couldn't have done.

I wasn't convinced that Shane really believed there was a fire. I couldn't help thinking that our ignoring him every time he called to the door might have been the real reason he broke the window. Although I was only following orders to ignore him like that, I was wracked with guilt so much so that cleaning up the broken blood-stained glass felt more like a penance than anything else.

Chapter 28

Gar

When I finished college in 2002, I got an apprenticeship as a trainee solicitor in a large corporate law firm in the city centre which meant a substantial improvement in my wages from what I had previously earned from my various part-time jobs through school and college. Ever since I had started caddying as a fourteen-year-old, Caroline had taken a third of all my earnings and that summer, just before I started my apprenticeship, Caroline informed me that the standard monthly 'rent' was being dramatically increased to €400 a month.

At this stage I was already considering moving out of the house but Caroline's rent hike acted as a spur for me to act quickly and I soon found a double bedroom in a friend's apartment in a great location that was also €400 per month. Coincidentally, my friend had spent a few months living with us in the spare room in our house when he was in between leases a little while before (his parents lived in Scotland). I had mentioned to Caroline that my friend needed somewhere to live for a while and was prepared to pay his way. She invited him to move in at a cost of €50 a week for bed and board. My friend was happy with this arrangement as he could eat what he wanted for his €50. Of course, Caroline did not impose the limitations on him that she imposed on us. Fin and I did find it amusing though when Caroline gave out about my friend behind his back for *having the oven on all hours to cook his potato waffles*.

It was almost entertaining to see her have to restrain herself from reprimanding him because he was a paying guest.

When I told Caroline that I had found somewhere else to live that was also going to cost me €400 per month she was not happy. She reminded me that her price included *free dinners* which I would have to pay for in my new place. I told her, with some satisfaction, that I could afford this on my new wage as a trainee solicitor. She seemed to get in a strop at this and was more unfriendly than usual in the few weeks before I moved out. My father tried to explain this to me by saying:

Your mother is just upset to see you cutting the apron strings.

I nodded to him when he said this but inside I was sceptical.

Once I moved out I knew I would be truly independent for the first time in my life. Emboldened by this impending independence, I began standing up for myself in conversations with my father. When I told my father and Caroline about the terms of my apprenticeship, my father nodded approvingly at how much I was getting paid and observed:

Now you can start paying me back for all the things I've done for you.

He said it in his half-joking way that was really quite serious.

He had made similar comments like this to me and to Fin before and they had always struck me as being perverse but I had been too afraid to question him. This time it was different though, I was moving out and I wasn't afraid of him as much anymore. I had also recently seen the movie *Guess Who's coming to Dinner?* and watched transfixed as Sidney Poitier had stood up to his father when he had made a similar comment about *all he had done for him.*

With Poitier's words buzzing in my head, I snapped back at my father:

What do you mean 'pay you back for all the things you've done for me'?

He stared at me when I said this, his sneer dying on his lips.

Well, he said, *everything you owe me for all the things I've done for you down through the years.*

Like what? I asked him.

He was beginning to get unsettled now. This was not like Gar to answer back.

He stared back at me. I knew I had to say what I wanted to say quickly before I lost my nerve so I blurted out as quickly and as authoritatively as I could:

I don't owe you anything, Dad. You are my father. I am your son. You brought me into this world. When you did that you took on the responsibility for me to take care of me and to give me everything that I needed until I was old enough to look after myself. One day I hope to be a father too and when I am I will be responsible for my son and make sure that he has everything he needs until he can look after himself. And when he is old enough to look after himself he won't owe me anything. That's just how it works.

I stood there trembling, waiting for his reaction, but he just stared with a mixture of curiosity and amusement on his face. I think he found it amusing that after all these years the worm had turned and I had finally spoke up for myself. Before he could reply we were interrupted and the conversation ended.

****

A year or so later, I had arranged to meet my father in town for a pint after work on a Friday evening. As we walked towards the pub, we chatted and I asked him how Caroline was. By my father's reply, I got the distinct impression that things were not going particularly well between him and Caroline but this was, according to him, because Caroline was being unreasonable. In years before I would have just nodded my head and said nothing but as I was no longer living in the house, I decided to speak up and so I reminded him that he could be unreasonable too sometimes.

He stopped walking when I said this.

What do you mean by that? he said.

I hesitated for a second or two and then replied:

Well, I said, *do you remember that time you poured 7-Up on Caroline's head?*

He stared at me, apparently speechless. Eventually he found his voice:

No, I don't remember that at all.

Well, I said, *I remember it. I remember it clearly; it was outside Nanny's house.*

He stared at me for a long minute, before he clucked his lips dismissively and said:

180

Huh. So are we going for a pint or not?

I decided that given the way the atmosphere had changed, I no longer wanted to go for a father-son Friday evening pint.

No, I said, *I can't, I have to head home.*

He sighed in exasperation, as if I had just wasted his time.

Right then, he said, *see you around, kid,* and walked off.

As I watched him walk away, I inhaled deeply, trying to calm my body which was trembling uncontrollably.

Even though, predictably, he had just denied everything, it was still an exhilarating feeling asking my father about the past. The adrenaline coursed through my bloodstream as I journeyed home.

Fin

In November 2002, Caroline gave birth to a son, our half-brother Séan. At this time Shane was twenty-eight, Gar was twenty-three and I was twenty-one.

It was a happy occasion and we were all delighted. It seemed to bring us all together, with the notable exception of Shane. He seemed to disappear off the radar for longer than usual this time. I knew he was in St. James's hospital and I convinced myself it was the best thing for him. It didn't sit entirely well with me but I started to try and put thoughts of him to the back of my mind.

Gar seemed to be a lot more willing to speak back to my father, now that he was no longer living in the house. This was very unusual, as I had always been the only one, particularly in our teenage years, who had spoken back to them so Gar's talking back was strange but thought-provoking for me.

On one hand, I was a bit annoyed that he could now ruffle their feathers and then leave the house, leaving me with the aftermath. On the other hand, I started to think that he had obviously changed his mind about not talking back. He clearly didn't seem to think that our father was the greatest guy alive, which was how I assumed Gar thought when we were younger.

At first I reacted with self-preservation. The aftermath of Gar talking back to my father was usually my father questioning me as to what Gar was on about and *what Gar's problem was*. As with everything else, I nodded and agreed with my father. Gar clearly had *a problem*. This seemed to endear me further to my father and he started to treat me as if I was now the favourite son. I had spent years listening to how I should be *more like Gar* and now suddenly, it was how *Gar should be more like me*. For a few months I accepted this. I still lived in their house, so the better I was getting on with them, the easier my life was.

I was also getting on really well with Caroline. I was able to babysit Séan and she even sometimes asked my advice about baby stuff since James was only a few years older so I had recent experience. Since I was babysitting for her, when I had James over, Caroline offered to listen to the monitor for him if I wanted to go out. So the arrival of Séan had improved things between us two in many ways.

Chapter 29

Gar

In 2002, around the time Caroline became pregnant with Séan, our father finally applied to divorce our mother. Caroline had been agitating for this for years; ever since the prohibition of divorce had been removed from the law in Ireland in 1995, but our father always seemed reluctant to get divorced. The impending birth of his child seemed to finally persuade him to legally marry Caroline, which required him getting divorced from our mother first.

Séan was born in November 2002 and although I had moved out of the house at this stage, I knew from Fin that Séan's birth had made things easier for him, particularly in his relationship with Caroline, who seemed to have softened since she became a mother. I was very happy to see this and I hoped that Caroline would behave a lot more like a mother to Séan than she had to us.

Once the date for the divorce hearing was set, our father began preparing himself - and us - for the impending showdown with our mother. As part of the preparations, our father told us we needed to talk about what was going to happen on the day of the court hearing. One evening over a pot of tea our father told us his strategy for the hearing. It was pretty straightforward:

I want you to testify against your mother.

This was not a request – it was an order. Our testifying was akin to our patriotic duty to show gratitude to him for *everything he had done for us* by giving evidence against our 'evil mother' who he had *saved us* from.

It became pretty clear that not only did he want us to give evidence against our mother but he wanted to make sure that the evidence we gave was 'the right evidence' (i.e. evidence that assisted his case). To ensure this, we had a number of conversations whereby our father encouraged us to 'remember' episodes from the past which he felt made our mother seem a negligent and bad mother. One of these episodes was the weekend when he had sent us down to Carlow as punishment for having tea and buns with our mother – the last time we had seen her ten years' previously.

He asked us to remember that weekend. He asked us to remember how we had called him from the pub in Carlow and begged him to take us home - away from our mother. He looked at us and told us to *remember this.*

We nodded somewhat reluctantly in agreement at our father's version of events – we had little choice – Fin was still living under his roof and I had only recently moved out. We were both, to varying degrees, still under his spell.

Despite our misgivings (which we did not share with each other at this time), we nodded in agreement and told our father that if called upon, we would testify against our mother and give that evidence to the judge.

Despite the fact that Fin and I were now both adults in our early twenties, we were still our father's children. Even now, fifteen years later, I am still his child and he is still my father. Such is the nature of the father/son relationship. Because of this I obeyed my father like an obedient child. That being said, perhaps because I was now older and more independent minded, I had the first pangs of discomfort that my father seemed to be twisting the past to suit himself. This was the first time I recall seriously questioning my father's bona fides. I kept this to myself for the time being.

On the morning of the divorce hearing, we gathered nervously in a coffee shop on the quays near the family law courts building in Smithfield. Caroline and our father's brother were there to support our father and my girlfriend at that time was there to support me. When the appointed time came, Fin, our father and I left the others in the coffee shop to meet with our father's solicitor and barrister prior to the hearing. As the three of us went past Smithfield Square, I saw my mother for the first time in ten years.

She was sitting impassively on a small wall in Smithfield Square, completely alone.

She looked just the same as when I'd last seen her a decade before, but with grey hair. She had a very pensive and anxious look on her face. I felt my emotions well up inside when I saw her, so mixed up it was impossible to identify which specific emotions I felt. I knew that I did not feel hatred or anger.

The glimpse of her was fleeting and soon we were in an office in the family law courts' building and meeting with our father's legal team. After some discussion between our father and his solicitor, the solicitor said to my father that he wanted to speak with just me and Fin privately and invited us to go with him to a nearby coffee shop. Our father was reluctant to let us go with him but the solicitor insisted. We were a bit surprised by this but followed the solicitor out to the Brown Bag cafe. The solicitor smiled amiably as he ordered us cappuccinos and we made ourselves comfortable.

The solicitor then asked us a question which had a profound effect on how we viewed our father from then on.

He asked us:

Do you really want to testify against your mother, like your father says?

We just stared at him when he said this.

This was our father's solicitor. Surely, he knew that if our father wanted us to testify against our mother then what we wanted was of no relevance? We didn't know what to say.

Your father, he continued, *tells me that you are very keen to get into the witness box and give evidence against your mother. Is this true?*

No answer again. We were too stunned.

Because I just want to tell you, he continued, *that I think it would not be a good idea for you to do that. In fact, I am advising you not to do that.*

Now this was really shocking stuff.

Our father's solicitor was advising us *to act against our father's wishes.*

This was unprecedented. Nobody had ever advised us to act against our father's wishes. He continued:

Can I ask you why you would want to do such a thing?

I hesitated to answer and looked at Fin who looked back at me, equally stupefied. The answer, we both knew, was because our father had told us to do it and that was that. But we also knew that our father would not want us to say this to the solicitor so instead we didn't really answer his question. The solicitor considered this lack of response and said to us that we didn't have to testify if we didn't want to testify and that under no circumstances should we feel forced to testify. He also said to us that we didn't need to tell our father what we had talked about.

We nodded at him – our minds racing.

That solicitor probably did not realise what a profound effect his words that day had on us. At the time this conversation took place, I was in Blackhall Place training to become a solicitor and was becoming aware of issues such as ethics and the particular relevance of that to the practice of family law.

To the solicitor's credit, not only did he not accept his client's word at face value but he actually spoke to us in a way that encouraged us to behave against his client's wishes. He was acting entirely correct from an ethical point of view as it was incumbent on him to have cognizance not just for his client, but of course the children of his client whose interests may not necessarily be aligned.

It was the first time that anybody had told us we did not have to do what our father wanted us to do. It felt like an outsider had opened the door and looked into the room where we lived out our father's fiction day after day. He had shone a light in the dark. It would take years for that light to reach every corner but the illumination process had begun.

Following this conversation, we re-joined our father in the family law courts' building where our father was in discussions with his barrister regarding tactics to be adopted for the negotiations which were going on.

Fin and I observed these negotiations with a mixture of fascination and distress, so much so that our father's solicitor, backed up by his barrister, stepped in and advised our father that we should be excused from the negotiations and we should only be called upon if we were ultimately required. Our father hesitated at this; he seemed very keen for us to be there. However, our father was squirming a little as his barrister openly argued with him in front of us about how much money he should offer our mother and now his solicitor was giving him orders in front of us. Our father reluctantly told us we were excused but ordered us to stay nearby with my mobile phone on-call and to be ready for action.

As I was studying in Blackhall Place nearby, I took Fin to the bar there so that we could play some darts to take our mind off things. When we got there, one of my friends was throwing some solo arrows to distract himself from the day of studying. We quickly got a game of *cricket* (a darts game) going and passed the next hour or two with Fin and me keeping one eye on my mobile phone. After a couple of hours, my father rang to say it was all over and we were to re-join Caroline and the others.

We were very relieved to hear this and glad it was all over. As soon as we arrived we could tell from our father's Cheshire-cat grin that he had got a good result. He was positively glowing as he fist-pumped the air and told us animatedly how our mother had capitulated totally to his offer. Caroline was also grinning from ear-to-ear, her white teeth flashing in giddiness and relief.

The unrefined joy on my father's face caused my stomach to tighten as a wave of revulsion washed over me. As the day wore on and our father became more aggressively celebratory with each drink consumed, the waves of disgust intensified. Later, as our father tried to persuade us to stay for more drinks to toast his success over our mother, I called time on what had been an emotionally draining day and went home to bed.

As I drifted off to sleep that night, I felt that something significant had happened that day. I felt that my feelings towards my father had significantly altered and for this first time began to really wonder about the relationship I had with him.

Fin

I felt physically sick at the thought of giving evidence against my Mam. I wish I could say that the sickness was caused by the fact that I didn't want to hurt my Mam but it was not. I felt sick because I remembered a lot of things vividly and if I was asked in a witness box for the truth, I didn't think I would be able to tell my father's lies. I lied to him and Caroline all the time, but lying to a judge about these episodes, after putting my hand on the bible, seemed so wrong. I was worried that I might capitulate and actually tell the truth and I was afraid what my father's reaction would be to me if I did that. Unlike Gar, I had to go home to the same house as my father after the trial. The doors would be closed. I would have to sleep in his house at night. Although I wasn't a child anymore, I was still *his child*, and his potential reaction to my non-compliance with this particular order scared me greatly. Even when the solicitor spoke to us, I was so used to my father's mind games that I considered that the solicitor was testing us at the request of my father, to ensure that we wouldn't capitulate if we were called to give evidence.

After the divorce hearing, I didn't hang around too long and got the bus home. I couldn't stand being in my father and Caroline's company. My father's' boasting and self-congratulation was as sickening as Caroline's satisfied smile although she did look as though she wasn't as happy as he was. He was delighted with himself and was gregariously ordering drinks. He wanted us all to stay but I made my excuses and left. Just watching him celebrate his apparent victory reinforced my growing conclusion that he was a nasty man and the fact that he was my father didn't change that fact at all.

I went back to Fiona's and checked my emails on her computer to see if I had any new property rental alerts. There was nothing that looked promising. Following the divorce hearing, Caroline's general attitude towards me continued to improve.

As soon as Séan was born, I was considered an ideal babysitter since I was well able to change nappies, sterilise bottles and keep a baby happy. I was delighted to baby-sit when they went out and they usually offered to babysit James in return. They very much believed in *tit for tat*. I remember Caroline stating correctly that *there's no minding in James once he goes to bed as he always sleeps through until the morning*. She was right but I couldn't help noticing the contrast in her attitude from before she had become pregnant. She was in such good spirits these days that I no longer feared her mistreating James.

She was a mother herself now. As nice as it was to have seemingly buried the hatchet with Caroline, I couldn't stand my father anymore. I found it very difficult to humour him now that I had given up trying to convince myself that he was a good person.

Chapter 30

Gar

On the weekend of 4-5 July 2003, not long after the divorce hearing, and two weeks before my father and Caroline were due to get married, I was in Canada, representing the Law Society of Ireland at an international negotiation competition. The competition itself was a great experience and my negotiating partner and I were chuffed when Ireland was announced as the winning team. After the closing ceremony festivities, I did not make it back to my hotel until the small hours of Sunday morning. When I opened the door to my bedroom I noticed a piece of paper had been folded under the door. I unfolded it to see that it was a fax that my father had sent to me at the hotel wishing me luck in the competition. The 'From' section of the fax declared it to be from "*The Murphy Family*" and the fax read as follows:

"*Hi Gar*

Just to wish you best of luck. Remember if you're stuck, think of what your Grandad would do when he got stuck (which was not very often): "what did you say?" Pass it back..........

Let us know how you get on, talk to you later.

Dad"

Underneath the above typed wording, my father had then signed the fax: "*Dad, Mum, Séan, Fin and James.*"

There was no mention of Shane, despite the fax purporting to be from "*The Murphy Family*".

I felt a mix of emotions when I read the fax. I was touched that my father had taken the time to do something considerate, it was not like him to do that. But I also felt confused. I had moved out almost a year at this stage and the memories of the divorce case were strong. I was not sure what to make of it and cried confused tears as I feel asleep that night.

The next weekend of 12/13 July was the weekend of the *Witnness* music festival and I was back in Ireland to go to the festival with Fin. After successfully blagging two weekend camping passes, Fin and I camped in a small tent at the festival and had plenty of time on our hands to drink, listen to music and talk. Pretty early on in our conversation, I told Fin how brilliant it was living away from home. I was now almost a year out of the house and I explained to Fin the amazing feeling of freedom and independence that I had in no longer living under Caroline and our father's yoke.

Fin was very keen to move out but was not financially able to do so until he finished college like I had done. However, he was very keen to hear what I had to say about how transformative the entire experience was and the great relief and joy I experienced in no longer having to walk on eggshells around our father and Caroline.

After a while and a few more drinks, our conversation got braver. The topic soon turned to the divorce that had recently taken place and in particular the conversation that our father's solicitor had with us when he told us we did not need to testify against our mother if we did not want to. It had seemed so strange for the solicitor, who was being paid by our father and instructed by him, to clearly go against his client's wishes for the benefit of his client's children. Even though I could see that he was merely acting as any decent ethical family law solicitor would, he still did, without question, *the right thing*.

As we chatted, we reached the conclusion that our father, in ordering us to testify against our mother, was clearly doing *the wrong thing*. It was the first time we had openly agreed that our father wasn't right and it set a precedent between us that it was okay to have this view.

We spoke about our father's efforts to coach us prior to the hearing to get us to say what he wanted us to say. We spoke about how our memories of what happened in Carlow all those years ago were radically different to his. We both had a clear recollection of that weekend and of Geraldine and the videos she had got from Xtravision for us. We both recalled that we had not rang him begging him to take us home – quite the opposite. We recalled the disappointment we felt when we had to tell Geraldine that we were going home early and would not be able to watch movies with her as we had planned.

We concluded that either our father was mistaken in his recollection or else he was purposefully recalling events in a manner that suited him and more importantly suited the story he wanted us to portray before the judge. We reckoned it was much more likely to be the latter than the former.

From this the discussion moved to other thoughts about our father and Caroline. Even though we were open with each other and far away from our father and Caroline, we did not mention our mother that weekend. The control our father had over us in prohibiting conversation about her was still in force even though I had moved out and we were at a music festival far away.

We did talk about Shane though, and how we wanted to see him again. We wondered how he was doing in the hospital and if he was okay. We even went so far as to suggest that we might visit him against our father's wishes. With Fin still living under our father's roof we realised this would probably not happen until he had moved out.

The weekend seemed to take a turn for the worse when the announcement was made that Jack White had broken a finger and the White Stripes had cancelled their headline gig. However, in keeping with the positive events of that weekend, the Flaming Lips took their place on the main stage, a band we had never seen before. We listened rapturously to Wayne Coyne singing about love, kindness and being considerate and we both agreed we had found a new favourite band.

The seeds of rebellion against our father and reunification with our mother were sown that weekend to the soundtrack of "*Yoshimi Battles the Pink Robots*".

Fin

When I went to the *Witnness* music festival with Gar, I told him of my problems living in the house with my father and Caroline. He implored me to move out, citing his experience that leaving the house had lifted a weight off his shoulders. I told him about the difficulty with finances and not being able to move in with friends. He thought about it and even offered to pay a portion of my rent to help me. I told him I appreciated the offer but knowing he was a trainee solicitor on a modest income, that I couldn't accept that.

It felt nice that he had offered it but more importantly it showed me how strong his will for me to move out was.

As I drifted off to sleep with the noise of other revellers singing a bad version of *American Pie*, there was one thought that stuck with me. If Gar was willing to part with cash that he could ill afford to help me move out, then moving out must be something that I simply had to do. It was obvious that moving out had opened up Gar's eyes and he was willing me to do the same. He wanted me to also see the world for what it was. Until I moved out I would always be seeing the world with our father and Caroline's skewed perspective.

After some months of searching for a place to live, I was delighted that a place nearby became available that suited me. It was advertised as a one-bedroom apartment although the word apartment was being kind. Essentially it was a flat. It had a big double bed so I decided that James and I could share the bed when he stayed overnight with me.

The flat had a kitchenette and a cooker adequate enough for me to cook our meals. It had a tiny bathroom and a small sitting room. The cost was €650 a month. It was more than I could afford since I earned about €20,000 a year, but I had an MBNA credit card with a credit limit of €8200. I was so desperate to move out that I decided that I could pay with cash from that if I needed to. I had decided I couldn't stay with my father and Caroline anymore. I reasoned that whatever debt I built up could be paid off when I was earning more money.

Once I moved out I was free to get on with my life without constantly thinking about how Caroline might react to every individual action or decision. I could do simple things, like making a slice of toast, without worrying that Caroline would come home in a bad mood and start questioning why there was a smell of toast and have an argument about it. If it weren't for Séan and for James, I wouldn't have visited my father's house very often after I had moved out. But I loved seeing Séan and joking with him. He had a horse teddy that he called Dinky. I had great laughs asking him how *Stinky* was only for him to correct me and tell me adamantly:

It's Dinky!

He had a great appetite for fun, just like James. I remember playing piggy in the middle with the two of them and I was the piggy. I kept running at both of them, roaring like a monster. The two of them were both in tears laughing. They were both having so much fun. We all got on so well together. I saw enough signs over the first few years to indicate to me that Caroline felt a maternal bond with Séan. I convinced myself that she would treat him very differently to how she treated us. However, I wasn't convinced about my father treating him well.

Once I moved out, my father and Caroline seemed to have very little interest in James. They would be nice to him when we were up visiting but they rarely seemed to care whether we visited or not. My babysitting of Séan continued and I would stay the night in the house. Always in turn, they would babysit James, which was good to an extent. It did, however, begin to seem to me that they saw James more as a currency in the babysitting market. I felt bad for James but I also felt bad trying to make excuses for them. I would try to hide the fact that I was babysitting Séan to Fiona's parents because I wanted them to think that my father and Caroline had offered to babysit James because they wanted to spend time with him. I didn't want them to know that it was because they wanted a night out and babysitting James meant I *owed* them back, *quid pro quo*. I started to hint to my father and Caroline that people were noticing this. I was braver after I no longer lived in the house. I also presumed that they didn't like to think that people might be talking about them negatively.

As a result, Caroline attempted to improve things by offering to take James sometimes on Friday afternoons. This gesture lessened my pain. I had to make less excuses and so I greatly appreciated it. But it was not long before I was being asked to mind Séan in return for *that Friday that Caroline took James*. I liked minding Séan but I disliked the fact that it seemed be the only motivation for them wanting to see James.

Chapter 31

Gar

Just over a week after the *Witness* music festival, on Tuesday, 22 July 2003, Fin and I attended the marriage ceremony of our father and Caroline which took place in the Registry Office with baby Séan and my girlfriend also in attendance. Our father wanted me and Fin to be witnesses to the marriage. After the ceremony, we went for a short lunch and then I went back to work. My feeling about the marriage was that it was only formalising something that had been in place for a long time and that it was good for Séan.

I knew from experience that it was definitely something Caroline wanted. Over the years I had repeatedly heard her scream at our father:

If you die tomorrow, I'll get nothing.

Our father was like King Lear in the way he seemed to enjoy wielding the power he held over those hoping to inherit his estate. One day around this time, when Shane was a *persona non-grata*, my father made a point of telling me, with a show of sadness, that he was *writing Shane out of his will*. I had not seen Shane in a long time and his comment made me think about Shane and wonder how he was doing.

The year after my father and Caroline's wedding, in the summer of 2004, I had an unexpected meeting with Shane. I was cycling along High Street towards James's Street on my way to Blackhall Place to attend the summer course. As I cycled, I saw a dishevelled figure slouching along the pavement in my direction. The figure had wild, unkempt hair, wore filthy clothes and had a waxen face with bloodshot eyes. But as I looked there came a spark of recognition.

That's Shane, I thought. *That's definitely Shane.*

I immediately jumped off the bike and ran towards him.

Shane, I said, *it's me, Gar.*

194

He had to focus his gaze before he recognized me but when he did a wide smile broke across his face.

Gar, he said, *how ya keeping?*

Great, Shane, I said, *how are you?*

Ah, grand, you know the usual. How's Finjun? And Dad? And Caroline.

Great, I said, *they're all great.*

As I spoke to him, I could see that he knew who I was and for a brief few minutes we maintained a normal brother to brother conversation as if we had only seen each other the day before. But after those few minutes his eyes glazed over and as he spoke some spittle rolled down his cheek. He seemed heavily medicated.

I have to go, he said.

Where you going?

He rummaged in his jacket pocket and took out a stack of CDs.

Have to sell these he said.

Are they yours? I asked

Kind of, I got them in the hospital. I have to go; I have to go.

Before he left I instinctively went to give him a hug, which was unusual for us as we were not brothers who were encouraged to hug each other. But it just seemed like the right thing to do. He had that look about him of somebody who needed a hug and who had not been hugged in a long time, so I gave him one. He reacted a bit awkwardly but reciprocated the hug and then was on his way to urgently exchange his stack of CDs for much-needed cash.

I watched him walk away, slowly got back on my bike and thought to myself - *we have to go in and visit Shane in hospital. We have to restore our relationship with him.*

Later that day I told Fin what had happened and he was as concerned as I was to hear that Shane was in a bad way and we agreed that we wanted to go in and see him and we wanted him to be in our lives again. However, we also knew that if we did we would be explicitly disobeying our father's orders. Since we had both moved out, our father had told us very clearly that we should not visit Shane in hospital because although we were now living elsewhere:

It's up to this house he'll start calling again.

In other words, our father portrayed our visiting Shane in hospital as a selfish act that would have negative repercussions only for him. Despite no longer living under his roof, he still exercised considerable power over us and invoked sufficient fear in us, that for the next while we obeyed his orders and left Shane to his own devices in the hospital.

****

In late 2005, our father apparently had his own unexpected meeting with Shane. He described this meeting in an email he sent to me on 14 December 2005:

"Sent: 14/12/2005 16:51
Subject: fwd: Life, sometimes its…

Just bumped into Shane, Did not talk to him. Just looked at each other for a split second, I don't think he even recognised me. He looked OK, dyed blond hair, army jacket, the usual. I looked back to see if he was looking back also; no chance."

I was confused by this email. On one level, it seemed that our father felt some remorse about the fact that he had bumped into his eldest son on the street and both parties had acted like strangers. On the other hand, he was taking no responsibility as to how this situation came to be. He seemed to me to be blaming Shane for not looking back, yet at the same time he says that he doesn't think Shane recognised him, which begs the question - then why would Shane look back? From the email, our father seemed to make no effort to go after Shane and make sure he knew it was him. He watches him walk away and then fumes that Shane does not turn around.

When Fin and I read this email it gave us renewed determination to go in and see Shane. We both agreed what a sad thing it was that Shane had apparently dyed his hair blonde and we didn't even know this. A couple of months after getting this email, in early 2006, Fin and I decided to act.

Now that we were no longer under our father's roof or under his power, we decided we could defy him and that his potential anger was a risk worth taking to see our brother again. If our father gave out to us, then so be it. In early 2006, the two of us finally put our dilly-dallying to one side and met at the 123 bus-stop on Dame Street to take us to see our brother in the psychiatric ward of St. James's Hospital.

After we got off the bus at St. James's Hospital, we entered the hospital through the main entrance into the foyer area. We were pleasantly surprised by the newness and cleanness of the entrance hall in the hospital which had recently been refurbished. We looked for signs for the psychiatric ward and saw a sign pointing towards the Beckett Ward which we knew to be part of the psychiatric unit as Shane had told us years before.

The Psychiatric Unit itself was called the Jonathan Swift Clinic. The Beckett Ward was on the ground floor and was for those patients who were not a danger to themselves or others and were free to come and go during the day. Upstairs was the Fownes Ward which was a more secure environment for those patients who required stricter supervision.

Mingled in with our nervous anxiety about how Shane might react to our visit was a general nervousness of being in a psychiatric ward. As we walked down the corridor we saw an outside smoking area where a few patients sat smoking with vacant expressions on their faces. We arrived at the nurses' desk and a smiling middle-aged woman asked if she could help us. We told her we were there to see Shane Murphy and asked her if she could tell us which ward he was in. She smiled at us again and told us her name was Yvonne. She guided us down the corridor into a ward with six beds, some of which had the curtain drawn around them. She stopped at one such bed and drew back the curtain to reveal Shane lying on his back, fully clothed, fast asleep and snoring loudly.

197

Wake up, Shane, the nurse said, *you have some visitors.*

Shane slowly awoke as if from a coma. He opened his glazed eyes which took in the two of us standing at the end of the bed. He shifted his ample frame, slowly sat up and a smile broke across face.

How's it going? he said

Great, we said.

It's great to see you, we said.

It's great to see you too, he said. *Do you wanna go outside for a smoke?*

Sure, we said, *let's go. You lead the way.*

Shane swung his legs over the bed - *right so,* he said *follow me.*

We walked behind as Shane led us outside to the smoking area. Shane nodded and said hello to nurses and patients as we passed, he was clearly a part of the fixtures and fittings in the psychiatric ward at this stage. The nurses looked curiously at us following behind him and smiled encouragingly.

When we got outside we sat on a bench and Shane had a cigarette and we chatted about music and football and things brothers talk about as if was just another normal day. We had feared that Shane might be angry with us that we had left it so long to visit. We felt he could ask with some justification.

Where the hell have ye been for the last five years?

But he never asked us that. It became clear within ten minutes of meeting him that he didn't care where we had been. He only cared that we were here with him now and hopefully would be here with him again in the future. We chatted as if our last meeting had been only the week before and we were simply catching up as brothers do. As we chatted, I examined his physical appearance. He had put on weight and was carrying what appeared to be a beer belly but what turned out to be a Coca-Cola belly. As we quickly learned, he was addicted to the stuff and would regularly down two litre bottles of Coke a day. He had also shaved his head entirely, which in

198

conjunction with his medication-glazed eyes and scruffy facial hair, gave him an almost stereotypical look of a mental patient.

His look however belied his ability to converse normally with us and for half an hour we talked about everything and nothing before tiredness seemed to come over Shane and he said he wanted to go back into the ward. We followed him back down the corridor and as we passed another nurse, Shane stopped and introduced us to her:

Colette, he said, *these are me brothers, Gar and Fin. They came in to visit me today.*

He spoke with huge pride in his voice. I was pleased and a little embarrassed by his pride.

Lovely to meet ye, she said. *Hope to see you again.*

Oh you will, we said, *for definite.*

We meant it too.

As Shane swung himself back up onto the bed he smiled at us and thanked us for the visit and said he hoped we'd be in again.

We will, we said, *we'll be in soon. Look after yourself.*

Bye, he said. He was already half-snoring.

We left the ward and walked back down the sterile corridor that led to the hospital entrance hall. We walked in a swirl of emotion. We were delighted to have seen our brother again and relieved that he seemed so glad to see us.

There was also guilt. *Why had we left it so long? Was the nurse judging us,* we asked each other - *was Shane?* We concluded that they were not judging us. Both Shane and the nurse had welcomed us with open arms with no recriminations or questions as to where we had been or what took so long.

When we talked about it later that evening over a few pints, warmth glowed between us. Whatever way you looked at it, what we had done that day in visiting Shane in the psychiatric ward was unequivocally *the right thing to do*. Shane had been open in his feelings of happiness at our visit. Although we were concerned about Shane's physical appearance and his mental state, we agreed that having family visit him and restoring his relationships could only benefit Shane. No doubt the nurses thought the same as they greeted us with such encouragement.

That night we basked in the glow of knowing that we had done *something good*, despite the fact that we had disobeyed our father. We reflected on the fact that it felt good, even if it had taken us a little while to do it. We also laughed at some of the things Shane had said. Despite everything, he was still the same old Shane, our big brother who we knew and loved so well. We were excited about the prospect of having our big brother back in our lives again, even if it was, for now at any rate, through the prism of the psychiatric ward.

Fin

It was a huge relief to finally visit Shane instead of just threatening it like we had before. Once we made the decision to disobey our father's orders about visiting Shane, there was no longer any real excuse to delay but still we did for a few weeks. It was hard to actually go through with the visit as we knew we would have to face up to the reality of our brother's current condition. We weren't sure how bad or good this reality would be. Each week that passed without facing up to this reality only added to the feeling of guilt.

The night before we were due to go in, I kept thinking about the last and only time I had visited Shane in the psychiatric ward. It was also in St. James's about a decade before and well before its refurbishment. My father had brought me in as a teenager after some incident where I had angered him. He left me in no doubt that the objective of my accompanying him to visit Shane in the psychiatric ward was to see how I was likely to end up *if I didn't get my act together*. I remember there were food stains on the ceiling and I couldn't quite understand how that happened. When I pointed this phenomenon out to my father he responded by saying:
Yeah they live like fuckin' animals here and if you keep going the way you're going, this is where you will end up .....I'm telling you; he said firmly, *you'll end up just like Shane.*

So when Gar and I entered the hospital many years later, I was comforted immediately when I saw that it was clean and very well kept. I was still quite worried about how we were going to approach Shane. What if he shouted at us to get out? What if he resented the fact that we hadn't called in to see him in years? What if his condition had worsened? What if he didn't even recognise us? All these thoughts flew around my head as myself and Gar walked nervously up the long corridor towards the psychiatric ward.

As we reached the doors of the psychiatric ward, there appeared to be some security lock on the door that I thought might prohibit us from entering. I was almost ready to use this as an excuse to simply turn back; such was the apprehension I was feeling. I looked at Gar and we both nodded as if to say, *we're in this together.*

The door actually opened without resistance when we pushed it. We walked up the corridor, past the garden, past a few people who looked like they might have been patients. We found what appeared to be a reception desk and waited for someone to assist us. When a nurse appeared and directed us to Shane's room, we knew this was it, the moment where we could assess how good or bad Shane's condition was.

To see that Shane was wearing clean clothes was a relief. He had a shaven head similar to the one I sported at the time, but he was also wearing jeans and a t shirt that matched and seemed to be in an adequate state. Before he even acknowledged us, I saw the big cardboard box beside his bed filled with CDs. This brought immediate relief to me as I knew it indicated he still had his love of music, a healthy interest. When he glanced over and noticed us, the smile he wore made me almost cry with relief and happiness. He was positively beaming and just seeing that happiness in him told me that we hadn't left it too late; our big brother's condition had not diminished completely as I had feared. Better still, his condition seemed far better than I could have even hoped. As we embraced Shane, I looked over to Gar and we just looked at each other knowingly, *we had gotten our big brother back.*

Chapter 32

Gar

Not long after visiting Shane, it became obvious to us that our visits were having a positive effect on him. Within a few months, he had grown his hair back and had started to buy clothes for himself and take a greater interest in his appearance.

Throughout his teenage years and early twenties, Shane had always taken a great interest in his looks and his clothes in order to convey the rocker look to the rest of the world. We therefore knew it was a good sign when after a few months of visits Shane proudly showed off 18-hole burgundy Doc Marten boots he had bought in Temple Bar. A few months later, he had saved up enough to buy himself €200 black leather pants with a biker's jacket to match. While he may have looked incongruous dressed like this in the psychiatric ward, he didn't care.

You could never accuse Shane of being a slave to fashion.

Yvonne, the kind motherly nurse, was always quick to tell us that our visits helped Shane to progress. It seemed that Shane had a strong desire to not let us down and to make sure that the visits kept coming.

Sometimes we would visit Shane and he would be having a bad day, audibly sucking on chain-smoked cigarettes, eyes glazed over and totally non-responsive to any attempts at conversation. At the start, these visits were upsetting but before long we came to terms with the fact that these days were inevitable. We knew that these bad days were only tolerable when there were two of us visiting together and so we rarely visited Shane alone. A solo visit on a bad day was hard to take.

What was very heartening for us was that as the months went by Shane developed an awareness of when he was having a bad day and the next time he saw us he would say apologetically that he was *all over the place the last time* because of a change in medication or some other reason. We told him not to worry about it as the bad days were rare and becoming rarer as he continued to improve.

Sometimes, because of a change in medication, Shane would be very lethargic and would drool from the numbing effects of the medication. For a time, the drooling was so bad that Shane wore a plastic collar around his neck to collect the drool that involuntarily dribbled from his mouth. It was like the one a dog wears so it cannot scratch its head. While it was shocking for us to see Shane have to wear this collar, it was hard not to be impressed by the fact that Shane did not seem to care about the collar at all, and continued as if it was not there, smoking cigarettes, drinking Coke and chatting away to us. Within a few weeks the collar was gone and the medication seemed to improve his mood significantly.

The most marvellous thing we noticed about Shane was that despite everything that had happened to him; the crazy decade yo-yoing in and out of James's hospital, the Oliver Bond, the Mendo, St. Michael's Estate and the years of solitary abandonment, Shane had not changed at all from our big brother when we were younger. He was still pretty lazy and would try and pull fast ones if he thought he would get away with them but he was also still the same jovial, warm hearted and generous person he had always been. Shane's goodness was so obvious and so transparent that it was clearly at odds with the message we had got from our father and Caroline that Shane was a useless, aggressive and worthless person.

Seeing Shane as he was - good-natured, warm, gentle and loving - caused us to examine ever more carefully the judgement of our father who had warned us against Shane. Restoring our relationship with Shane bolstered our feelings that it might be best for us to talk to our father about our relationship and the events that had occurred in the past.

Fin

Shane often asked us about our father and it was awkward as we didn't want to discuss why our father wasn't coming in to visit him. It seemed Shane was almost jealous that we still had a relationship with our father and Caroline and he didn't. He spoke about how he would love to call up to our father's house and for all of us sit around the table with a cup of tea. I often wanted to tell Shane that he wasn't missing out by not seeing our father but it felt naturally wrong to discuss our father in any way with him, given his unstable mental state. Anger was obviously not an emotion we wanted to draw from Shane.

I wanted to believe that my father had changed his ways and I looked for and welcomed any sign that this might be case. If I saw my father being good with James or Séan (which he was capable of being), I thought perhaps he had become more in touch with his sensitive side and become more loving. I knew he wasn't one to apologise, but I speculated that he had maybe seen the error in his ways and changed, possibly only telling Caroline in some dramatic admission. This story I made up was one that I eventually convinced myself was possible. I spoke to Gar about the idea of letting our father know that we were visiting Shane. I alluded to the fact that our father was potentially somewhat nicer in recent times and Gar agreed that this was a possibility. From our discussions, it seemed to me that Gar also wanted to believe that this was true.

In the four years or so since Séan had been born we had gone from having one brother (each other) to having three brothers. We had our hearts bolstered with a new younger brother and then, even more recently, we had found our older brother again. We were almost lulled by love into forgetting our father's bad traits.

We decided that it might be a good idea to give our father the benefit of the doubt again and try to persuade him to come in with us to see Shane. When we told him we had been in to visit Shane, he squirmed a little but acted somewhat concerned about Shane's wellbeing. He seemed guilty that we had seen fit to go and visit Shane against his orders. As far as Gar and I were concerned, it was a relief that at least now he knew we had visited Shane and we weren't hiding it from him any longer.

Gar

Shane's birthday fell within a couple of months of our first visit to the hospital. We decided that we would mark the occasion by bringing him in a birthday cake. We bought him a XXL sized Ireland rugby jersey and some CDs as presents. Like us, Shane had played rugby in the rugby club when he was younger and still followed the national team. On one of our first visits he told us how he had trials for Leinster when he was fifteen and how he could have played for Ireland.

We nodded at this – *of course you could have, Shane.*

He was also still as passionate about music as ever. He had a Sony CD Walkman and spent most of his waking hours listening to his favourite bands; *The Beatles, The Doors, Pink Floyd, Cream, Led Zeppelin, Soundgarden* and other rock favourites. The three of us had always been told we were good singers and Shane liked to utilise his talents to entertain or perhaps, torment the other patients around him by singing along with his earphones on. The nurses indulged him as an interest in music was seen as being healthy. Sometimes we would come in and Shane would be sitting at the piano that stood in a room close to his ward. Although he couldn't actually play the piano, he seemed to believe that he could and he would randomly hit the keys and sing along.

When we arrived in the ward for his birthday, we had the cake and presents wrapped up so as to keep it as a surprise for Shane. We spoke to Yvonne, the kindly nurse. Shane had confided in us that she reminded him of our Nanny from Crumlin. We both noticed the resemblance in that she had such a good nature. She was delighted to see Shane getting visitors, gifts and cake for his birthday – probably for the first time in years. We told her of our plan to light the candles on the cake and to sing Happy Birthday to Shane when we brought the cake in. She thought this was a great idea and told us that she would arrange for a canteen of hot water and tea and coffee to be brought into the TV room to have with the cake. She also rounded up the other patients so that they could join in Shane's birthday celebrations. We could then come in with the cake and candles and sing *Happy Birthday.*

When we were all gathered in the TV room, I distracted Shane while Fin went outside to light the candles on the cake. We had picked up the candles in a pound shop and Fin plugged the entire packet onto the cake to give Shane plenty to blow out.

When Fin had the candles lighting, he came in to the TV room holding the flaming cake aloft. There were *ooohs* and *aaahs* from the patients and from Shane as Fin carried the cake ceremonially towards where Shane sat. I gave the nurse the nod and we launched into a stirring rendition of *Happy Birthday.* The other patients joined in enthusiastically albeit in a number of different keys. Shane's face was filled with anticipation as we held the cake out in front of him.

He was the centre of attention and he loved it. He looked around the room and took his time, milking the moment for all it was worth. With great ceremony he sucked in as much air as he could manage and with great puffs of breath blew out the candles one by one until they were all extinguished. A great roar went up from the patients and Shane drank in the applause as Fin and I led a spirited rendition of *For He's a Jolly Good Fellow.*

Just as Fin and I exchanged victorious glances – *this was going rather well* – the mood in the room suddenly changed. Instead of singing, the patients started gasping and a shriek of terror rent the room.

We looked at each other - *Jesus Christ, what the hell is going on?*

As we looked frantically around for the source of the anguish, one of the patients, a skinny elderly man with a moustache, pointed at the cake and let out a blood curdling cry –

The candles, he screamed, *they're lighting back up again. By themselves!*

The entire room now pointed, moaning and gasping at Shane as he held the haunted cake in his hands and the candles one by one re-lit themselves to their growing horror. Shane's face had turned deathly white and for one horrible moment I thought he was about to throw the ghastly cake across the room.

Fin and I looked at each other and immediately recognised what had happened.

Oh bollocks. It's the candles – they're those re-lighting ones!

We had to extinguish the candles immediately before someone had a breakdown. We grabbed the cake from Shane's trembling hands and put it on the table and I extinguished the candles in a little pool of spit I made in my hands while Fin doused them in one of the cups of tea. Once they were all extinguished, a sense of order eventually returned. The cake was cut up and fresh tea and coffee was dished out to everyone.

When the commotion had died down, we gave Shane his presents which he rapturously received. He greeted the rugby jersey like an excited child, immediately putting it on and proclaiming –

Watch out Brian O' Driscoll.

The CDs; Led Zeppelin and the Doors, were equally well received. So much so it became obvious to us that Shane was pretty keen for our visit to conclude so that he could start listening to them in earnest. We happily took the hint and said our goodbyes to Shane and the nurse and the other patients.

Over a pint that night we laughed at the whole episode but vowed never to bring re-lighting candles into the psychiatric ward again.

As we reflected on what had been an emotional and eventful afternoon, my father called me on my mobile phone. A few months had passed since we had told our father about our first visit to see Shane again. We had told our father in advance that we are going in to see Shane for his birthday so he was now calling me to see how we had got on. When I told him what had happened with the candles and the presents, he laughed and sounded genuinely happy that Shane had had a good day. He sounded emotional like he had a couple of drinks taken. When I told him how happy Shane had been with the cake and the presents my father said:

Fair play to ye. Your Nanny is looking down on ye and smiling for looking after Shane.

It was an unusually heartfelt and touching thing for our father to say.

I reminded my father that Shane very much wanted to see him again and would welcome him if he visited Shane in the hospital. He paused - said he was really thinking about it and that he would like to see Shane again. I told him he would be glad if he did and Shane would be glad too.

With our encouragement he visited Shane within a few months of the birthday party and maintained visits to him. Within a year or so of these visits our father began to take pride in his visits to Shane and started boasting to friends and family of his dedication and devotion to his eldest son. We listened to these recitations with mixed feelings as our father's telling of the story conspicuously omitted the many years in which Shane languished alone in the hospital.

Before long, our father's story developed to include a detailed first-person account of the episode with the magic re-lighting birthday candles in the TV room. Fin and I had to bite our tongues as we listened to this – our father seemed to have deluded himself that he had actually attended the birthday party. We resisted the temptation to point out to our father's audience that he had not in fact been at that birthday party at all and in actual fact his policy at that time was to cut Shane out of his life (and out of his will). Of course, our father would not have been pleased if we had ruined his *Dedicated Father* story so we kept our mouths shut. Afterwards, however, we reflected on it and agreed that it reinforced this feeling that our father was not to be trusted. It also brought into question his entire motivation for visiting Shane. Was it for Shane's benefit, or was it for his own?

Chapter 33

Gar

An unintended consequence of us having broken our father's rule not to visit Shane was that it helped us see that our father could no longer control us completely. However, he did try to hold onto some of that control. He remained as adamant as ever that we should continue to regard Caroline as our mother and maintain the fiction of us as one big happy family. In around 2005, while in my mid-20s, I received a text from my father on the morning of Mother's Day with a simple three-word instruction:

Ring your Mom

I was angered and upset by this almost arrogant text-order. It seemed to me that any considerate person would have realised that for me and Fin - who had not seen our mother in over a decade - Mother's Day might be a difficult day.

Instead, our father continued to use Mother's Day as an excuse for him to reinforce the Happy Family fallacy and also to reassert his control over us even though we had at this stage moved out of the family home.

I rang Fin after I got this message and he confirmed he had got the same message. At this stage we were not yet prepared to argue with our father over this and so ultimately, we made the Mother's Day calls to Caroline and the charade continued for another year.

Another episode occurred in 2006 when I was visiting my father and Caroline with my girlfriend at the time that showed the unpleasant effects of maintaining my father's fiction. My girlfriend and I had been going out about five years and I had become very good friends with my girlfriend's mother. Her mother was a kind and caring woman who had separated from her husband and had moved into a new house with her three children. She had a strong personality and had weathered the storm with gusto and thrown herself into all kinds of new activities and made lots of new friends.

As I had been going out with her daughter for so long, I suggested that she might want to meet my father and Caroline. She said she would love to meet them and I decided I would mention it to my father and Caroline the next time I was over.

That occasion arose a few weeks later when my girlfriend and I were eating dinner with my father and Caroline in their house. I only went up for dinner to their house every now and again; despite Caroline putting on the fake niceness, it always seemed totally forced to me. My father and Caroline rarely invited me up and I rarely invited myself up and that seemed to suit all parties. However, on this occasion, I had wanted to go up as I wanted to suggest to my father and Caroline that they might want to meet my girlfriend's mother who I described to them as a lovely, friendly person. I waited until we were sitting around the table having dinner, my father in his usual seat at the head of the table and Caroline at her usual seat nearest the kitchen. I thought my suggestion might be well received. I was wrong.

My father's immediate reaction was to mutter something along the lines of *'maybe sometime in the future'*. I was a bit annoyed about this lack of enthusiasm particularly as my girlfriend was sitting at the table as a guest. Even just out of manners I felt my father could have been a little bit more enthusiastic. I said again that I thought it would be a good idea and not too much trouble and that everyone would get on very well but as I spoke I was suddenly cut off by Caroline slamming her plate on the table, standing up and screaming and crying and running into the kitchen, slamming the door behind her. My father looked at me like thunder and said angrily:

You've upset your mother now.

I stared open mouthed - thoroughly confused and embarrassed, as was my girlfriend who sat beside me. She stared intently at her plate, not sure where to look.

I finished off my dinner as quickly as I could and we left shortly afterwards. I didn't know what to say to my girlfriend so I just didn't talk about what had happened. When next I saw my girlfriend's mother, she asked again about a meeting and I told her it was being organised and I would get back to her with a date soon. I couldn't bring myself to explain that in reality, a meeting seemed out of the question.

Fin

By this stage, Fiona, James and I had moved into a little two-bedroom house close to where Fiona's parents lived. We were delighted to have the three of us living permanently together.

In the meantime, my father and Caroline were making less and less time to see James. I was getting tired of making up excuses to James and to Fiona's family about them. They didn't even bother to make up reasonable excuses themselves; it always seemed to be something about a horse. One Wednesday evening when I was supposed to be calling up with James, I got a phone call from Caroline to say that they were too tired after their weekend in Kilkenny. Considering they usually came back on Sunday, I considered this to be a pretty poor excuse. I told Caroline in an angry abrupt way that it was fine and after I hung up the phone, I sat back to think of a different excuse I could say to Fiona's family. I was getting annoyed. Not for the first time, I considered that merely being in any kind of a relationship with my father and Caroline was a burden.

In July 2005, on the evening of James' sixth birthday, I had texted Caroline to subtly remind her that it was his birthday. She then rang an hour later to wish him a Happy Birthday. I didn't tell Fiona or her family at the time that I had reminded them.

Fiona and I were very happy in our new home and we rarely argued. But when we did, it was usually an argument about my father and Caroline's negligent grand-parenting. Fiona saw through my made-up excuses and was quite rightly annoyed if I wasn't being honest with her. She was right and I knew that I couldn't be dishonest with her so I began to be honest and share with her the real excuses used. She made it clear to me what she thought of my father and Caroline which was an eye-opener for me and made me realise that what I had accepted as *normal* behaviour because it was so familiar to me, was anything but.

****

By July 2006, my father and Caroline's negligent attitude to grand-parenting had reached the stage where I was no longer willing to remind them of James' upcoming birthday.

211

On the day of his birthday, we had a fun day with James at the zoo, but my enjoyment of the day was dampened as I constantly checked my phone to see whether Caroline had called. I didn't think there was a remote chance that my father would call. As the evening drew to a close with no phone call, I was upset. I tried to hide it but Fiona noticed. She assured me that my 'parents' indiscretions were not a reflection on me. This was something I was so conflicted with. It was as if I had vouched for them down the years and they kept letting me down.

I also felt that this wasn't fair on James. I wondered did he notice and I hoped he didn't. I wondered should I have just sent a reminder for his sake, like I did last year. I didn't want to tell Fiona I had to send my 'parents' a reminder and I also didn't want to go behind Fiona's back even if I tried to justify it to myself by saying that it was for James' benefit. Again, their lack of consideration was causing me to question whether I was wrong in what I was doing and made me feel constantly guilty.

In the end I held firm and sent no reminder. They didn't ring. They had forgotten their only grandson's birthday.

At least there was something good to come from it. I was now in no doubt about my father and Caroline. The way they had treated me as a child had, at least subconsciously, always felt to me like it was in some way my own fault. It was always in the back of my mind that maybe I was that *useless lazy bastard* that Caroline always said I was and that maybe I deserved the treatment from her and my father. But they were showing me now that they could treat a child such as James with similar disregard for his feelings. I knew James wasn't a *useless lazy bastard*. He was a wonderful child; bright, amusing, well-mannered and well behaved. They spoke about how he was their only grandchild and yet they weren't bothered to see him most of the time. They didn't even remember his birthday. It was becoming clearer to me now that the problem was not with me but with my father and Caroline.

I realised that their behaviour was possibly having a detrimental effect on my son. For the first time I publicly announced (to Fiona) that my father and Caroline were selfish people. I felt a sense of relief. It felt right being honest with Fiona and with myself.

A few days later, Caroline rang apologising for not having called. I think the excuse was horse related again. I wasn't afraid to show her my disgust. In the past, I might have humoured her and told her that *these things happen*. But I was now at the point that I wished I could find a real reason to cut all ties with them. I wanted nothing to do with them. If it wasn't for Séan, I think I would have let the relationship between myself and Caroline and my father drift apart from that point on. But I wanted to see my little brother.

As the year progressed I became more vociferous to Caroline about them letting James down. She seemed to attempt to make more time for him. Meanwhile, my father just seemed to make more excuses.

Chapter 34

Gar

In May 2006, my girlfriend and I travelled down to Kilkenny to stay the weekend with my father and Caroline and to celebrate Caroline's birthday in the house in Kilkenny that they had recently bought.

We had an enjoyable day horse-riding but on the way back to the house I discovered that my father had not bought a cake for Caroline's birthday. This was not a big surprise to me and I told him it would be a good idea for him to get one. I said that I had made a CD of 80's music that Caroline liked that we could listen to it later and have a party. With all the fuss of a selfish man doing something uncharacteristically selfless, he manufactured an excuse to go to the shops where he bought a cake and hid it in the fridge so it would be a surprise later.

After a barbecue and a few drinks, we danced around to the CD in the kitchen, produced the cake and sang *Happy Birthday*. Caroline seemed genuinely happy and touched by the CD and the cake. Eventually, she and my girlfriend retired to bed to leave my father and me to stay up. We made small talk before my father cracked open another can of beer. He offered me a can and I refused, taking a glass of water instead. This seemed to offend him. His glazed eyes narrowed and he stared at me for a few moments before asking me belligerently:

So why have you been taking pot-shots at me recently, huh?

The tone of his voice was threatening. I quickly detected the threat and realised that this conversation was unlikely to end in a warm and loving embrace between father and son. I stared back at him.

What do you mean? I asked, although I had a fair idea of what he meant.

You know what I mean. The way you've been talking to me, answering me back.

I knew from his aggressively glazed eyes that he wanted to have it out with me right there and then. I foresaw drama. I foresaw voices being raised and a drunken shouting match. Thankfully I was sober enough to foresee this.

I knew I needed to extricate myself from the situation as soon as possible so I stood up and turned for the door.

Goodnight Dad, I'm going to bed.

He looked at me with a mixture of shock and disappointment. He seemed to have been waiting for such an opportunity to arise for me and him to have this argument and he seemed disgusted that I was just walking away from it. Before he could say anything, I turned my back on him and closed the door behind me and went to bed.

I trembled in bed for a while afterwards, knowing that I had avoided what would have been a very unpleasant, drunken confrontation with my father. I was glad that I had been in the position to recognise the danger and exit stage left.

I did not sleep much that night and my mind raced the next morning as I lay in bed thinking what the conversation might be when I saw my father. When we went downstairs he was merrily cooking breakfast and welcomed us into the kitchen and served us scrambled eggs and sausages as if nothing had happened. I realised immediately that that was how my father wanted it to be-*nothing had happened*-and at that time that suited me too. My father was ruddy cheeked from all the booze the night before but in ebullient mood. He even gave us a lift to the train station, an act of kindness so uncharacteristic that I knew he was trying to make up for something.

Fin

I kept at Caroline about the problems with her and my father and their relationship with James. She seemed to act concerned when I told her how bad their behaviour was. She always talked like she wanted to make time for James.

Therefore, I was delighted when Caroline and my father invited us all down to stay with them in Kilkenny for a weekend. This meant that James would have a weekend with his grandparents and it would improve my father and Caroline's image to Fiona and her parents.

We went to Kilkenny and had an enjoyable few days. Caroline suggested that she and my father would baby-sit if Fiona and I wanted to go for a drink. I was delighted because this was the type of thing Fiona's mother did all the time. I felt I could hold this up as at least one example of my 'parents' doing the same. I remember hearing Fiona telling her Mam on the phone and I was delighted that everyone would think my father and Caroline were okay grandparents. We went out and had an enjoyable few drinks together.

The next day, all of us went to the local pub, including the two children. After a short period, Caroline suggested that she and Fiona would go back to bring the children home. My father and I stayed for a few more pints. Although I was still suspicious about him, this had been a nice weekend. He was being remarkably friendly to me and I once again contemplated that despite everything, perhaps he wasn't so bad. It was as if offering this weekend to us was a way of making up for his previous selfish acts. I was once again taken in, some part of me wanted to just forgive and forget. I'm not sure why but this seemed to just be the natural thing to do. Almost like the commandment in the Bible "Honour thy mother and father" which doesn't carry any stipulations, my natural tendencies didn't either. To this point, I never really felt like I could just decide that because I didn't like him, I could just tell him that I wanted to cut ties with him. Phrases like, *"you can choose your friends but you can't choose your family"* somehow reaffirmed that I had to just get on with it with my father. Of course, the irony was that my father had chosen precisely which members of my family I could see and couldn't see throughout my life but that was only really starting to occur to me.

We chatted away about everyday things. My father commented that when I went up to the bar that some of the local lads were quick to move out of my way. I had a shaved head at the time and my father was saying that I looked tough. I laughed because I wasn't the type of guy to get in a bar-room brawl but I could tell that my father was saying all these things in an effort to flatter me.

After a few pints, we returned to the house. We had a few more cans of beer in the fridge so we started on them. Fiona and Caroline had gone to bed, leaving my father and myself. I suggested that we each take turns picking songs from my iPod and playing them. My father agreed and we continued drinking cans and playing tunes. At first, I was deliberately playing songs I knew he liked just to be nice. But then, when I was picking another song, I saw my father out of the corner of my eye. He was looking at me as if he was contemplating something. After a song or two, he turned to me and told me that I reminded him in many ways of himself when he was younger.

I knew my father had such a high opinion of himself that this was supposed to be regarded by me as the ultimate compliment. I just found myself cringing. Everything about the remark sounded so contrived. It sent a warning signal to me that he was being overly nice now and that there was some reason behind it. With the drink on board, I looked at him, almost in disgust. He seemed oblivious to my look and he tried to go further. He tilted his head as if he was pondering something and said:

We've had some great times together kid.

He looked at me smiling. I didn't agree with him but I just kept my mouth shut. I was curious to see where he was going with this. I soon found out. He fixed his paternal gaze on me and smiled as he said:

Do you remember when youse asked me could you call your Mum "your Mum" and not Caroline anymore?

Watching him smile as he said that really annoyed me. This was blatant lying. I remembered how we came to call Caroline *Mum* only too well. It was one of the memories of my childhood that I wished I could forget. I figured that he was used to the old *Me* that used to *plámáse* him because I had to. The old *Me* that felt trapped - I had to say what he wanted or I would be kicked out of his house. But I was no longer trapped. I thought back to the divorce case in 2002 and how he had contorted the truth and made me feel like I had to repeat his lies under oath for him. I thought of my Mam sitting outside the courtroom, timid and harmless-looking, a far cry from the evil money-hungry woman he had painted her as, and more like the mother I remembered as a child.

The anger in me rose and I tried to keep somewhat calm but I could feel the anger piercing from my eyes. I stared at him, still having not replied to his comment. He looked old and slightly dishevelled, particularly after the drinks. For the first time I realised that I wasn't

217

in any way afraid of him anymore. The days of him holding me up against the wall roaring at me were well and truly over. Finally, I spoke with an air of authority:

That's not what happened at all, I said firmly, growing in confidence.

He seemed taken aback and looked at me anxiously as if he wanted to backtrack. He sort of nodded and said:

Oh right, yeah in a very worried manner as he straightened himself up in the chair.

Even with the drink on board, I didn't expand on my first sentence. As angry as I was, I was wary of having a huge row with him, especially with James and Séan asleep upstairs. I was also keenly aware that my emotions were heightened with the drink so I needed to be careful.

It was a strange few moments, as we both seemed to be looking at each other, almost in silence, weighing each other up. The chats and pints we had prior to this were probably the best we had gotten on in ages. But his 'Mum' comment made me despise him for what he was doing, I knew right then that my relationship with him would never be the same again.

He seemed to sense my animosity. He suddenly moved away from talking about anything relating to childhood and started talking about horse riding. This was a topic I found boring but again had often previously humoured him on. But I was in no mood to humour him, I didn't see the point. I actually really wanted to go back to the conversation about referring to Caroline as *Mum*. I thought of the song that in a strange way, always made me think of my Mam. I picked up the iPod and spun the wheel to select the artist:

Tupac.

I knew he hated rap music so this was ideal. I spun the wheel again to select the song:

Dear Mama.

I hired the volume up a bit and sat back. I looked at him. He was looking sheepishly back at me. I glared at him and thought about how he screwed up our childhood. I had anger in my eyes and he actually looked quite scared. I was staring intently at him He sat opposite me, almost cowering in his seat. I had never seen him scared before and I found it interesting. I was surprised but felt empowered. For the first time ever, I felt like I was in control between the two of us. As Tupac belted out his regrets about his and his mother's *beef*, my father motioned as if to say something. I butted in, momentarily forgetting the two kids asleep upstairs.

Before you start with your shit, this song doesn't remind me of Caroline in any way, alright?

Oh right… yeah, he muttered, nodding meekly.

He even went on to praise the song, which was unusual for him. After the song I went out for a smoke to calm myself down. As I stood out the back, I considered having a real heart to heart with him. But I was aware we were both drunk and it probably wasn't the best time to have an emotional conversation. I came back in still trying to decide whether I would remind him how we had really started calling Caroline our 'Mum'. Still drunk on beer and empowerment, I rudely instructed him that it was his turn to pick a song. In another uncharacteristic move, he stood up and said.

No, I'm heading to bed.

Ordinarily, he never went to bed leaving beers in the fridge so I knew he wasn't enjoying this moment.
You finish the cans, he said in a generous tone, clearly humouring me. After he went, I opened up a can and put on an album by *the Strokes*.

As I sat there listening to the upbeat music, I realised that I had stood up to our father. Not properly or fully or to the extent I wished I had. But I had somewhat followed in Gar's footsteps in questioning my father. I felt like my father had provided the perfect opportunity but all the same I didn't wilt like I might have done in the past. I felt proud that I wasn't being a mug anymore. I vowed to myself that I would no longer play along and that I would stand up to him in future. I even decided that the next day, I would pull him to one side and we would have that conversation about calling Caroline *"Mum"*. It would be good to do that sober. That was the plan.

But the next morning, my father was in a very friendly humour. Caroline and Fiona were talking. James and Séan were playing. I was sober. The booze that had given me the Dutch courage to stand up for myself was gone. I couldn't keep the bravery up once the morning came. Perhaps if my father had reacted differently and we had had a row, I would have continued it the following day. But it seemed harder to justify being angry and cold to him there in the morning with everybody else present. He was acting particularly nice to Fiona and James as if he was the nicest guy in the world. This made it all the harder. I reverted right back to my old self and smiled and even slightly humoured my father as if nothing had happened the evening before.

****

For weeks after that trip to Kilkenny, I couldn't stop thinking about my father's apparent memory of how we came to call Caroline our 'Mum'. I couldn't just dismiss it or park it like I used to with my father's other misdemeanours. He had misremembered the past in his own way before, but I was really hung up on this calling Caroline *Mum* thing. I was 26 years old and I was still calling Caroline *Mum*. I knew I had a *Mam* out there who I hadn't seen properly since I was a small child. I was afflicted by that fact as it was. I had been considering having a chat with Caroline to see would she be offended if I didn't call her Mum anymore because it was so uncomfortable.

I was also unwilling to allow our father to make up bizarre memories in place of what really happened when we were growing up. I was willing to forget the past. I didn't even require an apology, or even an acknowledgment, although I would have welcomed one. I couldn't, however, deal with my father gloating about past incidents that didn't happen the way he claimed. The more it sunk in, the worse I felt. I remember a week or two later, waking up in the morning and feeling good and then it hit me that my father asked me two weeks previous if I remembered asking to call Caroline *"Mum"*. I immediately felt sick and angry. His lie was haunting me.

I started to distance myself further from my father. I considered at this time whether there was any possibility of us actually cutting ties

220

permanently with our father. I didn't think it was a realistic possibility, particularly with Séan around. It was as if the birth of Séan had given our father a new excuse to be as much as a selfish arrogant man as he wanted to be and there would be no repercussions.

I genuinely felt like my mind was so all over the place at this time that I was starting to doubt my own sanity. I thought that I might end up in St. James' hospital with Shane if I wasn't careful. Nothing was clear and I wasn't sure what I believed or didn't believe anymore. I became paranoid and distrustful to almost everybody. Fiona noticed it and alerted me to it. I immediately knew and admitted that she was right. I knew that one step I needed to take to maintain sanity was to not see my father.

Since cutting all ties with him didn't appear to be an option in my mind, I chose something of a compromise. I still maintained a relationship with them but I started being more and more obviously distant with both Caroline and my father. I didn't call them and try to arrange a time to go up and visit with James, which I would usually have done prior to this. I decided that the one-way traffic was over. This meant I saw less of Séan which was a wrench but I had my own young son to think about and I felt that it was a difficult compromise I had to make for myself and my son and partner.

After I had ignored a few texts from Caroline, asking me to ring her, I got a call from her. Her father had obtained some free tickets to *The Who* gig in Marlay Park and none of her family were keen on going. I was delighted and gladly accepted the tickets. I scolded myself that it was a bit mean of me to be giving out about her only contacting me when she wanted something now that she had proved otherwise.

She and my father made a big deal of the fact that she got me the tickets despite the fact that they cost her nothing and it was really her father who was giving me the tickets. I was happy with the idea that she was being nice to me so that I just laughed it off.

Chapter 35

Gar

After the *pot-shots* episode in Kilkenny, I took great strength from my ability to stand up for myself against my father, so much so that I eventually even screwed up the courage to ask him about our mother. The first time I did this it was by way of a joke. Our father had mentioned our mother in some small derogatory way. He was talking about having met her when he was only eighteen and how he regretted that. I told him that I held no such regrets because if he had not met her I would not have been born five years later. It was my way of mentioning her in a context he could accept. He laughed a puzzled laugh at this.

I then moved on to telling him how sometimes I wondered where she was – pretending it was just out of curiosity. My father was clearly uncomfortable with this line of questioning but he told me a few weeks' later that he had driven past my mother's family home in Carlow and said that she was living in a caravan beside her mother's house. It turned out that the house they had bought in Kilkenny was only a short drive from my mother's family cottage. He told me this with a degree of finality as if that was really the end of the matter.

However, I was now more curious than ever and soon afterwards mentioned her again. This time his reaction was to remind me *how she had abandoned us when we were kids*. He then made some allegations about her personal hygiene as if he was letting me in on a big secret. I was disgusted by his sharing this with me and my curiosity about my mother and her whereabouts only increased.

****

Although I was no longer afraid to stand up to our father I had not yet arrived at the point where I felt it might be better if he was out of my life. It was at the end of that year, Christmas 2006, that I realised definitively that my father was not someone I could rely upon for love and support when I needed it most. This realisation came from a deeply upsetting event that occurred to me when my relationship with my girlfriend of six years broke down in particularly painful circumstances on Christmas Eve morning.

Despite the fact that we had been going through a bad patch, the break up was unexpected and as far as my friends and family were concerned, it was totally out of the blue. We had just bought an apartment together in Sandymount the year before. After we broke up on Christmas Eve morning, I called my friend who drove around to me and gave me a lift up to Fin's house. Fin, my father and I were scheduled to visit Shane that day to give and receive Christmas presents and although my heart was not, in it I decided to go along to distract me.

We were due to get a lift to the hospital with our father so Fin called him beforehand to tell them what had happened with me. Fin called him from the other room and told me the conversation he had later. He said when he told our father that we had broken up, our father's immediate reaction was to say that he was glad because *she had never given this family the time of day*. Fin told him that was not the kind of thing I needed to hear at this particular moment in time.

However, Fin and I both knew that this reaction was characteristic of our father as he viewed everything through the prism of how it would impact him. The reality was our father had never had much time for my girlfriend, so he seemed relieved to hear that we had broken up, despite the impact it might have had on me.

Shortly after, our father rang to say he was outside in the car. We went outside to him. I was feeling weak and in turmoil and as I approached our father he opened his arms uncharacteristically to offer me a hug. I gratefully moved to accept this but as I walked towards him I noticed that he was beaming uncontrollably from ear-to-ear. As he tried to comfort me, I noticed a tone in his voice of unrestrained glee. He could not hide his happiness. The rebellious son firing off *pot-shots* was now coming home to papa.

For the entire journey and throughout the visit to Shane I kept asking myself the same question incredulously:

Is it just me or is my father happy that I have just had my heart broken?

By the time he dropped me off at Fin's house after our visit with Shane there was no doubt in my mind that he was more than happy, he was delighted with this unexpected turn of events. I was wounded and broken from what had happened and I needed care and love and my father was happy to give this to me but only in his own peculiar gloating fashion. It was like I had flown too high with my college degree, apprenticeship in a corporate law firm, girlfriend and *potshots* but now I had come crashing back down to earth and he was only too happy to welcome me back to the nest with my wings firmly clipped.

I was even returning to his house for Christmas day the next day, which, when it came, was torture.

Waking up in my old bedroom in my father's house on Christmas morning, I felt like I'd stepped back in time to when I was a teenager and that the last six years had not happened at all. Hours after waking up, I eventually dragged myself out of bed and just as I did, the door opened. It was my little brother Séan who ran in excitedly singing *It's Christmas Gar, It's Christmas,* over and over again. There was something about his innocence that overwhelmed me. I fell to my knees and roared with tears. Poor Séan, uncomprehending, started to cry too before Caroline came in and took him away. After a while I managed to carry myself into the shower but when I stepped out and saw my reflection in the mirror, naked and helpless, I felt completely vulnerable again and curled up on the cold tiles and cried my eyes out.

By the time I went to bed on Christmas night I knew that I could not stay with my father and Caroline for one more night. When I woke up on St Stephen's Day I was determined to return to the apartment I had lived in with my girlfriend even though there was a sense of foreboding about that. I just could not bear the thought of another night under my father's roof. Fin came back with me to make sure I was okay and I spent the next few weeks back in the apartment surrounded by friends checking in on me. It was a sorry reflection of the relationship I had with my father that I chose to be alone in the apartment rather than in his company under his roof.

Fin

My father's selfish nature really showed itself that Christmas. His reaction to Gar's heartbreak made me realise that there was no limit to how selfish he could be. Perhaps he thought Gar was too distraught to notice or maybe he forgot that I was there. I was stunned to see him beaming, grinning from ear-to-ear, eyes twinkling as he offered Gar a celebratory hug. He was not commiserating, he was delighted. I remember trying to think of a good way to tell him that he should at least pretend to hide his delight in front of his heartbroken son. It was sickening.

It took a month or so for that episode to really sink in. I was more worried about Gar than my relationship with my father. But as Gar healed somewhat with time, I started to reflect on that day and my father's reaction. It told me one unmistakable thing - my father only cared about himself. Gar's tragedy was his glory.

One night over a few pints a couple of months later, Gar and I talked about the whole episode. I was relieved when he asked me did I notice anything about our father's reaction. I told him I did and we both agreed it was outrageous. I told Gar about his constant failures as a grandfather and the two of us both had a long chat about how time and time again, we seemed to be discussing the selfish nature of our father.

Chapter 36

Gar

Within a month of Christmas, things had already begun to look up. There was still heart-ache and the inevitable pain that comes from separating two lives that were once entwined but two things happened which helped me through this period. Firstly, by the end of January I had been called in to the office of one of the partners I worked for and asked whether I would be interested in doing a secondment in New York with a US based client for a year or so? I jumped at the chance. By March 2007 I had been interviewed and was all set to go to New York in June of that year.

The other thing which helped me through that difficult time was my new hobby - cycling. It was serendipitous that just before Christmas I had committed to going cycling in the Alps the following June with a group of friends so when I found myself single in January and needing a distraction, there was a hobby ready-made for me. I soon found myself cycling every weekend around the Kilkenny Mountains with my friends, with the occasional solo spins over the Sally Gap to engage in some primal scream therapy shouting into the wind and the rain at the top of my voice.

The fresh air, exercise and camaraderie was just what I needed at that time so when it came to my boarding the plane in late June for a new life in New York I was physically in good shape and mentally in significantly better shape than I had been six months' previous. Before I left, I called up to my father's house to say goodbye to them and to Séan. I took the opportunity to go for a quick spin in the Dublin Mountains before calling in and when I arrived I left my bike out the back garden with my cycling shoes, helmet, gloves and sunglasses. I went inside and had a cup of tea and when I went back out to my bike I saw Séan, who was four years old, standing proudly beside my bike with his little feet in my size eleven shoes, his little hands in my gloves, with my oversized helmet on his head and wearing my sunglasses which looked like novelty sunglasses on his little face.

He was grinning happily:

Can I go cycling Gar? he asked me.

I grinned back at him.

Well, I said, *let's see if you can ride my bike.*

I lifted him up and put him on the saddle. He reached forward with his gloved hands and was just able to grip the handlebars.

Look, Gar, I'm riding your bike!

You are, I said, laughing, *you are.*

I got Caroline to take some photos of me holding Séan aloft on the bike, both of us grinning at each other. I was delighted that I had some great photos of my little brother to take to New York with me.

****

Within a few days of arriving in New York, I found myself a cosy one-bed apartment in Greenwich Village on Tenth Street between Sixth and Seventh Avenue that became my home for the next sixteen months. I had also started working with the client in New Jersey and did the reverse commute on the Path train to Newark every day. I had been to New York before and had a good friend in my Uncle Tony (Caroline's younger brother) and some new friends that I made through contacts when I got over there.

Once I got myself set up in an apartment in NYC and bought myself a new Trek road bike, I felt a wonderful feeling of liberation from the ghost of my ex-girlfriend and the shadow of my father and Caroline. I became acutely aware that I was now thousands of miles away from my father and Caroline's sphere of influence. The vastness of the Atlantic Ocean filled me with reassurance about my own independence. Unfortunately, I was also aware from daily conversations with Fin that I had left him in the spotlight, so to speak, in dealing with our father and Caroline face-to-face while I was far away.

Fin

When Gar got his opportunity to live and work in New York, I received the news with mixed feelings. From a selfish point of view, I considered that I needed him more than ever before as he understood the rigours of being related to our father and Caroline more than anyone. I also remember thinking that the one decent and all functioning member of my family that I grew up with was now going to be across the Atlantic Ocean. I felt a bit like I was going to be left with the problem of my father and Caroline without him to lean on. Of course, I had Shane as well, but with his temperamental condition, there was only so much I could talk to him about.

Despite these thoughts, I knew that for Gar's sake, it was a great thing. Not that he had any doubts but I told him he should grab the opportunity with both hands. It was a chance for a fresh start. We agreed to set up Skype accounts and talk and IM regularly. This alleviated my worries and I was delighted that he was getting to live in the greatest city in the world. Before he had even left, I had started looking up flights for myself, Fiona and James to go over and visit him.

Things didn't change much back in Dublin. I knew the visits to Shane would be a bit harder without Gar. Even the additional conversation topics he provided helped break the ice on Shane's bad days. I knew I had to be extremely disciplined with the visits. Some of the visits could be great but other times, Shane might be in a bad way and it was pretty depressing watching my older brother mumbling to himself in a frustrated manner and chain smoking. It would have been easy to sit at home the next week and make up an excuse not to go. I made a promise to myself that I wouldn't make any excuse to miss a weekly visit to Shane. I vowed to work around any other plans; bad weather or any other obligations for as long as Gar was away in order to keep this promise. I felt like this was very much my responsibility now that Gar was working in New York.

It was so obvious that the visits from us had improved Shane's condition, so I wanted that improvement to continue as if Gar hadn't left. As much as I wanted this for Shane's sake, I also didn't want Gar to be regretting being in New York if Shane's condition was to deteriorate in some way, simply because I had missed a few visits. I wanted him to enjoy New York knowing that I could keep things running smoothly back home.

On some of the weekly visits to Shane, I brought James in with me. On one such occasion, a poorly dressed man with a female companion pushing a buggy came into the garden where the three of us sat talking. Shane was telling James to practice the drums for the band's sake. James was agreeing politely. The pair with the buggy looked somewhat suspicious. I noticed Shane seemed to be annoyed by them. When I enquired further, he told me that the guy was always in trying to persuade Shane to buy cannabis. Shane said he just kept telling him to *fuck off* but that the guy was persistent.

It transpired the man was not visiting any patients but merely came in as a drug dealer from the nearby Basin Street flats. He didn't arouse suspicion with his female companion and buggy. Once inside the psychiatric ward, he tried to sell drugs to the psychiatric patients. I was disgusted by this but very aware that I had James and couldn't really start an argument with the guy. I also wasn't in the habit of arguing with criminals. I stared at him angrily, hoping he would catch my stare and perhaps start to worry that he had been rumbled by a non-patient and leave.

I urged Shane to tell someone in the hospital about this guy but he seemed very wary. It appeared to me that he might be scared. The visit didn't go great after that as Shane was distant and seemed worried. I thought it was because of the drug dealer. I tried to convince Shane that I would think of a way to make sure he wouldn't be back without any bad consequences for Shane. However, as I was trying to reassure Shane, I realised it wasn't the drug dealer that was annoying him. I was in mid-sentence when he just came out with an unrelated direct question:

Any idea where Dad's been? he said, staring at me inquiringly, *He hasn't been in for weeks.*

No Shane, I've no idea, I responded.

Shane looked at the ground, seemingly disappointed with my answer. He looked worried. I tried to tell him that our father was probably busy with something. Once again, I found myself lying and making up excuses on our father's behalf. I was just willing to say anything to try and cheer Shane up.

As I got the bus home, I thought about getting on to Gar about the drug dealer but at the same time, he was all the way across the Atlantic. I thought that this was possibly an unnecessary incident to contact him about. I didn't want him worrying about Shane after only a short time in New York. But I wanted a second opinion on what I was going to do and I knew he would rather I contacted him if he could offer an opinion. I decided to e-mail him.

As I reflected on the visit that evening, it struck me that in a normal family, the first person you would contact in a situation like that would be a parent. Yet, I didn't even consider contacting our father about this incident with the drug dealer. As Shane had reminded me, our father wasn't even bothered to visit him half the time. His hit and miss visits were more of a hindrance to Shane's wellbeing as far as I could see, as Shane's expectations were raised and then shattered repeatedly. It was always in my mind that Shane had, after all, been abandoned by his father before.

It was always much easier for me to see what a selfish man my father was when his selfish acts were against somebody else who I loved and not against me and in July 2007 an incident occurred in relation to James that was almost the final straw for me with both Caroline and my father.

It began with what seemed an improvement on the two previous years, when our father and Caroline had rung James on his birthday and even promised that Caroline would bring him out on the Tuesday three days after his birthday as a treat for him. I had told James this and he was very excited as an eight-year-old would be. On the Monday evening, as I was sweating away the weekend's badness in the gym, my father rang. As my father only rang for favours I was immediately on alert when I answered.

Fin it's your Dad

I know, I said coldly, *I have caller ID, it's 2007.*

Ha ha he responded, *very funny.*

Despite my remark, he remained 'friendly'. I therefore immediately knew what was coming.

Listen kid, we are down in Kilkenny and your mother wants to try out a horse and tomorrow is the only time to do it, he said.

The only time? I blasted, *well she won't be able to do that if she is bringing James out tomorrow for his birthday will she?*

Listen kid, she really likes this horse and it's now or never. She will bring James out another time.

Fair enough, I said and hung up the phone. I knew it was pointless arguing and my feelings at the time were that I didn't want to have to persuade him that they were once again being selfish and mean. If they couldn't figure that out themselves, what could I possibly teach them? They were lost causes. I was done with them.

Over the next day or two, I got a few texts from Caroline

Ring me, love Mum xx

I ignored them. Eventually, she rang me and asked me when she could take James out for his promised birthday treat. She suggested a day that Fiona's sister had promised to take James out. When I told Caroline this day didn't suit, she couldn't hide her annoyance.

Soon after this, I received an unusual offer from my father for tickets to go to an Ireland Rugby World Cup game with him in France in September. He had some contact that could get us tickets. Although he never offered to pay for the tickets, I suspected that he would consider the mere 'getting' of tickets as enough to mean that I was in his debt and that James's birthday and anything else I was angry with him for, should be forgotten.

But as much as I had been a mug in the past, it was different when he was being selfish only to me. Seeing his meanness towards my son and to Shane all in the same week and only a few months after his complete lack of sensitivity towards Gar was finally enough. He could have offered to bring me to the final of the World Cup on the half way line and I would have turned him down.

I sent him a text politely declining the tickets. I didn't want to tell him the reason, I thought he should realise that himself. If I told him the reasons, he would try to talk all sorts of sweet talk to convince me that I was wrong and he was a great guy. I was sick of listening to his sweet talk at this stage. I didn't want to give him any more chances to talk me around.

He rang a day or two later and I was still angry. I confronted him about not visiting Shane. It was bizarre, I felt as if I was the father and he was the son. He was making excuses about horse-riding in Kilkenny and I told him he could at least ring the hospital to tell Shane he wouldn't be in. I offered him the number and in a tone of indifference he told me he already had it but never thought to ring. I told him it wasn't fair on Shane. He seemed shocked that I would scold him.

I got off the call and emailed Gar to fill him on what was going on:

Sent: Tuesday, July 17, 2007 06:46 AM
Subject: ahoy

ahoy!
whats the crack man- any news, nothing much here- eventually answered a call to them last nite, prepared for questions of "why do u not answer our calls?" instead got the friendly jazz, attempts also made to rebuff their reasons for staying in Kilkenny. i acted indifferently on the phone and threw in that Shane was wondering why he hadnt heard from dad. he said cos they were in Kilkenny and blah and so I said "well why dont I give u his number if that happens again u can ring him" and after some hesitance he said he had his number but never thought of ringing him. Than Caroline, in an attempt to lighten the mood said would she take James on wednesday for his promised b-day stuff. as monica had already organised to take him i told her that that was not an option so she than said she was busy on tuesday and thursday and than they were heading back to Kilkenny friday and suggested an evening. i said id get back to her. they were well aware that i was not impressed by it all but dad was trying to keep it together. however Caroline wasnt handling it as well and i cud sense her starting to fume a bit(as far as she is concerned this is all hassle she cud do without and for me to be awkward about it, how dare me?) only to be calmed by dad asking to speak to James. i put James on for a bit and they talked to him for a minute before it being handed back to me. than i said i was putting James to bed and had to go......got the cheery and cheesy "bye, bye bye bye"

*from her and "see u kid!" from dad felt like saying
"dont "KID" me" but just hung up instead.*

*I havent got back to them about an evening for James.
dont really want to deprive him of a present so i
probably will but reluctantly. in other news, while in
with Shane i found out that a complete scumbag from
basin street is going into the psychiatric ward and
trying push drugs on the patients(Shane included). Shane
and this girl (from dalkey, seemed sound enough, Shane
and her best mates!!) were giving out about him. than
the lad came in, with scanger girlfriend and kid in
buggy to toe(to make it look like they are in visiting,no
doubt). looked a real howya, i was just going at this
stage and he was tryin to be very friendly, i just looked
at him(if James wasnt with me, i think i mite have tried
to deck him, my blood was boiling).*

I felt a bit bad emailing Gar and reminding him of the burden of our
father and Caroline and the bad times. I was relieved when he told
me that he was glad I had emailed him because he hadn't forgotten
them at all. Unfortunately, this was because despite being in New
York, he was still continuing to have his own problems with our
father and Caroline even across the Atlantic.

Chapter 37

Gar

As I read Fin's email, I felt guilty that I was thousands of miles away and not able to help him. This guilt slowly changed to an appreciation that perhaps because I was thousands of miles away I was in a position to help us both by finally taking a stance - buffered as I was by the Atlantic Ocean. My resolve to act was strengthened a few days later when I rang my father and he asked me to change my cell phone operator from Verizon to AT&T because if I did so he and Caroline would have free texts to my phone. He was being charged twenty cents a text to the US. I told him there had been an extremely difficult process in getting my cell phone set up in the first place, the US requirements including a $400 deposit and minimum twelve-month contract among other things.

He simply persisted that I do whatever it takes. I realized that I was wasting my time. I had just moved to a different continent on my own. I moved because I had got my heart broken six months' previous and was trying to put that difficult episode behind me. I was living in a whole new city that had a reputation for being a potentially lonely place despite its abundant population. And yet here was my father telling me to change my cell phone provider so that he and Caroline would not have to pay the twenty cents or whatever it cost to send a text message to me. Just like in our youth, my father and Caroline seemed to remain hell-bent on us not costing them anything financially.

I realised this and wearily told my father that I would see what I could do and let him know.

A few days later on 24 July, I got an email from my father but which purported to be from Caroline, as follows:

Subject: frrst email
Sent: Tuesday, July 24, 2007 08:16 AM

Hi Gar, mum here trying to send my first e-mail was thinking of you we all miss you let me know if you get this as this is a test run. Love mum dad and Séan xx"

As I read the email I wondered why Caroline was sending me an email from my father's email account. I wondered why the subject title was *"frrst email"* when I had received many emails from this address before. I wondered why Caroline had not simply set up and used her own email account.

I wondered whether this was their solution to the 20c text charge.

As I re-read the email I became suspicious; how could I trust this email was even from Caroline at all? The tone and content of the email (as well as the address, of course) had my father's fingerprints all over it.

I sent the email on to Fin and he agreed that it appeared to be disingenuous. We discussed how I should respond and we decided that this email was the opportunity for us to finally say something to our father and Caroline about our relationship with them. The fact that I was in New York and essentially 'out of harm's way' from any backlash was too good an opportunity to pass up. As we both knew that some reaction was inevitable, we agreed that we would frame the email as being from me alone and that I would ask them not to react to Fin. The reality was though that I was sending the email on both our behalves and the feelings expressed in the email were shared by the two of us.

After we discussed the content of the email, I sent my reply the next day, 25 July, as follows:

"Sent: 25 July 2007 17:02

Not quite sure what is being tested exactly as you are sending from Dad's address which has always functioned well as far as I know?

Either way thanks for email! I recommend you open your own account.

As you both have probably guessed by now due to the fact that I have not called, emailed etc I am going through what you might describe as a contemplative stage of my life. Being here alone has given me an awful amount of time to think about life, love and all the other little things that make up being a human being. It has also given me an opportunity to reflect on relationships that I have with others, including your good selves, with a little more objectivity than when I am at home in Ireland.

So to cut an awfully long story short I want to grasp this opportunity for contemplation of the past and my approach to the future. In order to do this properly I want to give myself not just geographic space but also emotional space. I feel that this will be best achieved if we don't keep in regular contact over the next while. You can take it that things are fine unless you hear otherwise.

I have no idea what you might think of my decision but I urge you both to also take this opportunity for reflection and do not allow it go to waste. Perhaps this comes as a surprise to you both but realistically, it shouldn't. I think we all know that things have been drifting over the last few years and now I feel is a perfect opportunity to gain some space and hopefully some perspective.

Also please don't interrogate Fin as he has enough on his plate as it is.

Suffice to say all of my love to Séan, I have shown the photos of him on my bike to half of New York at this stage!
All the best
Gar"

I felt a rush of adrenaline and euphoria when I sent this email and expressed this euphoria when I forwarded the email on to Fin under the heading: *"bombs away!"*

I waited with trepidation for the reaction which I knew could be aimed at Fin or at me.

Fin

When Gar first told me what he wanted to say in the email he was going to respond with, I was a bit taken aback. The email was a massive step in us suddenly saying that we weren't willing to just roll over and fall for their games anymore. It was going to be an admission that we were alert to the deceit in what they did, even if Gar said he would be subtle about that. Also, despite the fact Gar was sending the mail, I was well aware that some of the flak would fall back to me because I was easily accessible. As with everything with my father, I knew I could either choose to say I was with him or against him. I could not stand neutral.

I wasn't sure what to expect initially but after Gar sent the email, neither of us were contacted by our father. Instead, five days afterwards, Caroline showed up unexpectedly at my door. She said she wanted to know what Gar's email was all about and so I told her. I emailed Gar the next morning with the details of her visit:

"Sent: Tuesday, July 31, 2007 07:08 AM

Whats the jazz. So it was an eventful evening last night. There is me making changes to my fantasy team, happy as Larry when the doorbell rings. I really wasn't expecting anyone so when Fiona answered the door and Mum was standing there, I knew there were troubles ahead. She was crying and saying she didn't know what to do? She said she got the e mail and wanted to know did I feel the same way, did i not want to talk to her anymore. I said to her that it wasn't so much her but more dad that we had the problem with but her and dad combined were not exactly our favourite people. I told her that the reason u sent the email originally was that u felt that she didnt really give a sh1t as u felt that anyone elses mother would have learnt how to use the internet long ago to speak to their son. she said she was looking into getting an 086 sim card to be able to text u and that she genuinely didnt know how to use the internet and that she was constantly asking paulie how u were etc. I told her that that was between yourself and herself but that i felt that that was just the tip of the iceberg- as she was saying that that specifically is not a good reason to cut all ties with your parents(which on its own probably isn't). so i started by telling her about our problems with dad , starting with him talking about our childhood and the split/getting with her as being some sort of triumph. I told her we didn't see it as a triumph and further from that we didnt look favourably at all on our childhood. I told her how i remember dad

237

, first telling us nicely that if we wanted to call her mum we could, and then yelling at us for not doing it.i told her how hard it was to call her mum, and not fully understanding why it was so hard. i told her that we look back and feel sick when we think of the day we went to the cinema with joe [I still referred to my real mother as Jo, as our father ordered] and there was blue murder because we stayed out an hour too late(this was in response to her saying that they always said we can go and see joe) i told her that every mothers day dad sends us a text telling us to send her a text or call her and that it upsets us because we do think "what must our biological mother in Carlow be thinking" . i told her that although i felt we(i specified myself as i didnt want to speak for u on this but im sure u feel the same) had a bond with her(Caroline) it wasnt a maternal bond, which i didnt blame on her as she couldnt have one, but felt it affected how she treated us as in we were treated differently to how she would treat, for example Séan. she said she knows she gave out a lot but she felt it was for our own good and that she was only 21 moving in and she didnt know what to do. in response i told her that i didnt think it was particularly fair on her that she moved in at 21 and i said that i would probably give out a lot if, at 21, i moved in with 3 slightly or otherwise disfunctional kids. i told her i didnt think she particularly did a bad job, but that we didnt see it as being this great childhood that dad seems to go on as if it is. i than told her that to sum it up- i hated childhood, and that i look back on childhood now and am extremely glad that its over. she said she didnt like hearing that and i told her i was just being honest. i told her that i liked b-days, xmas;s and holidays in general and that she always made them special and i appreciated that but that i hated it in general. i told her that when we saw joe at the divorce case it was hard for us, and that dad telling us to testify against her was wrong. i told her that if i ever tried to tell dad a lot of the above ,. he would go on the defensive and pretend none of it happened. i took for example the calling her mum story and told her how i remember recently him relaying the story as " remember yous asked us could you call your mum, mum" and that i felt he had deluded himself into believing that things happened in a magical way that only he knew and that no-

one was affected in a bad way and that contradicting that would only make him flip out.

I told her it upset me that they prioritised on Kilkenny on James' birthday and that me having to tell him that they werent showing up was not on let alone having to explain to Marie [Fiona's mother]. i said that nothing should have stopped them from coming home and taking James bar a death- i also said that the fact that it was a year after them not remembering to ring made it even more sickening. she accepted this and u cud tell she already knew it was a bad thing when it happened.

that really is the jist of it. Looking back i know i left a lot out as well but im sure that wont be the end of it. I told her that for James sake i wud be happy to move forward and not cut ties- but live for the future. i told her this relied on dad never bringing up the past again the way he does. and i told her i wasnt sure dad would be able to do this. she asked what she thought she should do about u. and i told her that i would be talking to u and that i wasn't going to bullsh1t her, that i would be telling u exactly what happened and that we would see what happened. she half suggested putting dad on a plane to NY so beware!! ha ha"

It is very evident from my email that I am being very careful to include everything that was discussed. I knew from years of experience dealing with my father and Caroline that for my own sanity I had to ensure that nothing would be unclear to me in the future about this visit.

After the visit, I actually felt relieved that I had had the conversation with Caroline and had explained why I wasn't against Gar's email. It was also a big thing for me to finally tell her some of the truth about how I was feeling and how I had felt over the years. I thought she was being sincere and genuine in her reaction and her tears. I expected her to go back and tell our father and I awaited a call perhaps stating that we should all meet up and discuss it all.

I received no such call.

For the next few weeks I heard nothing from my father but I spoke occasionally to Caroline. She led me to believe that we could talk freely to each other, almost as if the argument was solely between our father and Gar and that she wanted to be some kind of mediator. Gar and I were curious as to why there was no response from our father. We were concerned and determined not to be manipulated by him so we tried to judge what his next move might be. Knowing his propensity to play mind games, we figured his silence was one of them. When we thought about it, we considered the fact that it would be Séan's birthday in November and our father probably knew that we would be keen to give Séan a birthday present and wish him happy birthday. We were aware that our father's modus operandi would likely be to wait for this opportunity to welcome us all back as if nothing had happened.

He was choosing to *not to speak to us*, leaving us to self-analyse our actions to this point.

Gar and I continually discussed our actions. There was an inevitable self-doubting that occurred. No matter how bad our father was, it is still difficult to justify breaking that relationship completely. Particularly now that he had us wondering if *he* was now the victim of *our* misunderstanding.

However, the two of us were able to reassure each other that we had done nothing wrong, despite the pangs of guilt that we felt. We had no intention of permanently breaking our relationship with him. We were simply attempting to set the record straight on the past. We felt we were entitled to do this. We were now quite sure that we were being manipulated to try and ensure that we could not achieve that goal. We were committed that if our father thought that we would concluded that we should never speak of the past or question him again after this episode, he was wrong.

I know it couldn't have been an easy thing for Gar to write the email that set the sequence of events in motion. What Gar had done by writing it and sending it was that he had created an opportunity for us to finally face up to our past. We did not want to lose that opportunity. We were very keen at this stage to discuss the past and ensure that our father's twisted tales were never again put forward as if they were facts.

On 11 September 2007, I belatedly received an unexpected call from our father when I was in work. Our father was angrily demanding what Gar's email back in July was all about. He seemed frustrated and asked why I had not contacted him earlier about Gar's email.

I started to tell our father that we needed to sit down and talk properly about this and that since I was on my mobile in my open plan office, that this was not ideal. Our father responded with rage and anger. I was completely flustered, not least because I was aware that others in my office could hear me. I told our father that I had to go and the call ended. I made some excuses in work to get out and once outside, I rang Gar and told him that the silence had been broken. Given the extent of the anger in my father's voice, I must admit I was worried. He sounded like a madman. I had to go home later on my bike to my house which was not too far from where he lived. I joked to myself that if by chance my father drove past me while I was on my bike, he might swerve to hit me. I didn't laugh though because it was a genuine fear I had.

My father's tone on the phone sounded like he wanted to show me that I shouldn't have *fucked with him*. I was even reasoning to Gar how I hadn't really done anything since it was Gar who had sent the email. Gar reassured me and said that he would ring our father and try to talk to him.

Chapter 38

Gar

After Fin received the angry call from our father, we agreed that I would call him from the safe distance of the USA and see if he would agree to have a discussion with us about our past. We had a rather forlorn hope that he might have taken up my offer in the email to contemplate our relationship and after the passing of six weeks or so he might be in a position to want to talk to us.

Judging by his tone on the call to Fin, it now appeared that he had spent the previous six weeks seething rather than contemplating. We both expected that realistically if I did call him, he would explode with anger and vent his spleen down the telephone line. A conciliatory chat was not expected, but we still hoped.

As we contemplated his reaction, we started to see a pattern to the way he acted in certain situations. Fin began to research his behaviour on the internet, which in turn led him to finding a link to a website about "psychological manipulation" which he sent on to me. The contents of the page were like a revelation to us as it explained so accurately our father's behaviour as a manipulator and the vulnerabilities he exploited in us.

Once I had finished reading this I called Fin immediately and went through it with him line by line, each of us taking time to marvel at the total accuracy of what we were reading. There was a feeling of wonder at how we had not recognised all of this before but also of empowerment that at least it was clear to us now.

Notwithstanding this knowledge, I still had to mentally steel myself for the call with my father. I reminded myself that there were over three thousand miles of distance between us. I told myself I shouldn't fear him. So I felt incredibly calm when I picked up the phone to call our father having not spoken to him or communicated with him in any way since my email six weeks before.

As soon as the call was over I made an attendance note of the contents of the call and sent this in an email to Fin.

"D" refers to "Dad". The attendance note email reads as follows:

"Date: Wed, Sep 12, 2007 at 12:15 AM

Subject: for posterity

Me : I was talking to Fin he doesn't really want to talk anymore today

D Fin can talk for himself

Me yeah but he's pretty emotional you know

D he's 24 he's well able to speak for himself

Me OK then well do you wanna talk to me then?

D About What???

Me eh well the same things Fin is talking about??

D - What Things? I tell you what I got your email - need time to think! I couldn't believe it

I've had a pain in my arm the last three weeks I tell you from that

Me Well dad vie had a lot of pain over the years in my heart

D Ah Pain in me Arse!! I tell you when I got that email - I'm sick that I reared a son like you - to do such a thing - I thought only your mother would break my heart but no you did you broke it !!

Me Dad the intention wasn't to break anything...

Dad And I heard you made a Show of Yourself up in Tony's

Me Well if you mean by that I was lonely and I went to see some family and got drunk and let my emotions get the better of me then yeah that is what happened

Dad - hold on - family ?? you're forgetting - what about the Link to that family ?? Now hold on, I don't want to cause any pain here (sneering) but what shall we call her - Mum or mam or Caroline??

Me - Yeah Caroline's grand.

243

D – fuckin' hell Good Bye Gar

Slams down phone"

I listened to the tone buzzing in my ear for a few seconds before I slowly put down the receiver. I recall feeling extremely calm despite the torrent of anger and vitriol that had just poured down the line. Sadly, he had reacted exactly as we had predicted he would. There was not going to be any attempt at reconciliation or understanding.

He was never going to ask-*can we talk this through?*

After all the years together and our new-found knowledge on manipulative tactics, we knew our father very well and we knew that there was only one way he was going to view the email I had sent him: as an unwarranted attack on everything he stood for. The insolence of me to question him, even in a general sense, was something our father could not abide. His response was best summed up in three words:

HOW DARE YOU?

Once my call with him was over, I immediately called Fin to tell him how the call had gone. He listened without surprise as I took him through the gist of the conversation. When I told him that he had said goodbye and hung up the phone on me, Fin's response was to tell me that he was envious that I had had such a clean break. We both laughed at this as we knew it was true. It felt like his goodbye was some closure on a relationship I was more than happy to end.

Fin

When I hung up the phone to Gar I felt happy for him, but it was a strange happiness. Gar was now effectively free from our father. Our father had ended the relationship with Gar and not the other way around. That made it harder for our father to play the victim and in turn make Gar feel guilty. It was the perfect break. I was glad that at least one of us was somewhat free.

But I couldn't help feeling envious. As I digested the news, I wondered did this make my life a lot more difficult. I now had to either maintain the relationship with my father or be the one to end it. With our father's ability to guilt me about nothing, I could only imagine how much he would try to guilt me if I told him I didn't want to maintain any relationship with him. I considered that Gar and I had been together dealing with the problem. I wondered if this new twist might mean I was now on my own with the problem. Of course, I wouldn't have been, but panic was setting in making me think quite unreasonably.

I still felt that Caroline was a sort of mediator and I felt obliged to fill her in on events. I rang her and told her about our father's phone call to Gar and how I considered that this was the end of the relationship between the two of them. It appeared to me that she was aware of roughly what was said but seemed surprised when I said it with the tone of disgust that I felt it deserved:

Well he has just told Gar in not so many words to fuck off forever, I told her.

When I said this, she seemed stunned and defensive.

I don't know what is going on or what was said, she said defensively.

It seemed as if she wanted to distance herself from our father's call to Gar. I considered that wasn't an unreasonable stance to take, to perhaps save her relationship with Gar. But when I told her I considered that there would be no comeback from that for Gar and our father, she got annoyed. Because of her reaction, I thought she presumed I was exaggerating. In order to emphasise the point I followed that up by saying that if I got a phone call like that from our father, I would consider that our relationship was over. I was very firm as this was exactly how I felt. She seemed extremely taken aback by this. She then told me that she had to go urgently and that we would have to talk about later. She hung up the phone.

As I thought about the significance of what had happened, I looked at my Nokia phone. It was on silent since I was in work so I casually pressed the red 'hang-up' button to light up the screen. I looked at the screen.

1 message
received

I paused before opening the message. I knew that there was a high probability that this message was related to what was going on. I felt as if I needed to sort of build myself up for it.

Right, here we go, I thought.

I tried to unlock the phone and in my anxious state, I wasn't properly hitting the centre of the menu button and it wouldn't unlock straight away. Eventually it lit up with:

'keypad active'

I clicked again to open the message. I saw at the top of the message that it was from "*Dad*". I read it, almost in disbelief.

"Fin sorry to hear that you can't talk to me except through Gar, at your age that's sad. I just said goodbye to him so I suppose i should say the same to you. I would have preferred to talk but that's not going to happen."

I had to read the message a few times. I was astounded. The tone of vitriol and anger and manipulation coursed through every word. I read some of the lines again.

"*at your age that's just sad*"

That basically said to me: *Son, I think you're a fucking sad case.*

"*I just said goodbye to him so I suppose I should say the same to you*"

This made no logical sense. Why does saying goodbye to Gar mean he has to say goodbye to me?

"*I would have preferred to talk but that's not going to happen*"

This line was almost comical if it wasn't so horrendous. Why didn't you ask me to talk instead of going straight to "*goodbye*" if that was what you would have preferred to do?

I had 'spoken' with Caroline at length only a few weeks before and given her a fairly comprehensive summary of what I wanted to 'talk' about. It seemed most likely that she had relayed all of this back to my father.

Once I digested the text message, I realised that there was one good thing to come from it: I now had *my* closure. My father had said

246

goodbye to me forever, via a text message. It summed up what I meant to him really.

I rang Gar to tell him the news. It was the ultimate bittersweet feeling. I just kept saying to him:

A fucking text message.

I was laughing at the sheer outrageousness of it because if I didn't see the comical side of it, I would have had to give in to the anger and hurt I felt inside. It was all the evidence I needed that my father thought I was nothing.

A fucking text message.

It made me feel worthless, yet it made me feel free.

Gar

Despite all of our preparation we were both still surprised at the anger and bitterness in the text message to Fin. The reason for this was that Fin was essentially an innocent party. We had purposely planned that it would be me who would send the email as I had the opportunity to do so living, as I did, thousands of miles away in New York. I had purposely said in the email not to bother Fin and tried to disassociate Fin in that sense. Although Fin had obviously had the honest conversation with Caroline, Fin had not directly told our father that he did not want to talk to him nor had he sent him an email asking for some time for reflection as I had done. So our father's text to Fin was totally unprovoked.

Once we got over the initial shock of the text message Fin realised that he too had been set free as I had been. He was relieved that this was so. We both agreed that if it were us who had said goodbye to our father and hung up the phone on him or sent him a goodbye text message, we could not maintain that goodbye without feeling a certain amount of guilt.

The fact that our father had very clearly and deliberately said goodbye to us individually and without just cause made it a lot easier for us to feel like having him out of our lives was a good thing. He had inadvertently done us a favour.

Chapter 39

Fin

I didn't expect it but I felt I deserved at least a call from my father to apologise for the text message. I knew he didn't *do* apologies but if ever there was a time for him to break the habit of a lifetime, I felt it was now.

Of course, I never received any such call. That wasn't surprising but I was somewhat surprised that I didn't receive any calls or texts from Caroline. It was our father and not her after all who had sent me the text. My last conversation with Caroline, although heated, was somewhat amicable.

I didn't contact her either. I was getting the feeling that she was simply pretending to be concerned on my behalf to fish for information and report her findings back to our father. I couldn't help noting that she left our last phone call rather hurriedly after I told her how I would react to such an angry tirade from my father like Gar had endured. I wondered had she tried to stop him sending that text message but was too late.

It felt good to not have a relationship with them. I felt sorry for Séan not getting to see me, James or Fiona. I was also uneasy about the fact that his birthday was in two months. I wanted him to know that we still loved him and that none of this was anything to do with him. Weeks went by. We did not get a call from our father or Caroline. We did not expect to.

November arrived, the month of Séan's birthday, and the problem of how we would get a present to Séan had to be addressed. Gar and I discussed the matter, at all times wary that our father and Caroline would most likely have been waiting for this day and had some plan in place to try and manipulate us into playing happy families again. We decided that the best thing to do to avoid this would be for me to call up to the house and leave the presents for Séan's birthday in the side passage. The side passage was a gated side entrance to the house where the wheelie bins were kept. We knew that the presents would be seen pretty quickly there. I chose to leave them there on the Sunday, which was the 18th of November. This was the day before his birthday but I knew that our father and Caroline would be in

Kilkenny so I didn't run any risk of bumping into them. As I walked home after the drop off I considered it was a success. I was happy that Séan would get the presents and confident he would like them.

The next morning, after two months of hearing nothing from our father or Caroline, I received a missed call and a text message from Caroline. The text message read:

"Hi Fin, tried to ring you could you give me a ring, love mum"

At least I knew the presents were received. But the message annoyed me. Firstly, I had told Caroline only a few months ago how much I disliked that we had been forced into calling her Mum and that I found it upsetting. Looking at her text, you would think that conversation had never taken place. In fact, looking at her text you might think that everything was normal and nothing had happened over the last few months.

I had purposely delivered the presents in a way that I could avoid my father and Caroline because I did not want them to talk to me and try to manipulate me. But once they saw the presents, Caroline seemed to use it as an excuse to contact me to re-open the conversation.

After two months of peace, I was once again back trying to analyse what to do without getting sucked into their manipulative traps. After discussing the situation with Gar, we both agreed that there was only one option that guaranteed that I wasn't sucked in. That was to simply ignore the text and the missed call. Séan had his presents and that was all that mattered.

Gar

A few days after this, Fin and I both received the following email from our father. It was the first time he had communicated with me since the 'goodbye phone-call' two months earlier and the first time he had communicated with Fin since his 'goodbye text message' the same day.

The email was sent on Wednesday 21st November 2007. It was addressed to Fin and copied to me and said:

249

"Wednesday, November 21, 2007 01:59 PM

Fin

This thing of leaving presents behind bins is not on. I am not allowing either Séan or James to be caught up in this emotional intrigue, something neither of us, nor either of them, know anything about. If you want to talk, ring me at 087******.

Gar,

We are in New York from Saturday 24 for a few days. The same invite to you."

As soon as I received the email I called Fin from New York. We were not surprised by the tone which begrudgingly offered Fin the opportunity to talk and extended this opportunity to me when they visited New York. We were equally unsurprised that there was no mention of the last few months or the conversations we had with him when he had said goodbye to both of us.

We mused on our father's apparent desire not to *"allow"* his son or indeed his grandson to be caught up in any *"emotional intrigue"* as he called it. This protective desire seemed to contradict his previous enthusiastic approach to my, Fin and Shane's involvement in all kinds of *"emotional intrigue"* in the past.

Fin was also less than impressed with our father's portrayal of himself as the moral guardian of Fin's son James, particularly our father's use of the word *"allow"*, as if our father somehow had control of Fin's eight-year-old son. It was also ironic to see our father portray himself in an email as his only grandson's great protector when in reality he rarely seemed interested in James' wellbeing.

As for me, I wryly noted that the invitation to meet in New York was almost an afterthought that had been spat onto the page. *"The same invite to you"* did not exactly strike a conciliatory chord.

After Fin and I spoke about the email for a few minutes I noticed that the mobile number our father had given to contact him appeared to be one digit short. Fin read it and confirmed that it was in fact the

250

case and we both started to laugh. The missing digit seemed to us to symbolise everything that was wrong with the email itself. The tone of the email was accusatory and unforgiving. It was an email from the heart of a bully who was used to always getting his own way. There was no reference to his angry diatribe against me on the phone or his totally unwarranted text to Fin. It was as if neither had ever happened. The invite to talk was framed in such a way that any such talks would only be had on the basis of him being the all-powerful father and our being his forever grateful children.

When we had considered this, we both agreed that the invitation to talk was so derisory that it should not be accepted. We agreed that we should both reply to the email separately to tell him how we felt. I sent my email first on the morning of Thanksgiving, 22 November, as follows:

"Sent: Thu, Nov 22, 2007 at 3:48 PM

Dad

It surprises me that you haven't mentioned in your email the last conversation (if you could call it that) that we had. I rang you in order that we could talk but I remember vividly that you were very clear in how you felt. There is nothing in your email to indicate that you recant or regret what you said, so I presume you still feel the same, that you are sickened to have me as a son/that I have broken your heart and, as you very firmly put it - Good bye.

Dad - these last few months, free from the mind games and the manipulation that seems to follow you around like a fog, have been refreshing. I am sick of manipulation, and I am quite sure I have had enough mind games to last me a dozen lifetimes.

Your 'offer' to talk - the way it is framed, the accusatory tone, the passing of the blame on to us, the attempt to induce a guilt trip, the complete lack of any remorse, the refusal to even acknowledge our last heart-breaking conversation and, most of all, the total absence of love is not what I regard as a meaningful attempt at reconciliation in any way and I intend to treat it as such.

251

It breaks my heart that I couldn't ring Séan on his birthday but I can sleep at night knowing that it is not of my making that this is the case, and hopefully I can make it up to him in the future."

Fin sent his email a few hours later:

"Sent: 22 November 2007 15:46

Considering you ended all contact with me by text message, I find it laughable that you now claim that you are not allowing either Séan or James to be caught up in it. What did you think was going to happen?

It would appear that you are using your usual manipulative techniques to resolve the issue. The use of Séan or James (who incidentally has not noticed the difference, we often had long periods without you seeing him) to guilt me into calling you, when you are the one who texted me to tell me that talk was "not going to happen", is as unsurprising as it is sickening. I have had enough of your manipulative ways and as you seem to know no other way of having relations with people I would rather we left it at this.

I will endeavour to send all further presents by post to Séan until there is a better alternative.

Fin"

As it was Thanksgiving, as soon as I sent the email I took the subway up to Yonkers to spend the day with my Uncle Tony. It was strange spending the day with a member of Caroline's family with everything that was going on but it was a great relief that it did not seem to make any difference to Tony who made me feel as welcome as ever.

I received no response to my email, as expected. I had a strange few days in New York from 24 November knowing that my father was somewhere in the city. The odds on me bumping into him were pretty low but that didn't stop me keeping my eyes peeled as I cycled around the Village at the weekend. I was relieved when December came and I could relax knowing he was back in Ireland. I wondered yet again how Fin managed to deal with living in the same neighbourhood as him under the circumstances.

Chapter 40

Fin

It felt good to tell our father that I was aware that he was manipulating me. I wanted him to know that his game was up. I thought there was a chance that it would make him reconsider using his manipulative techniques. But I should have known, to use his words: *that was not going to happen.*

The problem with living in the same neighbourhood as him was that I was easily accessible. While I got no response to the email I sent on 22 November, I received an unexpected visit from both Caroline and my father the following evening. Since Caroline was aware of the problems I had with them, I was half expecting that they had come to finally talk it through. I thought that they might see that enough absurdity had occurred and it was time to face up to what we all needed to face up to. I reasoned that it was the only way we could all move forward with our lives and relationships with each other. I even considered that our father's mention of James and Séan was, although twisted, still an acknowledgement that he knew that there were innocent parties involved who needed this controversy to be sorted out. I should have realised that my father cared little for innocent parties but I simply wasn't there yet. I felt like there was still a resolution, that our father could take a look in the mirror and change his ways and we could all move on.

When I opened the door, I could immediately tell that my father wasn't preparing for reconciliation. His brow was furrowed and he was walking quickly towards me. I noticed he was carrying some of the presents I had left for Séan. They were still wrapped. Caroline followed him to the door with the rest of the presents. They were returning the gifts without letting Séan see them. I realised that poor Séan would probably presume he didn't get any presents from us.

If you want to give Séan presents, you will come up to the house and give them to him properly.

I looked in disbelief. This loosely translated as:

If you want a relationship with Séan, you will have a relationship with us.

Of course I wanted a relationship with Séan, but this act of petulance was just confirming to me that I couldn't have a relationship with my father anymore. I looked at Caroline, she had a serious expression on her face, but in a way that it almost seemed put on. I decided to try to reason with her:

What about everything we talked about when you were sat on that couch?

She looked back at me and sneered:

What about it?

With that the two of them left and drove off. I was deeply disappointed. It seemed that Caroline had taken me for a mug again. It seemed to me now, that when I told her all about my childhood memories, she was merely on a *recce* to see exactly what we remembered from the past.

It hurt me to think that she did this. After all the things she had done to me when I was growing up, I should have cut all ties with her long ago. But instead, I tried to maintain some sort of a relationship. She surely remembered all those things she did to make my childhood a misery. She pretty much admitted it during what I thought was our heart-to-heart conversation about it. When she left that day, I believed she was remorseful about it. After this most recent visit, I no longer believed that to be the case.

Over the previous few years, I had listened to her and comforted her when she rang with her problems with our father. I gave her advice. I listened to her stories about horses and competitions. I acted like a friend to her, despite her past treatment of me. And in return, she slyly lulled me into a sense of trust, only for me to pour my heart out to her. She sat there crying, nodding, almost sympathising. Inside she was merely taking notes. Her sneer was as if to mock me for being fooled by it all. It struck me that she was still playing all the mind games she used to play when I was young.

I unwrapped Séan's presents and put them with some of James' other toys but they were for a younger child and he wasn't too interested in them. I thought about throwing them out. It was like a dagger in my heart looking at the toys that I had spent time choosing for Séan. One evening I was sitting on the couch alone and I saw one of the presents and I allowed myself to cry. I felt guilty looking at the toy and thought about why this was.

I felt that my father had given me a choice that was incredibly simple to understand but incredibly difficult to decide.

> I could call Caroline and tell her that we should forget the argument and I could go up and see Séan and pretend that nothing was wrong. I could bury the past deeper and deeper and hope it never resurfaced. I could give in.

> *Or*

> I could never speak to them again, finally ridding my life of them. I would be free from their constant manipulative ways. As a consequence, I would never be able to see my little brother, the innocent and delightful Séan, at least not until he grew up or I thought of a better plan.

It was a tough choice. The type of choice only a manipulator like my father would have you make. I tried to reason what the best option was.

I knew that if our father loved me and if he loved Séan, he would allow us to have a brotherly relationship without the condition that I would have to see him and Caroline too. He would not alienate his son from his brothers. It was already pretty evident at that stage that he didn't love me but I didn't like that the evidence suggested that he didn't love Séan either. We had been pawns in his games when we were younger. Years on and now he was using Séan as a pawn to try and ensure that he wouldn't ever have to face up to the past. Poor Séan would have no knowledge or control over this. Only he knows what he thought when his brothers suddenly stopped coming to visit him.

At this stage of my life I was very certain of the following:

I had seen my father's selfishness directly hurt and hinder Shane. I had seen my father's selfishness directly hurt and hinder Gar. I had seen my father's selfishness directly hurt and hinder me. Now I could see my father's selfishness directly hurt and hinder Séan.

Biologically he was a father but physically he was simply a cruel and selfish human being who didn't deserve the privilege. All he seemed to care about was himself.

Taking everything into account, Gar and I decided that at least for now we needed an extended break from the two people who had made our lives to this point as difficult as they possibly could make them. We discussed all kinds of hare brained ideas where we could meet Séan but we knew that our father would never allow it without seeing them. I knew that if I had to see either my father or Caroline that the manipulation would flow.

It was such a wrench that we wouldn't see Séan but we kept telling ourselves that we would think of a plan to see him at some stage. The choice to break free from our father under these conditions was as horrible and difficult to make as I'm sure he wanted it to be.

Personally, I also had James and Fiona to think about when making this choice. At this point, I was a bit of a mental wreck. For a few months, I found it hard to sleep and was waking up constantly, screaming. I was paranoid about everything, questioning everyone and anyone's actions or inactions as if they were an attack on me. Fiona was getting the brunt of it. I had somehow decided that she had fallen out of love with me. I think subconsciously I kept searching for ways to prove just that. I perceived quite usual actions of hers as being an action against me. Thankfully, she was patient. She knew that the stress of all that was going on with my father and Caroline was what was causing this. She convinced me to think about some of my more ridiculous accusations and it became clear to me that I wasn't thinking rationally. I realised that my father's manipulation was very close to making me have some sort of mental breakdown.

I was determined not to let that happen, not only for myself and for Fiona, but also for James. I also didn't want my father to have succeeded in breaking me.

With Fiona's help, I analysed things rationally and managed to see that my paranoid thoughts were just that, paranoid thoughts. Most of them were nonsensical. After a while, it seemed to fade away. With every day that passed that I didn't have any contact with my father or Caroline, the stress and anguish also faded away. But, of course, there was and still always is the niggling sorrow that we could not maintain a relationship with Séan because of our father.

Chapter 41

Gar

On my birthday in April 2008, I received a short email from my father. I was still living in New York after having had no contact with him for six months since the previous November. He used the same subject as the last email he had sent in November, except this time, he had corrected the typo in *"frrst"* to *"first"*, as follows:

Sent: Tuesday, April 08, 2008 04:20 PM
Subject: RE: first email

Happy birthday and many happy returns.

And "Have a Nice Day".

That was it. There was no mention of his or my name.

I tried to ignore it as best I could as I celebrated my birthday that night.

Fin

I had a brief encounter with our father in late July 2008. Shane had asked me to attend a meeting with his doctors and psychiatrists. He also warned me that he had asked our father to come too. Since I was very interested to hear the views of the doctors on Shane's progress, I didn't let my father's presence deter me.

I was, however, nervous about being in the same room with him. I refreshed my memory by reviewing the internet pages describing the various manipulation techniques the day before it so that I would be on guard. I spoke to Gar, who was still in New York, about it too and he gave me a good pep talk.

I wanted the meeting to be what it was supposed to be about, which was Shane. I arrived early so I waited in the TV room to be called in. Shane came out after a few minutes and called me in. I think there were eight people in the small room. My father was one of those people. He didn't look at me as I walked in. I barely glanced at him.

One of the doctors spoke about Shane's improvement in recent times. They allowed Shane to speak without restrictions. I laughed to myself as I knew that allowing Shane the floor and an audience was not a smart move, especially if they had any other plans for the rest of the day. Shane took his opportunity and gave his opinions on a number of issues, some related to this meeting and other issues far removed. Eventually one of the doctors saw a pause in one of Shane's speeches as an opportunity to end the meeting. I hastily said my goodbyes to Shane and quickly exited the building. I was very keen to avoid any pleasantries with my father. I was relieved when I was successful at doing this.

The next communication I received was from Caroline in late August 2008, nine months after they had returned Séan's presents:

"hi Fin I think it would be nice to meet up and have a chat as I think about you everyday Séan misses you terrible keeps talking about you James and Fiona xx"

It was almost a year since we had spoken. I missed Séan and it tugged at my heartstrings to hear that he missed me. I still didn't trust Caroline but it seemed a genuine text.

I decided to give her the benefit of the doubt. I liked that she didn't sign off as "mum" although that could have been because of lack of space. I was wary but I decided I wanted to see Séan so much that I considered my options.

Of course, despite all of this, my most recent communication with Caroline had been when she sneered at me after our discussion about my childhood memories. But I decided to take a chance to see Séan so I texted her back.

"Hi I only got your txt now.my fone is broke. iv got exams until end of nxt week so il call u then and maybe arrange something. I just want to focus on these for now".

I cursed my luck a bit that this had happened when I was doing exams for my degree. I needed my mind to be fully focussed on study.

On the morning of one of the exams, out of the blue, my father sent me this message.

"Good luck in the exams kid"

This was the first text message I received from him since the one where he told me goodbye. I got the feeling that my agreement to meet Caroline was their cue to act as if nothing had ever happened. It was hard at this stage to believe anything he said was genuine.

After the exams, I called Caroline and arranged for her to drop up with Séan to my house. She said in the text that she wanted to chat so I welcomed the idea, thinking it was a chat regarding reconciliation. When she came up, Séan greeted me as if I had just seen him yesterday. I gave him a big hug. I was delighted to see him. Caroline came in and I made her a cup of tea. We sat down and she asked about the exams. Fiona, James had recently moved house and Caroline began complimenting the décor. She seemed to be trying her best to act as if we had just seen each other last week. I didn't think this was a good idea. I thought we should tackle the issues. But since she was acting so nonchalant, I found it hard to bring them up.

After a while, she said she had to go. I offered for her to leave Séan and I would drop him to the house later that evening but she declined. I then suggested that perhaps going forward, she could drop Séan up and leave him in my house and I could drop him back afterwards, perhaps on a more regular basis. She indicated that if Séan was coming up, she was coming up. She used the line:

That's how it works.

When she left I considered her counter offer and decided it was merely the same as what our father had suggested. I imagined our father schooling Caroline on what to say to me to manipulate me. I imagined if I agreed to her demands that by Christmas I would be back in my father's house telling my father *he did a good job on the turkey*, back under their spell just like old times. I decided I couldn't allow that to happen. I spoke to Gar about it and he agreed.

I didn't call Caroline again.

Months went by and I received no calls or texts. This time, it appeared the relationship was really over. I found I had more and more free brainpower when I wasn't worrying about how I was going to get manipulated. I was free to concentrate on beneficial things. I was suddenly able to focus on mine and my loved ones' lives instead of trying to live my life around my father and Caroline.

One of the things myself and Gar had yet to achieve at this point in our lives was something we both dreamed of. Having successfully resurrected our relationship with Shane, there was another person we wanted to resurrect our relationship with:

Our Mam.

Chapter 42

Gar

I lived in New York until September 2008 and visited Fin in Ireland and Shane in the psychiatric ward at Christmas 2007 and again in May 2008 when I was home for a wedding. In my absence, Fin had taken the responsibility upon him to visit Shane every weekend and would let me know of his good progress which I saw for myself on the occasions when I returned home.

By the end of 2008, when I was back living in Ireland, Shane had improved greatly from when we had first started to visit him in the psychiatric ward. Although he was still prone to occasional bouts of staring into space and mumbling incoherently to himself, these episodes occurred less and less frequently. Sometimes Shane had to overcome physical ailments as well as psychiatric, such as when he contracted tuberculosis (TB), presumably from another patient. When we were informed of this, Fin and I were surprised as we had both thought that TB was something which had been eradicated in the 1950's. However, we were informed that it was being brought back into Ireland by immigrants from other countries which had not yet eradicated it.

As a safety precaution, myself and Fin then found ourselves in the waiting room at St. James's Hospital with other possible TB carriers awaiting our name to be called so that we could be tested. As we waited, we watched while a man was brought in handcuffed to two Gardaí before being led out again when his name was called. We looked at each other, eyebrows raised. Happily, after we were tested, both of us got the all clear.

Shane spent a month in the isolation ward confined to his own room whereby all visitors, including us, had to don a surgical mask and apron in order to visit him. He showed us how he had his own shower unit which importantly had an air extraction duct on the ceiling through which he could illicitly smoke cigarettes when the doctors were not watching. Thankfully within a month or so, Shane was clear of TB and back in the psychiatric ward.

Shane continued to progress so well that during one visit the nurses happily informed us that the doctors had decided to send Shane to a place called *Woodlands* on a trial basis one night a week. Woodlands is a big old house on the Grand Canal owned by the Department of Health which had been turned into a supervised community care house for psychiatric patients. The house was specifically set up so that up to eight or so patients could live there away from the negativity of the psychiatric ward and with a much greater degree of independence within the local community.

A psychiatric nurse attended the house and prepared meals and administered medication to the patients. The nurse tried as much as possible to minimise interaction with the patients so as to allow them lead a relatively independent life. There was a security fence around the perimeter of the gardens of the house, which were extensive, but each patient had a security card in order to come and go relatively as they pleased throughout the day.

Fin and I were obviously delighted at this development and talked with Shane about what a great opportunity it was for him. Shane was somewhat apprehensive about spending his first night there but reported back to us afterwards that the house was great and that he really enjoyed staying there. After many months of consistently good behaviour Shane was moved from one night in Woodlands to two nights, then to three nights and ultimately, and much to our delight, he began to spend seven nights a week in Woodlands.

As soon as we could, we started to visit Shane in Woodlands and not in the psychiatric ward, so as to encourage him to stay in Woodlands and to get to know the other patients and nurses. It was immediately apparent to us that the environment in Woodlands was significantly better than in the ward.

It was a massive boost to Shane's self-esteem to be living in a house and not in a hospital anymore. We happily congratulated Shane on the big improvements he had made and reminded them of the great leap he had taken from the dark days of the psychiatric ward. All of the patients in Woodlands were there because they had achieved the level of stability required in order to be invited to live there. This meant that Shane had to up his own game in order to achieve the same levels of stability and not risk being returned to the psychiatric ward as sometimes happens if the patient's condition deteriorated.

Since moving out of the psychiatric ward into community care, Shane has just gone from strength to strength. After a few years his condition improved so much that we felt confident taking him to see gigs again. We started out with a Led Zeppelin tribute band we knew, who performed a family friendly afternoon matinee as well as a late-night gig in the Sugar Club. So Fin, James, Shane and I went to the matinee to see them play Led Zeppelin IV in its entirety and Shane was in his element. He even engaged in banter with the lead singer who didn't seem to realise that Shane was liable to say anything. Happily, although Shane aired his many views to the crowd, nothing was said to spoil the family fun.

****

Over the years, we got to know the other patients in Woodlands very well and it was sad to see that some of them did not appear to have many or indeed any visitors. Shane was immensely proud of the fact that he had regular visits from Fin and me and was always grateful to us for calling in.

Our father maintained contact with Shane and occasionally visited him in Woodlands too, for a time, Shane seemed to want to get the family back together again like the old days. He would sometimes mention to us that our father was visiting on a certain day and maybe we should visit that day too but we always politely demurred. It was hard to explain to Shane why we didn't want to see our father without reminding Shane of what we had gone through in the past, which we did not want to do. In the end our father ended up cutting Shane off again, just like he had done many years before.

While Shane was not successful in reuniting us with our father, he was ultimately successful in his efforts to reunite us with our mother, which brings us back to the start of the book and our train journey to Bagenalstown in March 2010.

Chapter 43

Gar

When Fin and I first broached the subject of meeting our mother again, we did so with a certain amount of apprehension. We did not know where she was. We did not know what she now looked like. We did not know if she wanted to see us. We did not know what her mental condition was. We did not know what her physical condition was. We did not know what effect meeting her might have on her and on us and whether it was in fact a good thing to happen.

We vacillated over acting on our intention to visit for a couple of years after we had stopped speaking to our father. It took this long for us to realise we were independent and the only thing stopping us now from visiting her was ourselves. Eventually we articulated this desire during a visit to Shane. Once we did this, Shane made it his business to ensure that the reunification took place as soon as possible.

Shane told us how he had kept in touch with our mother throughout his stay in the psychiatric ward either through visits by her to the hospital or from him visiting her in Carlow. We were curious about these visits and her condition and relieved when Shane told us that she was in great form and *the same as usual*. He was extremely enthusiastic about the idea of us taking a trip down to Carlow to visit her and immediately proposed that we get the train the following weekend. He had the timetable for the trains from Heuston Station to Bagenalstown in Carlow as he had visited her by train before and proposed the eleven o'clock train.

While we were both keen to see her, we needed a little bit more time to come to terms with what was going to happen and so we postponed Shane's plan for a few weeks.

However, Shane was like a dog with a bone and every week proposed a visit for the next Saturday morning. After a few weeks we committed to making the trip to see her. I asked Shane if he had a telephone number for our aunt Geraldine, our mother's sister, who had been so kind to us in the past. I thought it would be a good idea to call her in advance of the visit and make sure it was the right thing to do. I put her contact details in my phone and called her the following day.

As the call rang and I waited for her to answer, I felt like I was stepping back to my childhood as I had not spoken to her since that weekend in Carlow all those years ago. I wondered whether she still thought about the time we were supposed to watch those movies with her but our father had made us go home. When she answered, I told her about our planned visit and she said she thought it was a great idea and that our mother would be delighted to see us. I asked how our mother was as we had not seen her in so long. She told me that *she was doing grand now* and was much better than last year when they had to fly to Asia to bring our mother back from Vietnam.

I was a little taken aback by this and asked her what our mother was doing in Vietnam to which Geraldine replied matter-of-factly that she was over there *to see the temples*. Our mother had disappeared a year after travelling to Vietnam and Geraldine had called the Irish embassy in Vietnam and asked them to watch out for her. She was told that it was unlikely she would appear on the embassy's radar unless she came to the attention of the authorities. As it happened she did just that when she was admitted to a Vietnamese psychiatric ward. The Irish Embassy was contacted and they in turn contacted Geraldine. Geraldine arranged for herself and her brother to fly to Vietnam to bring her back but they were told that she would only be released if under the care of a psychiatrist.

They scoured the internet and located a service provider in Paris who, for a fee, flew a psychiatrist to Vietnam to take custody of our mother and bring her back to Dublin where she was met by Geraldine and brought straight to the psychiatric ward of a hospital. Geraldine told me it had been a stressful time for her and that her hair had almost fallen out but that she was home now and everything was grand.

Geraldine said that she would meet us with our mother at the train station in Bagenalstown and we would go together to her sister's house for lunch. I thanked her for her help and told her we would see her that coming Saturday.

When I relayed this conversation to Fin we both felt a mixture of concern regarding our mother's foreign adventures and relief that

Geraldine was looking after her. Either way, the conversation only heightened the excitement, apprehension and suspense surrounding Saturday's proposed visit.

Saturday morning arrived bright and breezy. We had arranged to meet at the coffee shop in Heuston station half an hour before the train left. When I arrived, Shane was already there, full of excitement about the adventure that lay ahead. I was very nervous and was anxious for Fin to arrive to help me settle down. Shane however did not appear nervous at all and proceeded to engage a French man in a conversation that was half French, half gibberish but that the Frenchman seemed to understand exactly. I could only look on and marvel, grateful for the distraction.

After a few minutes, Fin arrived and we boarded the train. The three of us sat around the table and Fin and I drank coffee while Shane drank Coke. Despite the tension, Shane's presence meant that the hour-long train journey passed by quickly as he made us laugh with jokes and observations. He was clearly very pleased with himself that he was reuniting the family after so many years apart. We were pleased too, but apprehensive.

Finally, the announcement came over the intercom:

Next stop, Muine Bheag, Bagenalstown.

Here we go, said Shane, grinning widely.

Fin and I exchanged glances and I looked out of the window to see a flash of a figure that might have been our mother on the platform. The train came to a halt and the three of us disembarked. There, twenty yards away at the end of the platform, was the unmistakable figure of our mother with her sister Geraldine by her side. As we walked towards her, her features became more recognisable: her brown eyes, the shape of her nose, her nervous smiling mouth and her grey hair. When we reached her, we stopped and stood to attention in front of her, like two little boys presenting themselves for inspection.

Our mother looked at me and then Fin and then looked back at me and said:

Fin?

I laughed nervously.

No, I said, *that's Fin. I'm Gar.*

Well, she laughed, *nice to see you both.*

We laughed together and the three of us embraced, finally defying our father's order from all those years before.

Epilogue

Gar

Six years later, on 10 June 2016, I was on a call to a customer service line when I was jolted back to the past by the customer service agent asking me, quite matter-of-factly:

What is your mother's maiden name?

I inhaled deeply at this question. It was a question that had caused me inner turmoil ever since the late nineties when I started using the internet and this became a common security question. At that time, I still lived by my father's story, so I always answered _Fox_ to this question, Fox being Caroline's maiden name. But during the years when I was questioning my father, I had sometimes used Fox and sometimes used Hogan, my mother's maiden name. Since 2010 when we restored our relationship with our mother, I had only used Hogan. The problem with this particular account was that I knew I had set it up around ten years before, during the questioning period, so I had no idea which mother's maiden name I had used. I would have to guess.

I tried my mother's maiden name first:

Is it Hogan? I ventured.

_No,_ came the reply, and an awkward pause.

I tried again.

Is it Fox?

Yes sir, came the somewhat relieved reply, _Fox it is sir._

Sorry, I said, _it's a long story._

When I hung up the phone I thought back to that period of my life when I was so confused I didn't even know how to answer a very simple question: _what is your mother's maiden name?_ I thought about the last six years spent rebuilding my relationship with my mother, who is still the same kind, gentle and loving person I remember from my childhood.

I thought about how I would have no hesitation in answering that question now.

There is no turmoil and there is no confusion.

I know exactly who my mother is, was, and forever shall be.

My mother is, of course, *my Mam*.

Fin

I saw my father recently when I was bringing my youngest son over to his grandparents' house where he stays on Mondays and Tuesdays while my wife and I are at work. I was waiting to cross the road with my son in his buggy and he was pointing at the cars and babbling away like any healthy one-year-old baby.

There was a lot of traffic on the road and the vehicles heading towards the city centre were moving with the green light. As I waited for them to stop, I noticed the familiar SUV that my father drove. It was stuck in traffic exactly where I was crossing. The light went red for the vehicles and so I pushed the buggy across the road, walking directly behind his SUV.

I looked in at the back of my father's head through the back window. I could see that he was looking through his rear mirror at us. His face was expressionless. He seemed pleasantly unconcerned. He watched me, his son, who he hadn't spoken to in seven years, and his one-year-old grandson, who he has never met, walk behind his vehicle as he was stuck in traffic.

He saw us yet he didn't react. As I walked on I watched him pull off as the lights went green. Even after everything I went through with him, I was surprised at his lack of emotion. There is only one man I know that could have had such a heartless non-reaction.

That man is my father.

Dear Reader,

Thank you for taking the time to read our story. We hope that you connected with it in some way and that you found it an interesting and compelling read.

We also hope that you will realise from reading this true story that there are things that go on behind closed doors that are not spoken about perhaps as much as they should be.

We hope that our book will spark conversations and increase awareness of the issues raised in our book and will help to ensure that there are fewer childhoods like ours. Unfortunately, bad things happen when good people do nothing.

You are now in a position to help us in this regard and we would be very grateful if you would do so. Please share this copy of the book with somebody who will read it and encourage them to pass it on similarly. Also, please review the book on the Amazon website and spread your thoughts on the book to everyone you can via social media or simply by word of mouth.

We really appreciate you spreading the word!

You can also visit our website or Facebook page listed overleaf.

Many thanks

Fin & Gar Murphy

Manufactured by Amazon.ca
Bolton, ON